CONTENTS

C O N T E N T S

THE IMPACT OF THE DRUG TRADE ON BORDER SECURITY AND NATIONAL PARKS

MONDAY, MARCH 10, 2003

HOUSE OF REPRESENTATIVES,
SUBCOMMITTEE ON CRIMINAL JUSTICE, DRUG POLICY AND HUMAN RESOURCES,
COMMITTEE ON GOVERNMENT REFORM,
Sells, AZ.

The subcommittee met, pursuant to notice, at 10:21 a.m., in the Council Chambers, Tohono O'odham Nation, Sells, AZ, Hon. Mark Souder (chairman of the subcommittee) presiding.

Present: Representatives Souder and Shadegg.

Staff present: Nicole Garrett, clerk; Christopher A. Donesa, staff director and chief counsel; and Nick Coleman, counsel.

Mr. SOUDER. The Subcommittee will come to order. I am going to read an opening statement, then have a few comments and I need to clarify a little what we are doing here.

Good morning, and thank you all for coming. Today our subcommittee returns to continue its exploration of the status of security and law enforcement along the southern Arizona border.

Since the summer of 2001, this subcommittee has been making a comprehensive study of our Nation's borders, including a field hearing last February in Sierra Vista, AZ. The subcommittee has focused particular attention on the effectiveness of the Federal law enforcement agencies entrusted with protecting and administering our Nation's borders and ports of entry. Last summer the subcommittee released a comprehensive report on these issues, but our study continues. This is the report that was just released. It is a little over 100 pages, it is the most comprehensive study in the history of the government on the border.

Today's hearing is intended to focus on the problem of illegal drug smuggling across the southern border, and the related crime and damage caused by that smuggling. This hearing is not intended to focus on the related problem of illegal immigration, which is a much larger and even more contentious issue. We understand, of course, that the issue of illegal immigration is bound to come up today as it is so deeply intertwined with the problem of narcotics smuggling along the southern border.

This subcommittee also has jurisdiction over INS and immigration questions, but that is not our primary focus. As you probably know, Congressman Shadegg and I both have recently been appointed to the Homeland Security Committee as well. So we have multiple jurisdictions, but when we look at border issues, we look at narcotics, but then we also look at trade questions, we wind up looking at immigration questions and the more comprehensive—but particularly what we are looking at is the vulnerability of the southern border. Our primary responsibility in this subcommittee is oversight of narcotics questions, as well as authorizing the drug czar office and those regulations which we are in the process of doing in the next 30 days.

The southern border is still far more illegal—has far more illegal activity than the northern border, and it presents severe challenges for effective law enforcement. The southern border runs through deserts, mountains and rivers, through unpopulated areas as well as cities and suburbs, and through national parks, wildlife refuges, Native American reservations and even military bases. Questions of overlapping law enforcement agency jurisdiction can come into play, and we intend to address those issues today.

The particular problem of illegal cross-border activity in parks, refuges and reservations is illustrated by several incidents over the past year. In August 2002, Ranger Kris Eggle was killed by drug smugglers in Organ Pipe Cactus National Monument. The murder occurred less than a year after the U.S. Department of Interior's Inspector General released a report which raised serious questions about how well equipped and prepared park rangers and other Interior Department law enforcement personnel were to deal with increasing drug smuggling and other crime taking place at national parks and wildlife refuges. In April 2002, marijuana smugglers attacked four U.S. Customs officers on the Tohono O'odham Nation Reservation, wounding one of them. The Tohono O'odham Nation has reported numerous other incidents of cross-border violence, and even incursions by Mexican military personnel in support of drug smugglers.

Taken together, these incidents paint a stark picture of the challenges facing law enforcement and local citizens along the southern Arizona border. Drug smuggling and related crime have taken a toll on the environment and the quality of life for local residents, besides presenting a threat to the entire country. We are talking today about narcotics, but as we look at Homeland Security questions and the vulnerabilities you have when you do not control either of the borders, they are just incomprehensible. As I was out here yesterday trying to figure out how we would stop someone if they have a piece of a nuclear weapon and it becomes catastrophic. Short-term, that is not as an immediate threat on the south border as it is on the north border, but long-term, without control of your borders you cannot have a secure Nation.

These issues are all very important and extremely urgent, and we look forward to hearing from our witnesses today about ways to address them.

We want to first thank the Tohono O'odham Nation for agreeing to provide their facilities for this hearing. We greatly appreciate your courtesy in hosting this event and in providing four witnesses to testify: the Honorable Edward Manuel, chairman of the Nation, representing the sovereign government; Assistant Chief of Police Joseph Delgado, representing the Tohono O'odham law enforcement community; Ms. Fern Salcido and Mr. Augustine Toro, private citizens of the Nation who live in border districts. We look forward to learning more about the difficulties you face here in the Tohono O'odham Nation.

We have also invited representatives of the agencies primarily responsible for dealing with drug smuggling in this region; namely, the U.S. Customs Service, the U.S. Border Patrol and the Drug Enforcement Administration. The subcommittee is vitally interested in ensuring the effective functioning of these agencies, and we will continue to work with them and their staff to ensure the continued security and effective administration of our Nation's borders and its protection from narcotics.

We also welcome Mr. David Aguilar, Chief Patrol Agent for the U.S. Border Patrol's Tucson sector, who we have worked with in previous hearings. Mr. Hugh Winderweedle, Port Director of the U.S. Customs Service in Lukeville's Port of Entry and Mr. James Woolley, Assistant Special Agent in Charge of the Drug Enforcement Administration's Tucson Division Office.

As this hearing is particularly focused on the problems faced at our Nation's parks and wildlife refuges, we are also pleased to be joined by Mr. Dom Ciccone, Regional Chief of the National Wildlife Refuge System, representing the U.S. Fish and Wildlife Service and Mr. William Wellman, Park Supervisor for the Organ Pipe Cactus National Monument, representing the National Park Service.

I am also a member of the House Resources Committee on the National Parks and on the Fish and Wildlife subcommittees, so I have had many opportunities to visit our national parks and wildlife refuges and to meet with Interior Department personnel who manage them. We hope at this hearing to focus special attention on the law enforcement issues faced by your agencies, so we thank you again for your participation.

When examining border policies, we must of course also seek the input of representatives of the local community whose lives are directly affected by the changes at the border. We therefore welcome, in addition to Ms. Salcido and Mr. Toro, Ms. Jennifer Allen of the Border Action Network; Colonel Ben Anderson, a retired U.S. Army officer and local resident and Reverend Robin Hoover, president of Humane Borders, Inc.

We know that these issues can be very contentious, because they are a matter not simply of the quality of life for those who live here, but of life and death itself. We hope to have a courteous but frank discussion of these issues, and we thank everyone for taking the time this morning to join us for this important hearing.

It is an honor today to be joined by my friend and constant advocate for Arizona, Congressman John Shadegg, a previous member of this committee. As I said, we will be working together on border issues on Homeland Security. It is great to be in Arizona.

Mr. Shadegg.

[The prepared statement of Hon. Mark E. Souder follows:]

Opening Statement
Chairman Mark Souder

"The Impact of the Drug Trade on Border Security and National Parks: Field Hearing in Sells, Arizona"

Subcommittee on Criminal Justice, Drug Policy, and Human Resources
Committee on Government Reform

March 10, 2003

Good morning and thank you all for coming. Today our Subcommittee returns to continue its exploration of the status of security and law enforcement along southern Arizona border. Since the summer of 2001, this Subcommittee has been making a comprehensive study of our nation's borders, including a field hearing last February in Sierra Vista, Arizona. The Subcommittee has focused particular attention on the effectiveness of the federal law enforcement agencies entrusted with protecting and administering our nation's borders and ports of entry. Last summer the Subcommittee released a comprehensive report on these issues, but our study continues.

Today's hearing is intended to focus on the problem of illegal drug smuggling across the Southern border, and the related crime and damage caused by that smuggling. This hearing is not intended to focus on the related problem of illegal immigration, which is a much larger and even more contentious issue. We understand, of course, that the issue of illegal immigration is bound to come up today as it is so deeply intertwined with the problem of narcotics smuggling along the Southern border

The Southern border still sees far more illegal activity than the Northern border, and it presents severe challenges for effective law enforcement. The Southern border runs through deserts, mountains, and rivers, through unpopulated areas as well as cities and suburbs, and through National Parks, wildlife refuges, Native American reservations, and even military bases. Questions of overlapping law enforcement agency jurisdiction can come into play, and we intend to address those issues today.

The particular problem of illegal cross-border activity in parks, refuges and reservations is illustrated by several incidents over the past year. In August 2002, Ranger Kris Eggle was killed by drug smugglers in Organ Pipe Cactus National Monument. The murder occurred less than a year after the U.S. Department of the Interior's inspector general released a report which raised serious questions about how well equipped and prepared park rangers and other Interior Department law enforcement personnel were to deal with the increasing drug smuggling and other crime taking place at national parks and wildlife refuges. In April 2002, marijuana smugglers attacked four U.S. Customs officers on the Tohono O'odham Nation Reservation, wounding one of them. The Tohono O'odham Nation has reported numerous other incidents of cross-border violence, and even incursions by Mexican military personnel in support of drug smugglers.

Taken together, these incidents paint a stark picture of the challenges facing law enforcement and local citizens along the southern Arizona border. Drug smuggling and related crime have taken a toll on the environment and the quality of life for local residents, besides presenting a threat to the entire country.

These issues are all very important and extremely urgent, and we look forward to hearing from our witnesses today about ways to address them. We first want to thank the Tohono O'odham Nation for agreeing to provide their facilities for this hearing. We greatly appreciate your courtesy in hosting this event, and in providing four witnesses to testify: the Honorable Edward D. Manuel, Chairman of the Nation, representing its sovereign government; Assistant Chief of Police Joseph Delgado, representing the Tohono O'odham law enforcement community; and Ms. Fern Salcido and Mr. Augustine Toro, private citizens of the Nation who live in border districts. We look forward to learning more about the difficulties you face here in the Tohono O'odham Nation.

We have also invited representatives of the agencies primarily responsible for dealing with drug smuggling in this region, namely the U.S. Customs Service, the U.S. Border Patrol and the Drug Enforcement

Administration. The Subcommittee is vitally interested in ensuring the effective functioning of these agencies, and we will continue to work with them and their staff to ensure the continued security and effective administration of our nation's borders and its protection from narcotics. We welcome Mr. David Aguilar, Chief Patrol Agent of the U.S. Border Patrol's Tucson Sector; Mr. Hugh Winderweedle, Port Director of the U.S. Customs Service's Lukeville Port of Entry; and Mr. James A. Woolley, Assistant Special Agent in Charge of the Drug Enforcement Administration's Tucson Division Office.

As this hearing is particularly focused on the problems faced at our nation's parks and wildlife refuges, we are pleased to be joined by Mr. Dom Ciccone, Regional Chief of the National Wildlife Refuge System, representing the U.S. Fish and Wildlife Service; and Mr. William Wellman, Park Supervisor of Organ Pipe Cactus National Monument, representing the National Park Service. I am also a member of the House Resources Committee, so I have had many opportunities to visit our national parks and wildlife refuges and to meet with the Interior Department personnel who manage them. We hope at this hearing to focus special attention on the law enforcement issues faced by your agencies, so we thank you again for your participation.

When examining border policies, we must of course also seek the input of representatives of the local community whose lives are directly affected by changes at the border. We therefore welcome, in addition to Ms. Salcido and Mr. Toro, Ms. Jennifer Allen of the Border Action Network; Col. Ben Anderson, a retired U.S. Army officer and local resident and Rev. Robin Hoover, President of Humane Borders, Inc.

We know that these issues can be very contentious, because they are a matter not simply of the quality of life for those who live here, but of life and death itself. We hope to have a courteous but frank discussion of these issues, and we thank everyone for taking the time this morning to join us for this important hearing.

Mr. SHADEGG. Well thank you, Mr. Chairman and welcome to Arizona. We are thrilled to have you here. We know you spent the weekend here and we very much appreciate your coming here.

I am Congressman John Shadegg and I represent the Third District of Arizona. I am not a member of the subcommittee any longer, though I once was, but I have worked on border issues quite extensively with Congressman Souder. I want to welcome you here, Mark, and your lovely wife. I want to tell you that we appreciate your spending time in Arizona and looking at our issues with regard to the border and all of our issues with regard to drug enforcement. Mark spent part of his time on Saturday looking at our HIDTA in Phoenix and it wound up costing he and his wife their day's plans. So he has spent an aggressive amount of time here in Arizona working and not doing any recreation, but I hope we at least provided you with good weather.

I also want to thank the Tohono O'odham Nation and its chairman for hosting us here today. I want to explain that in part some of the groundwork for this hearing resulted from a visit I made to the border roughly 3 weeks ago, where we went to Organ Pipe Cactus National Monument and looked at the situation in that park. We looked at the location where Park Ranger Eggle was murdered, and began to take an accounting of the problems that we face along the border from Nogales west.

I want to point out—and I note this, Congressman, with some degree of tongue in cheek—that you and I both, I think, visited Nogales in January and did an extensive border tour there, including at that time their new truck facility and a helicopter tour there. We visited Sierra Vista in February and spent some time there and night time down on the border, helicopter work and also some ground work, looking at the new elevated stations for observing border crossings, and we are here in March. I wonder if I detect a pattern there? I do not see August or July in those months. [Laughter.]

Mr. SOUDER. What you neglect to mention is I have been here on other business with the parks in the hot season, so I decided not to repeat that. [Laughter.]

Mr. SHADEGG. Oh, I appreciate you inviting me only for your winter visits.

These issues are in fact very, very important. I want to note for the record and just make a comment for my friends from Arizona. Fellow Arizonans, that Mark is singularly devoted to two issues that I think are very important to us here in Arizona. One is the border issue in general and the importance of our Nation's borders and the importance of the security and law enforcement along those borders; and second, the issue of illegal drugs. He has worked aggressively on this issue. He has been around the globe looking at the drug issue. He is very personally dedicated to and concerned about the devastation of our young people in this Nation by illegal drugs and the damage they do. He has looked at interdiction in source countries, he has looked at interdiction in the transit regions and looked at our borders and has looked at enforcement within the country. I think that commends him well and he works very hard. The report that he has produced is a tremendously valuable asset and it catalogs the successes and the failures and the needs of our law enforcement officials at our borders and at our ports of entry.

I described to him my experience at Lukeville a couple of weeks ago and the condition of the fence at Lukeville and provided him with a book of pictures, trying to show to him some of the concerns. His only comment of note was that I seem to be in every picture. [Laughter.]

I also explained to him some of the issues here with the Tohono O'odham, and the very impressive information that the Tohono O'odham Nation presented to me when we were in Lukeville and over at Organ Pipe Cactus National Monument a few weeks ago in terms of the trafficking across the reservation, the damage that is done by that trafficking, the recent upsurge in drug trafficking across the Nation and the lack of resources that the Nation has to deal with that problem. I also described to Mark the genuine concern of the Nation for the fact that we have now appropriated funds to build an automobile barrier along the southern boundary of Organ Pipe Cactus National Monument, but we have not done anything to deal with the border either east of that location—meaning here on Tohono O'odham—or west of that location on the Cabeza Prieta National Wildlife Refuge. We have tried to give Mark some kind of an inkling of what he would find when he came here for this hearing.

I want to thank all of our witnesses for being here. I believe that this is a tremendous step forward for us to be able to present this information in a formal congressional hearing where it will get on the record. I would note that in his work on border issues and particularly on drug issues, Mark is acting at the personal request of the Speaker of the U.S. House, who shares Mark's passion about drug issues and about border issues because of the issue of drugs. So when you recognize this hearing and have an opportunity to put this information in the record, the problems that we face all along America's southern border, the particular problems we face here along the Arizona section of our southern border and the unique problems today that we face here in the Tohono O'odham Nation, at Organ Pipe Cactus National Monument and also at Cabeza Prieta. That information is going into the official record of the U.S. Congress and is being brought forward in a sense by a chairman who is working at the request of the Speaker of the House himself, which means that we have a chance to use that to try to make our case for the resources we need to deal with these issues.

With that, Mr. Chairman, I thank you for being here and for taking the time. I thank all of our witnesses and I yield back my time.

Mr. SOUDER. Before proceeding, I would like to take care of a couple of procedural matters. First, I would ask unanimous consent that all Members have 5 legislative days to submit written statements and questions for the hearing record, and that any answers to written questions provided by the witnesses also be included in the record. Without objection, it is so ordered.

Second, I would like to ask unanimous consent that all Members present be permitted to participate in the hearing.

Let me make a couple of introductory comments as far as how a hearing functions. This is not a town meeting. Generally speaking, even in Washington, often our hearings will have 1 to 2 Members present and maybe 5 to 10 people in the audience. It is not a participation meeting where people can ask questions, where they can make comments. There are designated witnesses, time periods of 5 minutes for a witness, which we try to stay as tight to that as possible and draw it out in the questions. Full statements are submitted for the record and additional material is submitted for the record, because it is a proceeding where we are building an official record as we work through different border issues.

Because there are not a lot of field hearings in hard-to-get-to locations, often people do not understand the difference between that and a town meeting, and I wanted to outline that a little bit before we got started with the hearing.

If you have comments that you would like to submit, you can submit them to the committee. We will work through, as best we can, to insert them into the record. That is not a uniform commitment that we will do so, but we will certainly consider that, and we consider the request, particularly if they go through the Congressman who represents you, who then can submit it to the members of the committee and go through—there is a legal process we have to work through for testimony as well, because one of the things we do in this committee is swear in every witness, and with handwritten statements you are not sworn in the same under oath, so we have to be careful. The reason this committee does that is we are an oversight committee. It is the only committee, I believe, in Congress—the Intelligence Committee may as well—that swears in witnesses. This committee is the one that does investigations such as on China and on Waco and the whole range of things like that, and we have had multiple perjury cases come out of this committee. So that is why submitted statements and random questions do not work in our field hearings because the people have to prepare that and have it cleared, and they should be prepared to be prosecuted if they give us false statements in a hearing. I am not threatening anybody, I am just saying as a factual matter that has happened in the committee. Our job is to figure out when the government is being effective in implementing the laws that Congress passed.

In recognition of the courtesy of Tohono O'odham sovereign Nation in hosting this hearing, we would like to first hear from their official representative. So would the first two witnesses, Chairman Manuel and Assistant Chief of Police Delgado, please come forward and remain standing because we'll need to administer the oath.

If you will raise your right hands. It is our standard practice, as I said, to have everybody testify under oath.

[Witnesses sworn.]

Mr. SOUDER. Let the record show that both witnesses have responded in the affirmative.

I also want to make sure that I put in the record that we have talked to a number of Congressmen to alert them of this. I talked to Congressman Grijalva approximately a month ago that we were coming. I believe he has representatives here today, but he was not able to be here. We always make sure that whatever district we are in, we approach that Congressman as soon as we have a confirmed date and let them know we are coming in, even if they are not a member of the committee.

With that, let me again say it is a great pleasure to be here. I drove through yesterday as we were heading to the park and back this morning from Ajo. It is absolutely beautiful country with the flowers and the cactus. It is not green soybeans like Indiana. It is not nice and flat where you can see the next two States like we can in Indiana, but what beautiful country. It is really a great honor to be here among you, and I look forward to hearing your testimony.

STATEMENTS OF EDWARD D. MANUEL, CHAIRMAN, TOHONO O'ODHAM NATION; AND JOSEPH DELGADO, ASSISTANT CHIEF OF POLICE, TOHONO O'ODHAM POLICE DEPARTMENT

Chairman MANUEL. Good morning, Congressman Souder, good morning Congressman Shadegg and staff persons. Welcome to the Tohono O'odham Nation. Also, I would like to welcome the public that are here this morning.

I am honored to appear before the subcommittee today to share my thoughts on the impact that the drug trade is having on Tohono O'odham Nation. We have many problems along the international boundary, such as homeland security, environmental and illegal immigrants. Today, I will confine my testimony only to the drug trade due to time limitations.

Let me share some background information on the Tohono O'odham Nation. The Tohono O'odham Nation is comprised of 2.8 million acres of land, an area the size of Connecticut. O'odham lands are contiguous to 75 miles of the international boundary and our Nation has approximately 28,500 members.

Cross-border drug smuggling is one of the most serious problems facing our community today.

It is important that you understand how the present crisis was created so that steps can be taken now to address the situation. We must avoid making these same mistakes in the future. In the past, the United States initiated several border programs such as Operation Gatekeeper and Hold the Line aimed at specific border areas. These initiatives were successful around the ports of entry, but had the unfortunate effect of forcing illegal activities away from the ports and unfortunately onto the land of the Tohono O'odham Nation. A shifting of resources is costly, time consuming and ineffective. Our land and our people have suffered tremendously. They have suffered collateral damages as a direct result of these policies and practices. We were never consulted.

Let me share with you some of the impact the drug smuggling is having on the Nation. In 2001, one of our Tohono O'odham policewomen, working alone, seized 450 pounds of cocaine with a street value of $4 million and arrested the two smugglers who had recently brought their load across the border. Last year, our police department seized in excess of 75 tons of narcotics. This level of drug smuggling has seriously strained our law enforcement resources and put our officers at great risk. Drug smuggling is big business. The Tohono O'odham Nation Police Department's drug seizures have resulted in significant financial losses to those businesses that engage in the importation of narcotics. We know that it is just a matter of time before the smugglers start to retaliate. Smugglers are armed with automatic assault type weapons, have armor-piercing bullets and have sophisticated communication equipment to detect our law enforcement presence. Our resources are diverted away from our community, our community-based policemen.

The people involved in the smuggling business on our lands come from all over the United States. They are not American Indians and we do not have legal authority to prosecute them in our courts. They recruit our children to transport the drugs, they lure our teenagers to experiment with drugs such as cocaine, heroin and crystal meth—drugs that never before were found in our communities. When our kids become addicted, we have no services to treat them, no residential care, and no detox beds. All too often, they end up in the intensive care units of Tucson hospitals.

These are just some of the tragic effects of cross-border drug smuggling—the question is what can we do? You and I both know that until demand in the United States for narcotic products is effectively dealt with, those of us who live and work along the border will have to deal with the effects of drug smuggling.

We are told that plans are in the works to build a vehicle barrier fence along the Organ Pipe Cactus National Monument, along its border. As a stand-alone project, this will simply divert more smuggling traffic into the lands of the Tohono O'odham Nation. The Tohono O'odham Nation stands ready to work in partnership with our neighbors, but it is not right to implement a project in one area, which only have the effect of making life worse for our communities and our people.

Protection of America's borders is clearly a Federal obligation. We hear a lot about homeland security and yet how secure is our homeland when tons and tons of narcotics cross our border every day?

I propose that the United States construct and maintain a road immediately adjacent to the international boundary from the west end to the east end of the Tohono O'odham Nation, the entire 75 mile length. Further, I propose that the U.S. law enforcement resources be stationed directly on the border and removed from our communities.

I know that these proposals are costly, but we simply must stop the massive importation of narcotics across the lands of the Tohono O'odham Nation. We can do this in one of two ways—either the United States can provide direct and adequate funding to the Tohono O'odham Nation and we will build and maintain the road and put our law enforcement personnel on the border, or the United States can build and maintain the road and station Federal law enforcement agents on the border. We must act now—regardless of which option we pursue. We must act in collaboration with the United States and our neighbors along the border. Not only does drug smuggling have major negative effects on the Tohono O'odham Nation, drugs go beyond the boundaries of the Nation into the Arizona communities and the United States. The grave danger faced by our law enforcement and the health and safety of our people in our communities require that we all work together to effectively address the issue of border crossing importation of drugs.

Again, thank you. I am pleased to answer any questions you may have.

Mr. SOUDER. Thank you, Mr. Chairman.

We would now like to hear from Assistant Chief Delgado.

[The prepared statement of Chairman Manuel follows:]

Testimony on the Effects of Cross Border Drug Smuggling

Presented by
Chairman Edward D. Manuel
Tohono O'odham Nation

Before the Criminal Justice, Drug Policy and Human Resources Subcommittee
Of the House Committee on Government Reform

March 10, 2003

Sells, Arizona

Good Morning Members of Congress, Welcome to the Tohono O'odham Nation.

I am honored to appear before the Subcommittee today and share my thoughts on the effect that cross-border drug smuggling has on our Nation.

The Tohono O'odham Nation is comprised of 2.86 million acres of land, an area roughly the size of the State of Connecticut. O'odham lands are contiguous to seventy-five (75) miles of the International Boundary and our Nation has approximately 28,500 enrolled members.

Cross-border drug smuggling is one of the most serious problems facing our community today.

It is important that you understand how the present crisis was created so that steps can be taken now to address this situation. We must avoid making these same mistakes in the future. In 1996, the United States initiated several border programs such as "Operation

Gatekeeper" and "Hold the Line" aimed at closing the border areas around Ports of Entry. These initiatives were successful around the Ports, but had the unfortunate effect of forcing illegal activity away from the Ports and onto the lands of the Tohono O'odham Nation. Our land and our people have suffered tremendous collateral damage as a direct result of these policies and programs. We were never consulted. In 2001, one of our Tohono O'odham policewomen, working alone, seized 450 pounds of cocaine with a street value of $4 million dollars and arrested the two smugglers who had recently brought their load across the border. Last year, our police department seized in excess of 75 tons of narcotics. This level of drug smuggling has seriously strained our law enforcement resources and puts our officers at great risk. Drug smuggling is big business. The Tohono O'odham Police Department's drug seizures have resulted in a significant financial loss to those businesspersons engaged in the importation of narcotics. We know that it is just a matter of time until one of our police officers is kidnapped, tortured, wounded or killed. We know it is just a matter of time. Smugglers drive humvees, are armed with automatic, assault-type weapons, use armor-piercing bullets and have sophisticated communication equipment to detect our law enforcement presence.

The people involved in the smuggling business on our lands come from all over the United States. They are not American Indians and we do not have legal authority to prosecute them in our Courts. They recruit our children to guard their loads. They lure our teenagers to experiment with cocaine, heroin and crystal meth---drugs that never before were found in O'odham communities. When our kids become addicted, we have no services to treat them, no residential care, and no detox beds. All to often, they end up in the Intensive Care Units of Tucson hospitals.

These are just some of the tragic effects of cross-border drug smuggling---the question is what can we do? You and I both know that until demand in the United States for narcotic products is effectively dealt with, those of us who live and work along the border will have to deal with the effects of cross-border smuggling. We are told that plans are in the works to build a vehicle barrier fence along the Organ Pipe Cactus National Monument southern border area. As a stand-alone project, this will simply divert more smuggling traffic into the lands of the Tohono O'odham Nation. The Tohono O'odham Nation stands ready to work in partnership with our neighbors, but it is not fair to implement a project in one area, which will only have the affect of making life much worse for our communities and our people.

Protection of America's borders is clearly a federal obligation. We hear a lot about Homeland Security, and yet how secure is our homeland when tons and tons of narcotics cross our border everyday?

I propose that the United States construct and maintain a road immediately adjacent to the International Boundary from the west end to the east end of the Tohono O'odham Nation, the entire 75 mile length. Further, I propose that all United States law enforcement resources be stationed directly on the border and removed from our communities.

I know that these proposals are not cheap but we simply must stop the massive importation of narcotics across the lands of the Tohono O'odham Nation. We can do this one of two ways: either the United States can provide direct and adequate funding to the Tohono O'odham Nation and we will build and maintain the road and put our law enforcement personnel on the border, or, the United States can build and maintain the road and station federal law enforcement agents at the border. We must act now—regardless of which option we pursue. We must act in collaboration with the United States and our neighbors along the border. The grave danger faced by our police officers and the health and safety of our people and our communities require that we all work together to effectively address the issue of cross-border importation of drugs.

Again, thank you. I am pleased to answer any questions that you may have.

Mr. DELGADO. Good morning, Members of Congress, welcome to the Tohono O'odham Nation.

The Tohono O'odham Nation has experienced a dramatic increase in the amount of smuggled narcotics across our lands from Mexico into other parts of the United States. The increase is simply beyond the Nation's control and due largely to the demand for narcotics. Nevertheless, the impact of this illegal traffic presents a huge cost for the Nations Tohono O'odham Police Department and prevents the police department from completing its mission to provide community policing for the Tohono O'odham communities.

TOPD estimates that it spends in excess of $3.7 million on interdiction of illegal traffic across the international border. In other words, fully 60 percent of the TOPD's budget is devoted to fighting the international drug problem.

During fiscal year 2001, the TOPD seized 45,000 pounds of illegal drugs. At the end of fiscal year 2002, the TOPD seized a total of 65,000 pounds. In April 2002 alone, the TOPD seized a record 15,960 pounds or one-third the total seized in 2001. A recent analysis by TOPD demonstrates that in 2002, we spent $642,880 in direct costs associated with international drug smuggling cases alone. That cost represents only the personnel time involved in such investigations; it does not include vehicle and/or other non-administrative costs.

Protecting the border and deterring international traffic in narcotics is the responsibility of Federal law enforcement agencies. The scale of the problem indicates a sizable hole in the border sufficient to threaten homeland security. TOPD attempts to plug the hole with limited resources, while we receive no Federal funding support for our efforts. Clearly, without Federal funding support, the TOPD will remain overwhelmed by the international border problem, much to the detriment of the Tohono O'odham members and our communities.

The $3.7 million cost of interdicting narcotics amounts to 60 percent of the TOPD's budget, and an effort which provides significant assistance to Federal law enforcement agencies. Other local law enforcement receive some Federal funds for similar efforts. TOPD should be accorded the same level of funding and resource allocation, if not more, considering the size of the international problem occurring on our land of the Tohono O'odham Nation. Federal funding support would reimburse both direct and opportunity costs of TOPD's forced involvement in border-related law enforcement and public safety challenges, which are a Federal responsibility. Few local law enforcement agencies face the scale of challenges before the TOPD. Local, community public safety needs of Tohono O'odham often are put at risk, if not compromised.

To better address the local need for TOPD's law enforcement services, while balancing the TOPD's assistance in illegal trafficking, TOPD requests $3,707,000 in Federal funds. Currently, operational costs for our efforts amount to $1.8 million, while personnel costs amount to $1.6 million and indirect costs at $326,790. Federal funding in this amount would cover personnel, vehicles, support equipment and operational expenses. Only through Federal funding support can TOPD continue to meet border-related challenges and protect the homeland security of the United States. Most important, these funds will allow TOPD to address the need for community-based police services.

Thank you. I am pleased to answer any questions you might have.

[The prepared statement of Mr. Delgado follows:]

Tohono O'odham Nation Police Department
PO Box 189
Sells AZ 85634
(520) 383 6418

Assistant Chief Joseph Delgado

Testimony On The Effects Of Cross-Border Drug Smuggling
Presented By
Assistant Chief Joseph Delgado
Tohono O'odham Police Department
Before The
Criminal Justice, Drug Policy And Human Resources Subcommittee
Of The
House Committee on Government Reform
March 10, 2003
Sells, Arizona

The Tohono O'odham Nation has experienced a dramatic increase in the amount of smuggled narcotics across our lands from Mexico into other parts of the United States. This increase is simply beyond the Nation's control and due largely to the demand for narcotics. Nevertheless, the impact of this illegal traffic presents a huge cost for the Nation's Tohono O'odham Police Department ("TOPD) and prevents the TOPD from completing its mission to provide community policing for Tohono O'odham communities.

TOPD estimates that it spends in excess of $3.7 million on interdiction of illegal traffic across the International Border. In other words, fully sixty percent of TOPD's budget is devoted to fighting the international drug problem.

During fiscal year 2001, the TOPD seized 45,000 pounds of illegal drugs. At the end of fiscal year 2002, the TOPD seized a total of 65,000 pounds. In April, 2002, alone, the TOPD seized a record 15,960 pounds, or one-third the total seized in 2001. A recent analysis by TOPD demonstrates that in 2002, we spent $642,880 in direct costs associated with international drug smuggling cases alone. That cost represents only the personnel time involved in such investigations; it does not include vehicle and other non-administrative costs.

Protecting the Border and deterring international traffic in narcotics is the responsibility of federal law enforcement agencies. The scale of the problem indicates a sizable hole in the border sufficient to threaten homeland security. TOPD, attempts to plug the hole with limited resources, while we receive no federal funding support for our efforts. Clearly, without federal funding support, the TOPD will remain overwhelmed by an international border problem, much to the detriment of Tohono O'odham members and our communities.

The $3.7 million cost of interdicting narcotics amounts to sixty percent of TOPD's budget, and an effort, which provides significant assistance to federal law enforcement agencies. Other local law enforcement receive some federal funds for similar efforts. TOPD should be accorded the same level of funding and resource allocation, if not more considering the size of the international problem occurring on the lands of the Tohono O'odham Nation. Federal funding support would reimburse both direct and opportunity costs of TOPD's forced involvement in border related law enforcement and public safety challenges, which are a Federal responsibility. Few local law enforcement agencies face the scale of challenges before the TOPD. Local, community public safety needs of Tohono O'odham often are put at risk, if not compromised.

To better address the local need for TOPD's law enforcement services, while balancing the TOPD's assistance in illegal trafficking, TOPD requests $3,707,000 in federal funds. Currently, operational costs for our efforts amount to $1.8 million, while personnel costs amount to $1.6 million and indirect costs at $326,790. Federal funding in this amount would cover personnel, vehicles, support equipment, and operational expenses. Only through federal funding support can TOPD continue to meet border related challenges and protect the Homeland Security of the United States. Most important, these funds will allow TOPD to address the need for community-based police services.

Thank you. I am pleased to answer any questions you might have.

Mr. SOUDER. Thank you both for your testimony.

Chief Delgado, is your department eligible for equipment under the drug czar's office—do you know or are you familiar with that program?

Mr. DELGADO. Yes, we are.

Mr. SOUDER. So you have been able to get Federal equipment through that?

Mr. DELGADO. We get very limited and very little equipment through them. I believe we got some night vision equipment once.

Mr. SOUDER. Have you applied on a regular basis?

Mr. DELGADO. We do talk to them.

Mr. SOUDER. Because that is the primary way we transfer technology to police departments around the country and we want to make sure in the legislation that we are doing that you are eligible. So you are eligible for that, which is the same as other departments. Are there particular programs where you think that other—it would be helpful if you could give us where you believe State and local police departments are able to apply for Federal funds in drug enforcement that you are not.

Mr. DELGADO. OK.

Mr. SOUDER. If you can talk to some individuals and maybe followup with the Tucson Police Department, the Arizona Governor's Office, could rather than actually complaining, actually give—I do not mean you, but the Governor's Office, rather than just complaining, give some specifics of how to help along the border. We certainly realize that you have one of the biggest segments of the border and that you ought, at the very least, have the same ability as everybody else to apply. It does not even make sense not to have that happen, and there probably needs to be additional efforts too. And I think your statement is helpful on that.

Can I ask you another question, on the amount of narcotics that you have seized, is most of that marijuana?

Mr. DELGADO. Yes.

Mr. SOUDER. Fifty percent?

Mr. DELGADO. Probably a little higher than that.

Mr. SOUDER. And then what is—by higher, two-thirds?

Mr. DELGADO. Probably about two-thirds.

Mr. SOUDER. And then cocaine, the next amount?

Mr. DELGADO. Yes and meth after that.

Mr. SOUDER. Is most of this coming in small back packs or are you occasionally intercepting groups, have you seen any of the mule trains that they have seen in other places?

Mr. DELGADO. All different things, we have seen mule trains in conjunction with like 8,000 pounds all the way to maybe 10 pounds, it comes in all ways, horseback. We have gotten reports of dropping it by airplane in different areas of the reservation, the airplanes come by and drop it. We got a report last week. So there are all different ways of bringing it across.

Mr. SOUDER. Chairman Manuel, you mentioned about a road. Would you support a continuation of the fence like is going through the park?

Chairman MANUEL. We looked at the one that they are proposing in Organ Pipe and believe the two districts that are adjacent to the international boundary are in discussion now and if they agree, we will support it.

Mr. SOUDER. One of the things where we have had some disagreement over in the Sierra Vista/Douglas zone, as well as on the north border, is I believe we need to be more aggressive at the border and as we gradually put the pressure at the border. But we are also going to need check stations beyond the border, merely because no matter what we do, people are going to come through and move toward the major highway areas. And I know that is controversial in those States, but there just is not any other way to do it because they will rendezvous. But the more we can catch at the border, the more difficult we make it, the better.

Now I am not an expert on this and I know it is an issue that we are going to talk about later today, but how would you see addressing a fence in the border regarding, I understand your Nation is also spread across the international boundary? Are there ways to track tribal members so that we would know who—so we would not have a formal border crossing there, but there would be a way to allow the flexibility within the tribe so we would still be able to protect American citizens? We have a similar case up in upstate New York.

Chairman MANUEL. We have three entries into the Nation from the international boundary that our members know about and they utilize it all the time for transportation for health purposes. So we are proposing that three remain open.

Mr. SOUDER. We have had a lot of discussion, less in the last year but certainly there are going to be discussions about what we need to do regarding immigration policies and guest worker policies and I know that you have proposals about citizenship questions, but at the very least, it would seem like this would be a way to do a pilot, if not citizenship, guest passes or maneuverability. Would you be able to identify who the actual members are on the Mexican side, so that they could be double-checked if they were, you know, picked up in a random mix or something, that we would know whether they are clearly a member of the Nation?

Chairman MANUEL. Yes, we have enrollment cards that our members carry and they cannot be duplicated. So that's how we know.

Mr. SOUDER. And they could be matched by name?

Chairman MANUEL. Right.

Mr. SOUDER. Because in my home State where the narcotics and illegal immigration, whether it comes through here or through Texas, back in Indiana, as we all know there are tons of places that make Social Security cards and green cards and all that kind of stuff and you cannot ask questions. So there would have to be some kind of a check thing. On the other hand, if we put a fence up, it divides a Nation, perhaps there could be flexibility on how to address that, and it would seem to me, just looking at it on the surface, that this might be a way to look at the full program to see whether in fact we can monitor proposals like guest workers and different immigration strategies that we are looking at at the Federal level.

I will yield to Mr. Shadegg for some questions.

Mr. SHADEGG. Thank you, Mr. Chairman. I want to thank both of you for excellent testimony, I appreciate it very much, I think it is very helpful.

Chairman Manuel, I want to begin by asking you about the drug issue and particularly about the impact of the drug issue on the Nation itself.

When we met over at Organ Pipe, information was provided to me about a concern of the Nation that its youth were being recruited by drug smugglers to take a part in the drug smuggling activity and being offered presumably large sums of money to do that. Is that in fact occurring and are you aware that it is a concern of the Nation?

Chairman MANUEL. Yes, it is happening. I believe the individual that was at the Organ Pipe meeting was one of the District Chairs and one of the comments that she made was that she had a daughter who has a friend and this friend had a new vehicle with sophisticated scanning and communication equipment in the vehicle and so she told her daughter not to associate because she does not have a job and to have that kind of gadgets in her vehicle. It is happening to members of the Nation, especially our young people because of the unemployment that is very high here on the Tohono O'odham Nation. So it is very lucrative when they get the money that they can get by doing that, but not realizing the consequences that they can get into when they are caught. So that is a problem.

And the person is here today if anybody wants to ask her any questions about that. We also know that there are other people that are involved.

Mr. SHADEGG. Assistant Chief Delgado, I noticed that in your prepared testimony, you mentioned that this diversion of so much of your financial resources to patrolling the border, dealing with illegal crossings, dealing with drug smuggling, dealing with other crossings that are illegal, diverts you from community policing. Are you also aware of an increasing tendency of your young people to be recruited or other damage being done here to the Nation itself and to the people of the Nation?

Mr. DELGADO. Yes. Predominantly out west, in the western part of the Nation, we have seen an increase in younger juvenile, even ages 12 and up, 14, 15, they are being recruited to be lookouts, watchouts, to watch for us, Police and Customs and other departments that are coming. We are also seeing younger drivers. There was a report that there was a kid as young as 13 years old that started running drugs at the age of 13—we have seen that.

Mr. SHADEGG. Speaking of drug runners, I presume that while some drug smuggling can occur in a backpack fashion, other smuggling occurs by vehicle crossing. Is it a concern to the Nation, and have you begun to look at how serious it would be if a vehicle barrier were built along the southern boundary of Organ Pipe, that that would drive vehicles bringing drugs across over here on the Nation?

Mr. DELGADO. Yes, it would be a great impact, just like that operation when they close down the borders in Nogales and other places creates a funnel to our Nation.

Mr. SHADEGG. Mr. Chairman, you mentioned that you have three crossings that members of the Nation use to go back and forth. I believe that when I was in Organ Pipe or Lukeville with you, there was some concern expressed that perhaps the Nation wanted to close, I do not know if it is one of those three or one of the more informal crossings, because of concern about trafficking across the border of either drugs or illegals. Is that in fact—is one of the Districts concerned about that issue?

Chairman MANUEL. The community that is I think about a mile from the border, the members were at the meeting at that time and they did propose that they close that gate, but I told them that it is really up to the District and they have to work with the District if they want to close that, because there are members that come back and forth for health purposes.

Mr. SHADEGG. Just one more question on the drug issue and then I want to move a little bit to homeland security for a moment. In terms of quantities of drugs, the statistics you have given us show a rather dramatic increase. Do you have reason to believe that increase is going to continue, and in stopping or interdicting any of the drugs, do you sometimes find drug drop points here on the Nation where drugs are brought in and then dropped and left and they could be found by members of the Nation or by youth of the Nation? Is that a concern?

Mr. DELGADO. Yes, it is. There are different ways they bring the drugs up. A lot of times, they store them at the locations and washes, in and around communities, around the houses and different areas. So we have had reports that people have found drugs and even some young people have found drugs and will call us and we will go out and pick them up. So it is a great concern.

Mr. SHADEGG. Do you get cooperation on those issues from DEA or Border Patrol or other Federal agencies?

Mr. DELGADO. Yes, we do, we work real well with Border Patrol and U.S. Customs, we all work together.

Mr. SHADEGG. In the materials that I was provided over at Organ Pipe, there was information about the issue of crossings not just by Mexican nationals, and there was this ticket that was explained. Since in part our focus here is homeland security, could one of you explain—I believe this is a ticket that showed a crossing not by a Mexican national, but rather by a individual with a Middle Eastern name. Are you seeing increase in crossing by non-Mexican nationals and can you explain to us exactly what that ticket was about and your concern on that particular issue?

Mr. DELGADO. That was an airline ticket, I believe?

Mr. SHADEGG. Yes, an airline ticket.

Mr. DELGADO. I believe it was an airline ticket that was found.

Mr. SHADEGG. I should have said this in the question—an airline ticket found last August for an individual by the name of Youssef Abdul Covare, that I believe you found just abandoned here on the reservation.

Mr. DELGADO. Yes, it was southwest of here along some of the trails where people with drugs and also illegal aliens come across. We turned it over to the FBI.

Mr. SHADEGG. And you have evidence—this is my last question and I will yield back to the chairman—you have evidence of increasing crossings by non-Mexican nationals in this area?

Mr. DELGADO. I am not sure, you may have to talk to Border Patrol.

Mr. SHADEGG. Mr. Chairman.

Chairman MANUEL. I am not aware of it, but it is a concern for homeland security purposes.

Mr. SHADEGG. Thank you. I yield back my time.

Mr. SOUDER. I wanted to followup with the chairman's testimony. You said that "The people involved in the smuggling business on our lands come from all over the United States. They are not American Indians, so we do not have legal authority to prosecute them in our courts." What happens if you apprehend someone?

Chairman MANUEL. If they are not Indians, they are turned over to Customs or the FBI.

Mr. SOUDER. And do you have—and I know we will get into this on the second panel that is going to be focused on the entire border, but this will be an opportunity to focus on the Nation in particular. Do you have agents that are close by or do they have to come from Tucson or where do they come from? If you apprehended somebody and you cannot prosecute them in your courts and you need to turn them over, what, in a practical way, happens here?

Mr. DELGADO. It just depends, because they are also overwhelmed with these same issues we are overwhelmed with on this border. So sometimes if they are close by, we have a 10 minute ETA. The other night we had something like 75 we had to house in our department and it took them approximately an hour to get here. Sometimes there's extended ETAs because like I said, they are overwhelmed. So it could be anywhere from a 5-minute to a couple hour timeframe to come and respond.

Mr. SOUDER. And it is the Border Patrol that always responds?

Mr. DELGADO. On illegal immigrants. On drugs, we work with Customs, U.S. Customs Service.

Mr. SOUDER. Does that vary whether they just come across the border or they are further in, or is it just assumed that they have come across rather recently, if they are in your Nation?

Mr. DELGADO. It is assumed they have come across very recently, depending on where we get them at. We have got them all the way as far as 40 miles up from the border, all the way up to Casa Grande area, all the way up by Silver Barrel Mine, and that could take a couple of days to get there.

Mr. SOUDER. On the south border—and pardon my ignorance on this—are there any other sovereign Indian nations along the border that have a similar problem, that you have talked with?

Chairman MANUEL. Not that we are aware of, I think we are the only one. There is only one other tribe in California that has land similar to the Nation, but I am not aware whether they face similar problems. But we do have Customs at the substation here on the Nation's land, so they are here 24 hours a day.

Mr. SOUDER. I guess we definitely need to look at even in housing, make sure there is—often in the law, we have to specify Indian Nation separate on these different things for law enforcement questions, for when we have people overnight, not to say that there is a lot of money, every single jurisdiction along every border crossing says they do not have enough to cover, but there needs to be some kind of focus.

Do you find that—you said you had 75 one night in your prison?

Mr. DELGADO. Yes.

Mr. SOUDER. Did they take them somewhere then or——

Mr. DELGADO. We housed them in our police station.

Mr. SOUDER. I mean after Border Patrol arrived, what happens?

Mr. DELGADO. They take control. I believe they brought a bus up and picked them and took them for deportation.

Mr. SOUDER. If you find narcotics and they are not part of your Nation, what jurisdiction do you have to seize narcotics?

Mr. DELGADO. Ourself and Customs works together and whether they are tribal or non-tribal members, we will seize them, we will also arrest them and present the case to the U.S. Attorney's Office for prosecution.

Mr. SOUDER. And if they are non-tribal members, do you have to wait until a Customs person arrives?

Mr. DELGADO. Yes and no. We do work with them, usually we are working hand-in-hand, so it is not a long wait for them, or we can start the case ourselves, we have our own narcotics team, and it is a two-man team that works with Customs. They have radios with Customs and I believe they are cross certified.

Mr. SOUDER. In the testimony, and we have also heard informally, about concerns that Mexican law enforcement or military have come across the border actually aiding the narcotics smugglers. Does this happen very often, is this confirmed or just the type of thing people are saying? What specificity do you have?

Mr. DELGADO. I believe it is confirmed. They show up with Mexican military or Mexican, whatever they are, but they are dressed in uniforms. We have had numerous incidences with them along the border. One of our rangers, they came up to him on our side, we just had a case about a month ago I believe it was, where we had a stolen vehicle and it went across the border. The Mexicans came across and were seen loading the dope from one side to the other side. So it does happen.

Mr. SOUDER. Pardon again my ignorance, on the Mexican side of the border, is there an organized Indian Nation and do they have lands or is it not set up exactly the same way? I am sure it is not exactly the same way, but how much of your parallel would there be and how many people are there and how intermingled?

Chairman MANUEL. We have about 90 members on the other side in Mexico, they are recognized as Mexican citizens.

Mr. SHADEGG. Mr. Chairman, I have a few followup questions. First of all, to your question about the Mexican military incursions, Chief Delgado, Chairman Manuel, when I was in Organ Pipe, we were presented this list of I believe five different incidents of Mexican military incursions that are recited by the tribe of incidents that were documented where Mexican military personnel came across. Is that an accurate list of at least some of those incidents?

Mr. DELGADO. Yes, it is.

Mr. SHADEGG. Mr. Chairman, perhaps we should put that in the record. It lists the date and the particularities surrounding the particular incursion.

I have just one other question, and Chief Delgado, you may be able to answer it. In the Arizona press, particularly in Phoenix, there has recently been very high profile coverage of incidents where INS was not able to respond or Border Patrol was not able to respond, following an apprehension; that is, a couple of incidents where EPS had apprehended large numbers of individuals, they had good evidence that they had crossed illegally. I do not believe either of the incidents involved drugs, but they were high profile incidents where INS was called and maybe Border Patrol was called, I am not sure, perhaps even some other Federal agencies were called, and in those instances the Federal agencies simply said we are too busy, we cannot respond, and the individuals were let go.

Have you had here on the Nation any incidents where you have called for Federal assistance but the Federal authorities, due to workload and other obligations elsewhere along the border have simply been unable to respond to your request for help?

Mr. DELGADO. Yes, it has happened in the past.

Mr. SHADEGG. Is that a frequent and ongoing problem? And Mr. Chairman, I know you seemed to want to respond to that as well, I will be happy to afford both of you an opportunity to respond.

Chairman MANUEL. Usually what their policy is, if it is a small amount of narcotics, they do not want to wait their time on it.

Mr. SHADEGG. I thank you very much for your testimony.

Mr. SOUDER. Let me make sure I get a couple of other questions in the record. Is the Nation participating in the High Intensity Drug Trafficking Area as part of the border HIDTA?

Mr. DELGADO. Yes.

Mr. SOUDER. You are. It is our understanding that stringent environmental regulations have hampered your ability to patrol certain areas along the border. Is that true, and do you think those questions could be resolved if we had a certain zone of possibly 2 miles in from the border that was a zone for security purposes?

Chairman MANUEL. I guess one of the reasons why we wanted the Border Patrol and Customs presence along the international boundary is because right now there is no presence because there is no road to travel back and forth along the international. Presently a lot of immigrants will come in through when a lot of the trust members are coming through, but we are also aware that some of them may still get through and we are aware that there will probably still be a need for Border Patrol in different areas of the Nation's land and I think that can be accommodated, it is not a problem. The problem right now is no protection of the international boundary.

Mr. SOUDER. On the question of environmental regulations, is part of the problem along the border, environmental regulations?

Chairman MANUEL. It is a problem because there is a concern on the environmental part because the people that come through, we do not know what they carry in backpacks or on their shoes and that is a major concern because of the damage that can create on our wildlife, on our plants, on the animals, domesticated animals, especially our cattle. And that is a major concern for our ranchers.

Mr. SOUDER. Let me pursue one other question, and I know this is a controversial question and we are going to hear from the third panel as well. One of the problems—and this is the huge dilemma because when illegal immigrants come through, it is partly because there is employment all over the United States that pays so much better, including in my home State, and we have to address the immigration question. Another is the narcotics that come through with a certain percentage of those illegal immigrants, who my guess is that in the last 2 weeks, we have had more people killed in Fort Wayne, IN with illegal narcotics that have come through the Arizona border than you have had people killed on the border. In other words, it is not a harmless matter that we have 30,000 deaths in the United States because of narcotics, 67 percent of which is coming across the U.S. and Mexican border. So it is a murder rate, related to murder rates all over the United States. We clearly have a compelling reason. We also have a huge problem with the people who themselves are often being victimized. They either are becoming dehydrated and dying or they are mugged along the borders or there is a safety question there. We have heard stories there about how Phoenix is just over the mountain, all sorts of things.

Two part question. One is some of the rescue groups have put water in to try to solve the third part of the problem, but the question is does that aggravate the problem, the second part of the problem, which is more illegals come in, more narcotics come in and therefore more people die. What is your opinion on that, particularly if it does not go through your Nation as a process. And second, are you doing or has the U.S. Government done anything in your area like is starting to be done in the park area that gives you explicit warnings—no water, rattlesnakes, you know, you are not close to Phoenix?

Chairman MANUEL. Again, we believe the solution is to intensify the surveillance along the border, that would decrease a lot of these people coming through and getting in the desert. So if we can get a lot more people along the international boundary, or some people at least along the international boundary, that would decrease a lot of the activity on the mainland of the Nation. But I think the overall issue is the border policy, that needs to be changed, because you are going to have these problems all over unless the policy is changed in some way to address this problem.

Mr. SOUDER. Is there a formal way people can come if they want to try to help address it through the Nation, to talk to you directly rather than coming and doing it independently?

Chairman MANUEL. I guess one of the problems that we are experiencing is the amount of activity that is created within ranches and if the people are not home, the people that come through help themselves to the food, even to the telephone. It is my understanding that one individual had a phone bill that came in for $500 for calls that were made to other parts of the country. That means these people came into their house at that particular time and made phone calls throughout the country.

So these are some of the things that we are hearing on a daily basis. And that is one of the reasons why our members do not agree as far as enticing, in some way enticing people to come this way because we will help them. Our members always help people who are in distress and they care for people. If they need help, they will help them, but the problem is when you have so many people coming through and some people are not home and they help themselves to whatever they need and that is a major problem.

So those are some of the concerns that they raise to me. Not only that, but also the drug problem that our kids are experiencing in the community because of drugs being available. So those are some of the concerns that we have.

Mr. SHADEGG. Mr. Chairman, I have a brief followup on that last question. We are going to get good testimony on the third panel, but Mr. Chairman, when I was at Organ Pipe with you, you explained to me much of what you said today; that is, that from a humane standpoint if you become aware of people crossing, you want to assist them, you do not want people dying on the reservation, dying of thirst or dying for lack of resources. At the same time, I was told by you and by officials of the Tribal Police Department that inducing people to cross the reservation and encouraging them to do that does not—is not consistent with tribal policies, that in fact the more people who cross, the more environmental damage there is, the more property crime there is and therefore the tribe has actively sought to work with groups who are concerned on the humanitarian side, not to encourage crossing of the reservation lands for those reasons; is that correct?

Chairman MANUEL. That is correct.

Mr. SHADEGG. And that is because you have seen property crime, drug issues and other environmental damage as a result of the volume of people who are induced to cross the border.

Chairman MANUEL. Yes.

Mr. SHADEGG. I thank you, Mr. Chairman.

Mr. SOUDER. Thank you very much for your testimony, this helps bring attention that when we address and respond to an urgent problem that is created at Organ Pipe, we have to make sure that we do not complicate your life and that the U.S. Government and people have a long time of being less than conscientious in respecting the rights of Indian people and Native American people and in this case, we have an obligation to do so and we will do what we can to help. Everybody wants more money than they get, but we will certainly do what we can. If we can target in some of the equipment programs, high intensity areas that are under particular stress, we will do so and we appreciate your willingness to sacrifice and help protect the rest of America with your tribal funds. I thank you on behalf of the people of Indiana for doing what you do.

With that, we will move to the second panel, thank you very much.

Chairman MANUEL. Thank you, Congressman.

Mr. SOUDER. If the second panel could come forward, Mr. David Aguilar, Mr. Dom Ciccone, Mr. William Wellman, Mr. Hugh Winderweedle, Mr. James Woolley. And if the Chief of Aviation Operations for Customs, Mr. Dennis Lindsay, could come up as well, I need to swear you in at the same time because I am going to have some questions although you do not have testimony.

If you will remain standing, if you could each raise your right hand.

[Witnesses sworn.]

Mr. SOUDER. Let the record show that each of the witnesses have answered in the affirmative.

OK, Mr. Aguilar, good to see you again. Go forward with your testimony.

STATEMENTS OF DAVID AGUILAR, CHIEF PATROL AGENT, TUCSON SECTOR, U.S. BORDER PATROL; DOM CICCONE, REGIONAL CHIEF, NATIONAL WILDLIFE REFUGE SYSTEM, REGION 2, U.S. FISH AND WILDLIFE SERVICE; WILLIAM WELLMAN, PARK SUPERVISOR, ORGAN PIPE CACTUS NATIONAL MONUMENT, NATIONAL PARK SERVICE; HUGH WINDERWEEDLE, PORT DIRECTOR, LUKEVILLE PORT OF ENTRY, U.S. CUSTOMS SERVICE; AND JAMES WOOLLEY, ASSISTANT SPECIAL AGENT IN CHARGE, TUCSON DIVISION OFFICE, DRUG ENFORCEMENT AGENCY

Mr. AGUILAR. Thank you and good morning, Mr. Chairman, committee members, welcome back to Arizona.

Mr. Chairman, and distinguished committee members, I am pleased to appear before you today to talk about the Tucson Border Patrol sector's initiatives to secure the border here in Arizona. My name again is David Aguilar and I am the Chief Patrol Agent for the Tucson sector of the recently established Bureau of Customs and Border Protection [BCBP], at the Department of Homeland Security.

First I would like to thank you and your colleagues for providing BCBP and the Border Patrol with the support, funding and resources required to bring better control and increased security to our Nation's borders. The challenges we face are significant, but we are confident that the creation of the Department of Homeland Security and including the Border Patrol in the new agency will help us to use those resources more effectively to secure our borders and protect the homeland.

In 1994, the U.S. Border Patrol developed a strategy to deter illegal immigration, the principal goal of which is to bring the border areas with the highest level of illegal activity under manageable control incrementally and effectively.

Forward deployment of resources is the key to our success in implementing this strategy, which we have now named Operation Safeguard in the Tucson sector.

The Tucson sector covers 261 miles of Arizona's border with Mexico. We have eight Border Patrol stations in four counties in southern Arizona and 1,701 Border Patrol Agents who cover the main Arizona corridors—Nogales, Douglas/Naco and the West Desert corridor.

Smuggling organizations exploit border communities in the Tucson sector as primary staging areas and transportation hubs to move their illicit cargo, including illegal drugs and unlawful migrants. To counter their activities we employ an operational philosophy that can best be described with three terms—gain, maintain and expand.

In the gain stage, we deploy resources to areas of highest activity to establish a foundation of operations and gain control. We then maintain the integrity of the controlled area by leaving sufficient resources in place as we then expand our focus outward from populated areas and highways leading away from the border.

This approach flushes criminal elements out of their comfort zones and away from areas most easily and profitably exploited.

The Tucson sector's operational response to illegal entries in more remote areas combines uniformed line presence, mobile interdiction, Special Response Team operations, Border Patrol Search, Trauma and Rescue Teams and Anti-Smuggling and Disrupt Unit operations. These agents and units respond to intelligence and reports from other law enforcement agencies and citizens in those areas.

The key asset in the Border Patrol's Operation Safeguard is the Border Patrol agents themselves. I am extremely proud of these men and women for their diligent efforts, commitment and professionalism in implementing the safeguard strategy. Their efforts continue to make a positive difference in the Arizona communities we serve.

Our agents' efficiencies and effectiveness are directly proportional to supporting enforcement infrastructure. The Tucson sector applies a mix of resources to support Operation Safeguard including surveillance technology, all terrain vehicles, horse patrols, vehicle barriers and other equipment. In addition, we have developed and applied deterrence technology in support of primary line teams and maintain deterrence in more active areas with fewer personnel.

Operation Safeguard was initially implemented in Nogales, AZ in December 1998 and the results have been dramatic. By February 28, 2003, reported attempted illegal entries were down in the area by 72 percent and local arrests have decreased by 70 percent.

We have also achieved substantial enforcement gains along the border in Cochise County in the Douglas/Naco corridor. Incremental operational expansion since late 1999 has brought manageable control to a large part of this corridor's border area. This was achieved with an aggressive and sustained forward deployment of personnel and the strategic use of force-multiplying deterrence equipment and technology.

Recorded attempted entries in the Douglas/Naco corridor through the first 5 months of fiscal year 2003 were 103,000 down 74 percent from the 397,576 recorded during the same timeframe in fiscal year 2000, which was the peak year for the corridor. Arrests in that corridor are currently at an 8-year low.

The West Desert corridor is Tucson sector's largest corridor and remains our greatest challenge. It includes 120 linear miles of border with Mexico, and compares in size in its entirety to Rhode Island, Connecticut and New Jersey combined.

The sheer magnitude of the corridor's terrain, insufficient road access and lack of deterrence technology and infrastructure, lead to illegal incursions that degrade environmentally and culturally sensitive lands. Increases we have seen in drug and immigrant smuggling in this corridor highlight our successes in the Douglas/Naco and Nogales corridors, but also indicate that great challenges lie ahead in the West Desert corridor in the future.

The best way to meet these challenges and establish deterrence in the West Desert corridor will be to create a certainty of detection and interdiction. To do this, we have adjusted our operations and redeployed assets and are working more closely with Mexican and

Tohono O'odham Nation counterparts and are enhancing our air surveillance operations.

Taken in combination, these steps should help us to gain the foothold we need to establish better control over the West Desert corridor.

We can safely say that the U.S. Border Patrol has achieved a number of successes in the Tucson sector, but that much work remains to be done. I am confident that with the necessary resources and the continued support of the Congress, our State, local and Federal partners, we will continue to expand manageable control of the border and enhance homeland security in Arizona.

Overall, Operation Safeguard has netted significant operational gains in the Tucson sector. We have achieved a reduction in arrests of 52 percent since 2000 and with the exception of a drop in activity immediately following the events of September 11, 2001, arrests in the entire Tucson sector are at an 8-year low.

I thank you for the opportunity to present this testimony and I look forward to answering any questions that you might have.

[The prepared statement of Mr. Aguilar follows:]

Statement of

David Aguilar
Chief Patrol Agent, Tucson Border Patrol Sector

Bureau of Customs and Border Protection

Before the

COMMITTEE ON GOVERNMENT REFORM
SUBCOMMITTEE ON CRIMINAL JUSTICE, DRUG POLICY, AND HUMAN RESOURCES
U.S. HOUSE OF REPRESENTATIVES

Regarding

Impact of Drug Trade, Status of Law Enforcement Along the Arizona/Mexico Border, and Ways to Improve Security

March 10, 2003
10:00 a.m. Sells, Arizona

Mr. Chairman, distinguished committee members, I am pleased to have the opportunity to appear before the Subcommittee today to speak to you about the Tucson Border Patrol Sector's operations and law enforcement initiatives to secure the U.S. border here in Arizona. My name is David Aguilar, and I am the Chief Patrol Agent for the Tucson Border Patrol Sector of the recently established Bureau of Customs and Border Protection, or "BCBP,"at the Department of Homeland Security.

I would like to begin by thanking you and your colleagues for providing the Bureau of Customs and Border Protection and specifically, the Border Patrol, with the support, funding and resources required to bring better control and increased security to our nation's borders. The challenges we face are significant, but we are confident that the creation of the Department of Homeland Security and the inclusion of the Border Patrol in this new agency will help us to utilize those resources more effectively to secure our borders and protect the homeland.

In 1994, the United States Border Patrol developed a strategy to deter illegal immigration into the country. The principal goal of this strategy was, and still is to bring the border areas with the highest level of illegal activity under manageable control incrementally and effectively. This strategy is designed to be flexible and have both enforcement and deterrence benefits.

The application of Border Patrol resources in a systematic, focused and effective manner is essential to the success of this national strategy. Forward deployment of resources in the Tucson Sector is a crucial element in the success of our efforts in Arizona to take away smugglers' means and motivation to use the geography and available routes of egress from the Southwest Border.

The Tucson Sector's area of responsibility covers 261 miles of Arizona's border with Mexico. We have eight (8) border patrol stations within 4 counties in the southern area of the state, and host a force of 1,701 Border Patrol Agent positions. We have divided the state of Arizona into three main corridors, the Nogales Corridor, the Douglas/Naco Corridor, and the West Desert Corridor.

Smuggling organizations exploit Southwest Border communities in the Tucson Sector as primary staging areas and transportation hubs for their movements of illicit cargo, including illegal narcotics and unlawful migrants. These organizations specifically target larger population centers with existing infrastructure and transportation capabilities -- on the Mexico side, these include the Cities of Nogales, Sonora and Agua Prieta, Sonora. On the U.S. side, these include the Cities of Nogales and Douglas, AZ.

The Tucson Sector's piece of the Border Patrol's national deterrence strategy has been named *Operation Safeguard.* I would describe our operational philosophy for *Safeguard* in three basic terms: Gain, Maintain, and Expand. In the "gain" stage, we deploy resources to the areas of highest activity in order to establish a foundation of operations and gain control. Once control of an area is gained, we "maintain" the integrity of the controlled area by ensuring that sufficient resources are left in place as we continue to redeploy and expand our area of focus. The next critical element in this deterrence-based operational approach is our ability to "expand" outward from populated areas and away from highways leading out of the border areas.

The expansion of primary deterrence assets on the immediate border, reinforced by operations that support our initial "gain and maintain" efforts, is what deters smugglers from exploiting border communities in Arizona as staging and transportation hubs. By taking this approach, we flush the criminal elements out of their comfort zones and away from areas most easily and profitably exploited

The Tucson Sector's operational response to address illegal entries in more remote and rural areas is a combination of uniformed line-presence, mobile interdiction, Special Response Team operations, Border Patrol Search, Trauma, and Rescue (BORSTAR) Teams Anti-Smuggling and Disrupt Unit operations. These agents and operational units concentrate on responding to intelligence and reports of illegal traffic and smugglers from other law enforcement agencies and citizens in those areas

The key asset in the Border Patrol's *Operation Safeguard* is the Border Patrol agents themselves. I am extremely proud of the men and women of the Tucson Sector for their diligent efforts, commitment and professionalism in implementing the Tucson Sector's strategy in *Safeguard.* It is their efforts that continue to make a positive difference in the Arizona communities that we serve.

While, operations are founded on the presence and operational response capabilities of our agents, their capabilities, functionality, efficiency, and effectiveness are directly proportional to the supporting enforcement infrastructure they receive. The Tucson Sector currently has a mix of resources that we apply in support of *Operation Safeguard.* Technology, including Remote Video Surveillance Camera Systems (RVS), Integrated Surveillance Intelligence Systems (ISIS), Long Range Operations Infra-Red System (LORIS) scopes, night vision goggles, sensors, all terrain vehicles (ATV's), horse patrols, vehicle barriers and other equipment complement and enhance agent capabilities and serve as force-multipliers. In addition, the Tucson Sector has aggressively engaged in developing and applying what we refer to as "Deterrence Technology." This technology is deployed in close support of our primary line teams and has permitted us to maintain deterrence in some of the more historically active areas, with fewer personnel.

The Nogales Corridor

The Tucson Sector's current strategy, *Operation Safeguard*, was initially implemented in Nogales, Arizona in December of 1998, and the results have been dramatic. By February 28, FY 2003, recorded attempted illegal entries were down in the area by 72%, compared to February of 1999 (the peak year for NGL). Arrests have decreased by 70% during the same timeframe. These are just a couple of measures of the significant increase in our overall effectiveness since the initiation of *Safeguard*.

Crime in the City of Nogales has declined 38% since 1999,. The Santa Cruz County Attorney reports that illegal aliens currently account for only 10% of felony crimes prosecuted in the county, compared to the estimated 75% of felony crimes prosecuted in the county prior to Operation Safeguard. Arrests in the Nogales Corridor are currently at a 9-year low.

The Douglas/Naco corridor

Since the implementation of Operation Safeguard, the Tucson Sector has also achieved substantial enforcement gains along the border in Cochise County. Incremental operational expansion since late 1999 in this area has brought manageable control to a large part of the county's border area. This was achieved with an aggressive and sustained forward deployment of personnel, and the strategic use of force-multiplying deterrence equipment and technology.

Recorded attempted entries in the Douglas/Naco Corridor through the first five months of FY03, were 103,046, down 74% from the 397,576 recorded during the same timeframe in FY00 (the peak year for the corridor). Arrests are currently at an 8-year low.

The West Desert Corridor

The West Desert Corridor is Tucson Sector's largest corridor and our greatest operational challenge. It is comprised of the Tucson, Casa Grande and Ajo Station areas of responsibility. It includes 120 linear miles of border with Mexico, extending west to the Yuma County line. It is comparable in size to the states of Rhode Island, Connecticut and New Jersey combined

The sheer magnitude of terrain in the West Desert Corridor, insufficient road access, an absence of deterrence technology, and a lack of infrastructure along the U.S./Mexico border lead to illegal incursions into and degradation of environmentally and culturally sensitive lands in this corridor. During the first five months of FY03, Border Patrol seizures of marijuana increased by 14% over FY 2002, to 62,271 pounds, and arrests of illegal aliens increased by 31%, to 29, 217. These increases are positive in the respect that they highlight our successes in driving illegal activity from some of the more populated and developed areas, but they are indicative of some of the challenges faced by Border Patrol agents and the Bureau of Customs and Border Protection in the West Desert Corridor.

I believe that the most viable enforcement approach to establishing deterrence in the West Desert Corridor will be to create a certainty of detection and interdiction. In order to do this, we have undertaken a number of operational adjustments and redeployments of Border Patrol assets, including the following:

- Agents from other sectors have been temporarily assigned to the West Desert Corridor.
- Sector Disrupt Unit operations, which target smugglers' staging areas and smuggling routes, have been directed to the West Desert Corridor.
- Special Response Team tactical operations in the West Desert Corridor have been initiated and will continue through FY03.
- The Sector Mexican Liaison Unit will continue to focus liaison efforts on the Mexican military and law enforcement presence south of the West Desert Corridor.
- A Sector Tow Initiative for identifying smugglers and vehicles operating in the West Desert Corridor was formalized in FY03.
- Close coordination with the Tohono O'odham Police Department in several aspects of law enforcement -- ranging from search and rescue, intelligence sharing, smuggling investigations, to scheduling -- and the establishment of a multi-use Remote Processing Facility on the Tohono O'odham Nation, have served to heighten deterrence and efficiency.
- Operation Skywatch, which will enhance air surveillance and tactical response to the West Desert Corridor during the summer months, is scheduled to commence in May of 2003.
- Joint operations with Yuma Sector, Ajo and Casa Grande Stations to conduct simultaneous "Camp" Details – in other words, maintaining continuous law

enforcement presence in high-trafficked areas difficult to access by regular patrols -- are scheduled to begin in March of 2003.

Taken in combination, these steps should enable us to gain the foothold we need to establish better control over the West Desert Corridor. The effort will need to be sustained and adequately resourced, but it is a worthwhile undertaking of which I will be proud to be a part.

To conclude, we can safely say that the United States Border Patrol has achieved successes in San Diego, California, El Paso and McAllen, Texas, and I would now include the Nogales Corridor and a majority of the Douglas/Naco Corridor among these positive achievements. Overall, *Operation Safeguard* has netted significant operational gains in the Tucson Sector – we've achieved a reduction in arrests of 52% since 2000, and with the exception of a drop in activity immediately following the events of September 11, 2001, arrests in the Tucson Sector are at an eight-year low.

Despite these successes, great operational challenges still remain and we have much work to do. But, I am confident that with provision of necessary resources and the continued support of the Congress and our partners in the surrounding communities, we will continue to enhance border security in Arizona as we expand manageable control of the border.

I thank the Subcommittee for the opportunity to present this testimony and I would be pleased to respond to any questions that the Subcommittee may have at this time.

Mr. SOUDER. I thank you. And let me just say here because it is not going to come up during the questions, that in our organization meeting in Civil Service, it is one of our priorities this year to do the law enforcement part to the Border Patrol, which has been neglected for so long, but we are committed to trying to get that done legislatively as soon as possible and also I believe and we hope, working with Secretary Ridge, that we can deal with some of the pay inequities. We had been dealing with it appropriations last year and it was blocked in the authorizing, but I think now we might have more luck appropriating it and authorizing it. Obviously the budget is tight, but we have had severe problems with the additional recruitment in the Border Patrol when so many agents are applying to much better paying jobs at TSA and other places, and it is unrealistic for the American people to think and demand out of Congress that we are going to be able to maintain our borders when it is difficult to maintain the men and women of the Border Patrol because they are treated inequitably in the pay system. And we are trying to address that question.

Mr. AGUILAR. Thank you, sir. On behalf of the men and women of the Border Patrol, thank you.

Mr. SOUDER. I am not sure who is next—Mr. Dom Ciccone. Did I say your last name correctly?

Mr. CICCONE. Ciccone [pronouncing].

Mr. SOUDER. Ciccone, OK, I'll make sure I get it. Thank you.

Mr. CICCONE. Mr. Chairman, thank you for the opportunity to discuss our agency's current efforts to protect the visiting public, natural resources and staff on national wildlife refuges located along the Arizona/Mexico border. I am Dom Ciccone, Regional Chief, National Wildlife Refuge System for the Southwest Region of the U.S. Fish and Wildlife Service. With me today are the three refuge Managers of the refuges along the Arizona border. Mr. Roger DiRosa supervises the Cabeza Prieta National Wildlife Refuge, Mr. Wayne Shifflett is the manager of the Buenos Aires National Wildlife Refuge and Mr. Bill Radke manages both the San Bernadino and Leslie Canyon National Wildlife Refuges.

The Fish and Wildlife Service is experiencing significant and lasting environmental damage caused by smuggling and illegal immigration across refuge lands throughout the southwest. Illegal activities pose a serious threat to the safety of refuge employees, volunteers, the public and our law enforcement officers. As enforcement efforts are increased around populated areas and ports of entry, there has been a dramatic shift in smuggling and undocumented alien crossings onto remote lands. Correspondingly, the amount of illegal drugs smuggled across refuges and other Department of Interior lands has skyrocketed in recent years, as has illegal immigration.

The Service has 21 refuge officers along the southwest border to cover over 1 million acres and 153 miles of border from California to Texas. Clearly, we have limited staff resources to conduct a very difficult and dangerous job. Refuge officers are routinely involved with drug and undocumented alien interdiction through their normal patrol activities. Only through effective coordination with other agencies are we able to meet officer safety requirements. Unfortunately, resource damage continues to be a huge problem and the ability to achieve our agency conservation mission is severely compromised. We are also being forced to restrict public use programs along the border due to safety concerns and access issues.

The Service has identified a need for an additional 33 refuge officers on the border.

Ongoing drug seizures and undocumented alien apprehensions on refuges in the southwest underscore the need to increase our level of preparedness along the U.S./Mexico border. At the end of 2002, over 100,000 pounds of marijuana, 508 pounds of cocaine and 22 pounds of methamphetamine were seized as they passed through border refuges. In addition, 100 vehicles were recovered, which was an increase of over 300 percent from 2001. The number of undocumented aliens apprehended increased 400 percent from 2001, totaling 86,000 in refuges in Arizona and Texas alone. In fact, Mr. Chairman, only a week ago, refuge officers assisted U.S. Customs and Bureau of Land Management officers in the seizure of drugs and transport vehicles that had traveled across the Cabeza Prieta National Wildlife Refuge and into the Air Force's Barry Goldwater Range. A total of 6,340 pounds of marijuana and three vehicles were seized. The drivers and occupants fled and were not apprehended; however, left in the vehicles were pouches for night vision goggles and radios for monitoring law enforcement transmissions.

Impacts on natural resources are also troubling. Hundreds of new trails and roads have been created in crossings on refuge lands. This proliferation of trails and roads damages and destroys cactus and other sensitive vegetation, disturbs wildlife and causes soil compaction and erosion. At Cabeza Prieta Refuge, sensors placed by the U.S. Border Patrol on known routes recorded 4,000 to 6,000 undocumented alien crossings per month during the busy migrating months of April, May and June. Between 20 and 30 abandoned vehicles litter the refuge at any given time. During 2001, the Border Patrol apprehended more than 400 undocumented aliens each month on the Buenos Aires Refuge. This trend accelerated in 2002 as other traditional crossings became less attractive due to increased security. At Buenos Aires, there have been 25 burglaries of staff residences over the past few years.

In a 5-year period on San Bernadino and Leslie Canyon National Wildlife Refuges, there have been 37 human-caused wildfires attributed to undocumented alien crossings.

In summary, even though we have increased the deployment of our available law enforcement resources along the southwest border, we are struggling to meet our obligations regarding public safety and resource protection. Like many other agencies, the Service will have to use available resources more efficiently to improve our law enforcement program. Reviewing and managing our priorities, identifying problems and seeking out creative solutions that involve neighbors and partners will go a long way to protecting our refuges.

Mr. Chairman, this concludes my statement, I would be happy to answer any questions that you and other members of the subcommittee have on the issue. Thank you.

Mr. SOUDER. Thank you very much for coming over today, and also bringing the different refuge managers. We know it is a tremendous threat to the resources and I look forward to asking some additional questions.

Mr. William Wellman. Bill, thank you for hosting us and touring much of the park yesterday, it was very informative and we learned a lot about the park as well as about your particular challenges along the border.

[The prepared statement of Mr. Ciccone follows:]

TESTIMONY OF DOM CICCONE, REGIONAL CHIEF OF THE NATIONAL WILDLIFE REFUGE SYSTEM, SOUTHWEST REGION, U.S. FISH AND WILDLIFE SERVICE, DEPARTMENT OF THE INTERIOR, BEFORE THE U.S. HOUSE OF REPRESENTATIVES SUBCOMMITTEE ON CRIMINAL JUSTICE, DRUG POLICY, AND HUMAN RESOURCES OF THE COMMITTEE ON GOVERNMENT REFORM, REGARDING THE IMPACT OF DRUG TRADE AND THE STATUS OF LAW ENFORCEMENT ALONG THE ARIZONA/MEXICO BORDER

March 10, 2003

Mr. Chairman, and members of the subcommittee, thank you for the opportunity to discuss our agency's current efforts to protect the visiting public, natural resources, and staff on the National Wildlife Refuges located along the Arizona/Mexico border. I am Dom Ciccone, the Regional Chief of the National Wildlife Refuge System for the Southwest Region of the U.S. Fish and Wildlife Service. With me are the three Refuge Managers who supervise National Wildlife Refuges along the Arizona/Mexico border. Mr. Roger DiRosa manages the Cabeza Prieta National Wildlife Refuge. Mr. Wayne Shifflett is the manager at the Buenos Aires National Wildlife Refuge, and Mr. Bill Radke is the Refuge Manager for the San Bernardino and Leslie Canyon National Wildlife Refuges. Although today's hearing is meant to focus on southern Arizona, we would like to take this opportunity to also relay information about our National Wildlife Refuges in California and Texas, which face similar issues.

Although the U.S. Fish and Wildlife Service has a variety of law enforcement responsibilities within National Wildlife Refuges, it is not the Federal agency responsible for international border security. Nevertheless, the natural resources that the Service are responsible for are experiencing significant and lasting damage from smuggling activities and illegal immigration across refuge lands throughout the Southwest. In addition, these illegal activities pose a serious threat to the safety of volunteers, the public, refuge employees and to our law enforcement officers. As enforcement efforts by the Department of Homeland Security's Bureau of Customs and Border Protection (BCBP) have increased around populated areas and ports of entry, there has been a dramatic shift in smuggling and illegal immigration crossings through more remote public lands along the border. Similarly, the amount of illegal drugs smuggled across refuges and other Department of the Interior (DOI) lands has increased in recent years. In fact, more than 100,000 pounds of marijuana were seized on refuge lands last year along the Southwest border. Illegal immigration across these same refuges has skyrocketed, with more than 86,000 illegal immigrants being apprehended in 2002 on our National Wildlife Refuges in Arizona and Texas alone.

In response to these problems, DOI is in the process of developing "The Southwest Border Strategy." This initiative will be designed to protect DOI visitors and employees from increasing levels of violent crimes and minimize natural resource damage caused by smuggling and illegal immigration.

In a recent report to Congress entitled, "A Report to the House of Representatives Committee on Appropriations on Impacts Caused by Undocumented Aliens Crossing Federal Lands in Southeast Arizona," which was prepared by DOI field station managers, the needs and concerns of the border refuges in southeast Arizona were specifically outlined. Similarly, managers on other refuges in Arizona, Texas, and California have also documented their requirements for border protection. Much of this information has been developed in response to requests for information related to Homeland Security and the National Drug Control Policy related law enforcement initiatives. Many of these needs and concerns center around the limited amount of resources that are available to the small number of law enforcement personnel responsible for refuges along our country's borders.

Current U.S. Fish and Wildlife Service Law Enforcement Efforts on the Southwest Border:

The Service currently employs 21 Refuge Officers along the Southwest Border at eight different National Wildlife Refuges in California, Arizona, and Texas. These refuges total over one million acres in size and have 153 miles of contiguous border with Mexico. The refuges along the border in Arizona account for the vast majority of this acreage, and share 63 miles of the border with Mexico. Clearly, we have limited staff resources available to conduct a very difficult and dangerous job within these areas. Refuge Officers are routinely involved with drug and undocumented alien interdiction through their normal patrol activities. Through effective coordination with other agencies we are able to meet officer safety requirements. Unfortunately, natural resource damage continues to be a significant problem and the ability to achieve our agency conservation mission has been severely compromised.

In addition, we are also being forced to restrict public use programs along the border due to safety concerns and access issues.

Also due to safety concerns, the Service recently eliminated scheduled solo patrols after nightfall. This alleviated some of our concern about officer safety when on patrol alone at night, but the consequence is that the overall number of patrols has now decreased.

The Service also employs Special Agents who support drug interdiction and eradication efforts on and off lands managed by the agency. They assist with illegal alien interdiction on DOI properties; assist Refuge Officers, participate in interagency enforcement task forces; and assist the Department of Homeland Security's Bureau of Immigration and Customs Enforcement (BICE) with smuggling cases. They routinely work on refuges and other DOI properties. In one recent case, a Service Special Agent rescued three Mexican citizens stranded in a remote region of Arizona. They were near death when discovered and would have died had they not been found. Currently, the

Service has one Wildlife Inspector stationed in Arizona and four Special Agents located in southern Arizona.

In addition to our law enforcement officers, we have refuge biologists and recreation specialists who conduct daily field activities on border refuges. We are concerned for their safety. On Cabeza Prieta refuge for example, our non-law enforcement personnel often conduct field work for extended periods of time in remote areas, which often involves camping in the field overnight. Cabeza's size and ruggedness negates the possibility that they can commute back and forth daily to their surveying sites. Additionally, our employees often have limited radio contact after business hours. We currently have a contract in place with the Bureau of Land Management to utilize their dispatch center for extended hours coverage, but this system still leaves many areas without service. We are currently discussing the possibility of extending our radio coverage by utilizing the Ajo Border Patrol Station and Organ Pipe National Park's radio network infrastructure.

The Service currently expends approximately $2 million of Refuge Operations funding to support the 21 Refuge Officers along the Southwest border. Thus far, additional funding in the amount of $24,000 has been provided each year by the Southwest Border High Intensity Drug Trafficking Area (HIDTA) Arizona Partnership for the payment of overtime costs for officers involved in drug and undocumented alien interdiction efforts on Arizona Refuges. Acquisition of HIDTA funding for overtime costs of $30,000 annually for officers at the Lower Rio Grande Valley National Wildlife Refuge in Texas is in progress.

The mission of the Southwest Border HIDTA Arizona Partnership is to facilitate federal, state and local multi-agency task forces and other partnerships to increase the safety of Arizona's citizens, by substantially reducing drug trafficking and money laundering, thereby reducing drug-related crime and violence. In 2002 the HIDTA program spent $47 million along the border area on task forces and coordination projects. This included $11 million in Arizona and California and $8 million in New Mexico, western Texas, and southern Texas.

In FY 2001, the Southwest Region received a one-time allocation of $1.3 million for law enforcement efforts. Of that total, $632,000 was spent on law enforcement enhancement and equipment projects specifically on the Southwest Border refuges.

Drug and Undocumented Alien Interdiction:

Ongoing drug seizures and undocumented alien apprehensions on refuges in the Southwest underscores the need to increase our level of preparedness along the US/Mexico border.

The following highlights some of the key statistics for 2002: At the end of calendar year 2002, over 100,000 pounds of marijuana, 508 pounds of cocaine and 22 pounds of methamphetamines were seized as they passed through border refuges. Additionally, there were 100 vehicles seized, abandoned, or recovered (an increase of over 300 percent from 2001). The number of undocumented aliens apprehended included 86,296 individuals (an increase of over 400 percent from 2001). Fortunately, there were only four known fatalities among border crosses in 2002, down from 14 in 2001.

During 2001 for example, the U.S. Border Patrol apprehended more than 400 undocumented Aliens each month on Buenos Aires National Wildlife Refuge. This trend accelerated during 2002 as other traditional crossings became less attractive due to increased security.

Examples of drug seizures on refuges are numerous. I would like to take this opportunity to outline a couple of the more significant seizures:

1) Texas: On April 4, 2002, U.S. Border Patrol Agents, in cooperation with the Lower Rio Grande Valley National Wildlife Refuge, were observing traffic on the refuge and noticed a truck and a sedan driving back and forth through the same area, which is consistent of narcotics smugglers. Agents set up surveillance about a 1/4 mile up-river from the Los Ebanos Port of Entry on the Lower Rio Grande Valley National Wildlife Refuge. Agents observed a white extended cab truck running with its lights off. The truck was found at a residence. The home owner flagged agents down to tell them that the truck had just driven in. The bed of the truck revealed 1,024 pounds of marijuana and a black duffel bag in the cab contained 34 pounds of cocaine.

2) Arizona: At San Bernardino National Wildlife Refuge, a special joint operation with the U.S. Customs during January 2002 resulted in the seizure of 1,960 pounds of marijuana, one transport vehicle, and five individuals arrested. Refuge Officer Drew Cyprian from Buenos Aires National Wildlife Refuge represented the Service on the operation.

3) Arizona: In May of 2002, at Cabeza Prieta National Wildlife Refuge, Officer Lyle Williams located and apprehended two drug smugglers with 936 pounds of marijuana. The U.S. Border Patrol assisted.

- These are just a few examples of our success in this area. It also highlights what our Refuge Officers and other agency personnel are up against on a daily basis. Unfortunately, there are many other smugglers that are not apprehended. These individuals continue to pose a serious threat to Refuge Officers, staff and visitors on our border refuges.

- As you can see, the trend for drug seizures and alien apprehensions has increased significantly. This is most likely a reflection of the Border Patrol's efforts in the urban areas to restrict the flow of aliens and drugs with increased officer presence and the construction of physical barriers. This forces illegal border crossings to federally managed refuges, parks, and private lands, which are remote and much more easily entered.

Impacts on Natural Resources and Government Property:

- The impacts on natural resources are just as troubling. At Cabeza Prieta National Wildlife Refuge the foot traffic on lands that have been set aside for wildlife is disruptive to the vegetation and the animals, including endangered species such as the Sonoran pronghorn. Sensors placed on known crossing routes by the U.S. Border Patrol record 4,000 to 6,000 illegal crossings per month during the busy migrating months of April, May and June. As the sensors only record at discrete points, the actual numbers of undocumented aliens passing through our wilderness is much greater. We estimate that between 20 and 30 abandoned vehicles litter the refuge at any given time, although the staff attempts to remove them as quickly as possible.

- Literally hundreds of new trails and roads have been created from illegal immigrants crossing through refuge lands. This proliferation of trails and roads damages and destroys cactus and other sensitive vegetation, disrupts re-vegetation efforts, disturbs wildlife and their habitat, and causes soil compaction and erosion.

- Within many refuges on the border, the International Border fence is torn down on a daily basis and in many areas no longer exists. This has lead to habitat destruction on refuges resulting from cattle, which come up from Mexico and trample the vegetation set aside for wildlife.

- In a five year period on San Bernardino and Leslie Canyon National Wildlife Refuges, there have been 37 human-caused wildfires presumably initiated by undocumented aliens crossing through these refuges.

- Refuge vehicles and other government property have also been vandalized. At Buenos Aires refuge, there have been 25 cases of burglary within the past few years at refuge houses where staff and volunteers live.

Cross-Agency Law Enforcement Initiatives:

- In an effort to best utilize law enforcement resources and ensure officer safety, several joint operation initiatives, Memorandums of Understanding (MOUs), and multi-agency agreements have been formed. Due to the remote locations in which they work, Refuge Officers must rely on other agencies' law enforcement resources for safety and assistance. One way to ensure better officer safety is to use joint operations to accomplish our mission of protecting the natural resources found on refuges.

- Agents from the Department of Homeland Security's BCBP and BICE routinely patrol and operate on refuge lands, as authorized by law. They work very closely with Refuge Officers whom they rely on for backup, support, and assistance. In turn, Refuge Officers rely on these agents for similar assistance, because they are generally the closest and most reliable source of help. The Service will continue to look for ways to forge cross-agency law enforcement initiatives in cooperation with the new Department of Homeland Security.

- An example of inter-agency cooperation is evident in a recent operation completed at Santa Ana Refuge in Texas during August, 2002. In concert with the U.S. Border Patrol, the Hidalgo County Sheriff's Department and the Lower Rio Grande Valley Refuge cooperated in detecting and interdicting criminal activity on the refuge. The officers conducted patrols and surveillance over a three day period which resulted in the apprehension of 17 undocumented aliens and two smugglers. From the statements of one of the smugglers apprehended, it was obvious that our remote public lands are routinely targeted for smuggling operations.

- The Refuge Managers from all border refuges in Arizona are actively participating in the Borderland Management Task Force, which includes representatives from the Service, Bureau of Indian Affairs, Bureau of Land Management, National Park Service, Department of the Interior, U.S. Forest Service, the Department of Homeland Security's BCBP, Luke Air Force Base, Arizona Game and Fish Department, BLM's Resources Advisory Council, and elected officials. The purpose of this task force is to proactively address issues related to drug smuggling and undocumented alien traffic along the border. The most recent meeting of the Task Force held on February 6, 2003, in Tucson, Arizona, addressed the following topics: employee and visitor safety; U.S. Border Patrol/Southwest Border Strategy MOU; a coordinated plan for Arizona and New Mexico; trespass livestock; and reduction of immigrant deaths.

Additional Personnel and Equipment Needs:

- In the previously mentioned Reports to Congress, the Service has identified a need for an additional 33 Refuge Officers on border refuges. The Service is currently embarking on a formal Law Enforcement Assessment and Deployment Needs Analysis which should be in place by 2004. This analysis will tell us how many officers we need and where we need to deploy them.

- To help address these law enforcement needs on refuges, the President's FY 2004 budget request includes an increase of $25.5 million for the National Wildlife Refuge System, $1.6 million of which has been specifically designated for law enforcement. The President's 2004 budget requests this funding to allow the refuge system law enforcement program to accelerate compliance with the Interior Secretary's directive to implement law enforcement reforms throughout the Department.

For example, to improve our capability to perform quality law enforcement, the Service will use the additional funding it receives to implement recommendations from the Secretary's Law Enforcement Review Panel Report and the International Association of Chiefs of Police Report, both of which call for the development and implementation of a Zone System and a Field Training and Evaluation Program (FTEP) for the refuge system law enforcement program. The mission of the FTEP will be to provide highly trained, fully functional, and positively motivated law enforcement officers on every refuge complex. The purpose of the Zone System is to centralize the law enforcement program in order to streamline operations, institute accountability and oversight, enhance training and evaluation, achieve the goals of the refuge system, and to promote refuge law enforcement as a national asset, not just a local event or necessity. The Zone System will be initiated in FY 2003, and be integrated with FTEP to provide a comprehensive law enforcement program by FY 2004.

In summary, we have increased the deployment of our available law enforcement resources along the Southwest Border, and are working to meet our obligations regarding public safety and resource protection. We have a statutory responsibility to protect these refuges for their wildlife resource values and for their use by future generations of Americans. An effective law enforcement program is a critical element in accomplishing that mission. We also have an obligation to work with sister agencies at all levels to support their missions and legal responsibilities. Like many other agencies, the Service will have to use available resources more efficiently to improve our law enforcement program. Reviewing and managing our priorities - both human resources and natural and cultural resources - identifying problems and seeking out creative solutions that involve neighbors and partners will go a long way in protecting national wildlife refuges.

Mr. Chairman, this concludes my statement on law enforcement on the border and cross-agency law enforcement initiatives. I would be happy to answer any questions you or the other members of the Subcommittee might have on these issues.

Mr. WELLMAN. Mr. Chairman, thank you for this opportunity to present the efforts being made by the National Park Service to protect visitors and resources in national parks and to mitigate the impact of illegal drug trafficking in border parks.

Protecting national parks along the Mexican border is no longer about simply protecting landscapes, plants and animals. Today, national park rangers are helping fight for America's security in a battle posed by illegal drug smuggling and illegal immigration. At stake is the safety of our citizens, our agency's own employees as well as the health of some of our Nation's unique national treasures.

Recently, there has been a lot of emphasis on what is happening in Organ Pipe Cactus National Monument, largely because of the death of Ranger Kris Eggle. This problem is not unique to Organ Pipe, it affects all of the National Park Service areas along the Mexican border. We have seven areas from west to east—Organ Pipe Cactus National Monument, Coronado National Memorial, Shamizar National Memorial, Big Bend National Park, Amistad National Recreation Area, Palo Alto Battlefield National Historic Site and Padre Island National Seashore. Altogether this comprises 365 miles of international border and 72 miles of seashore.

To give you some idea of what has happened over the last few years, in 1997 at Organ Pipe, the park rangers interdicted less than 1,000 pounds of marijuana. Last year, with basically the same staffing, park rangers interdicted over 14,000 pounds of marijuana. At Amistad National Recreation Area, in 2000, 1,300 pounds of marijuana was interdicted. By 2002, that number was up to 5,000 pounds. This year in January in Big Bend National Park, 6,000 pounds of marijuana was interdicted, which is more than the total for the previous year.

Because of what is happening in the parks in damage to our resources and threats to our visitors, the Park Service has made a commitment to strengthen our protection programs in the border parks. This fiscal year, using money appropriated by Congress, we are going to add nine rangers to the staff at Organ Pipe, which more than doubles our protection staff.

Seven million was also appropriated for a vehicle barrier along the entire 30 miles of boundary in Organ Pipe and 1 mile at Coronado National Memorial. We feel the place to start is by stopping the vehicles. In Organ Pipe, there are over 150 miles of illegal roads that have been created. The most dangerous and most damaging traffic that crosses the border comes by vehicle. In addition to that, we are increasing our ability with remote sensors.

At Amistad, although money was not appropriated this fiscal year, our regional office is providing funding for four additional rangers to deal with the increasing situation there as well as funding for additional seasonal rangers at Big Bend National Park.

One of the problems that we have not discussed yet along the border is the lack of communications. We are in very remote areas and communication is often a problem, not only between agencies, but with our own officers. This year, the National Park Service received appropriation to greatly improve our communications in southern Arizona with additional repeaters and radio equipment.

That appropriation will also allow us, by the end of this year, to have 24-hour dispatch service available.

Dealing with illegal immigration and border problems is not the primary mission of the National Park Service. The primary mission of the National Park Service is to protect park resources and provide safe enjoyable visits for the citizens that come to our parks. But with the level of illegal activity coming across the border in border parks, we cannot achieve our primary mission without being engaged in border protection activities.

We know we cannot do this alone, we look forward to working with the new Department of Homeland Security. In the past, we have worked closely with the Border Patrol, Customs, Immigration, State and county law enforcement agencies. To correct problems along the border will take the efforts of all of law enforcement agencies along the border. We intend to do our share.

The National Park Service has a statutory and moral obligation to protect our resources in the parks. Visitors and employees in the parks should be able to expect that if they need help, help will be available. We are trying to work toward those ends.

I will be happy to answer any questions you might have.

[The prepared statement of Mr. Wellman follows:]

STATEMENT OF WILLIAM WELLMAN, SUPERINTENDENT, ORGAN PIPE CACTUS NATIONAL MONUMENT, NATIONAL PARK SERVICE, DEPARTMENT OF THE INTERIOR, BEFORE THE HOUSE GOVERNMENT REFORM SUBCOMMITTEE ON CRIMINAL JUSTICE, DRUG POLICY, AND HUMAN RESOURCES, REGARDING THE IMPACT OF THE DRUG TRADE ON BORDER SECURITY AND NATIONAL PARKS

March 10, 2003

Mr. Chairman, thank you for the opportunity to present the efforts being made by the National Park Service (NPS) to protect visitors and resources in national parks and mitigate the impact of illegal drug trafficking on park borders. On January 20, 2003, Don Murphy, Deputy Director, National Park Service testified before the Senate Finance Committee on the subject of national parks and border security.

The NPS practices and policies are dedicated to preserving its natural resources and providing a safe, clean, and secure environment for its visitors and workforce. We have initiated programs and studies and undertaken actions to address many of the concerns and needs in these areas. The National Parks Omnibus Management Act of 1998, P.L. 105-391, Section 801 directed the Secretary to conduct a study to fully evaluate the needs, shortfalls, and requirements of NPS law enforcement programs. A study team of national park rangers and U.S. Park Police officers was assembled in February 1999 and the final report, The National Park Service Law Enforcement Programs Study, was presented to Congress on March 8, 2000, in two volumes. One addressed the U.S. Park Police and the other addressed the field protection rangers. Included in the study are suggestions to address shortfalls, justifications for all suggestions, and a statement of adverse impacts should identified needs remain unmet. The NPS is implementing a number of those suggestions as well as a series of law enforcement reforms directed by the Secretary in July 2002.

The NPS has Park Police and ranger forces who manage the law enforcement, resource protection and emergency needs of both people and parks. The following programs were identified as already in place or were put into effect:

- Drug enforcement funding, initiated in 1992 as a specific line-item in the NPS budget, has a base of over $9.5 million. Currently all but $2.1 million is located in the budgets of the parks and the U.S. Park Police. The $2.1 million is allocated annually from a central source to individual parks and regional offices to address emergency issues. For example, in September 2002 this funding was used in an investigation of marijuana gardens at Sequoia National Park, which resulted in the removal of over 100,000 plants and led to 20 indictments.
- The NPS has received funding from several regular and supplemental appropriations between 1997 and 2001 to cover the costs of anti-terrorism expenditures. Funding in the construction appropriation provided surveillance and monitoring equipment, perimeter fencing, physical barriers, and communication equipment at Mount Rushmore National Memorial, the National Mall, Independence National Historical Park and Jefferson National Expansion Memorial. Funds were provided in FY 2001 in the Park Police appropriation for one-time costs associated with the design of a visitor screening facility and a key system for the Washington Monument, as well as for the installation of alarm systems and closed-circuit television at other monuments on the Mall. Total funding provided was $11.6 million.

Protecting national parks along the Mexican border is no longer about simply protecting landscapes, plants and animals. At stake is the safety of our citizens and the agency's own employees as well as the health of some of our Nation's unique natural treasures.

While the NPS has the responsibility to enforce Federal laws within the borders of its parks, the NPS's primary mission is not international border security or drug trade eradication. The Department of Homeland Security's Bureau of Customs and Border Protection is the primary Federal entity responsible for international border security, while the Drug Enforcement Administration and Department of Homeland Security's Border and Transportation Security directorate are primarily responsible for the elimination of drugs entering the country. To better meet the responsibilities of these respective agencies, the NPS is working to develop closer lines of communication and cooperation with the Department of Homeland Security, the Drug Enforcement Administration, and other Federal, state, and local agencies. The NPS is creating lasting partnerships so that each agency can accomplish its mission in the most logical and cost-effective manner. We look forward to working with the new Department of Homeland Security to establish plans of action and responsibility for ensuring appropriate border security in parks along the border.

The NPS manages seven National Parks along the United States-Mexico international border, including Organ Pipe Cactus National Monument and Coronado National Memorial in Arizona; Amistad National Recreation Area, Big Bend National Park, Chamizal National Memorial, Palo Alto Battlefield National Historic Site and Padre Island National Seashore in Texas. They hosted more than 2,780,000 visitors in 2000. They share approximately 365 miles of the international border with Mexico and 72 miles of seashore and are directly impacted by increased illegal border activity. Other parks nearby including Saguaro National Park, Chiricahua National Monument, Fort Bowie National Historic Site and Tumacacori National Historical Park also feel the effects of illegal border activity and can document indirect impacts.

Great attention has been focused on one national park unit, Organ Pipe Cactus National Monument, where Ranger Kris Eggle was murdered and where threats and illegal activities originating outside the United States grow in numbers. The problems in this park are emblematic of how increased enforcement on the part of U.S. Customs and U.S. Border Patrol, now part of the Department of Homeland Security, at traditional, urban crossings have pushed more border crime onto adjacent public land. In light of this situation, efforts on the ground to contend with the rising tide of undocumented aliens and drug smugglers require ongoing coordination between the NPS and other Federal agencies, including the Department of Homeland Security's Bureau of Customs and Border Protection and Bureau of Immigration and Customs Enforcement. Without communication, without advance intelligence and information and without these Federal partners, NPS would be unable to protect the lands with which it is entrusted. Organ Pipe Cactus National Monument, Cabeza Prieta National Wildlife Refuge, managed by the U.S. Fish and Wildlife Service, and other Federal agencies have a long history of working together.

Because most of these parks were originally established to preserve some of this country's most unique natural and cultural resources, they are filled with irreplaceable treasures contained in a very fragile environment. Illegal border activity can threaten park visitor and employee safety and damage natural and cultural resources within national parks. In addition, the job of controlling illegal activities is compounded by logistical difficulties. Coronado National Memorial is circled on three sides by ridges rising over 2,000 feet above the valley floor. The terrain itself hinders radio communication inside and outside the park and slows law enforcement backup.

In 2001, the U.S. Border Patrol estimates that 250,000 undocumented migrants entered the country through parklands with over 200,000 through Organ Pipe Cactus National Monument alone. The explosion of impacts from these human and vehicular intrusions is already causing serious damage to park resources. Hundreds of miles of illegal roads and trails have been created and huge amounts of trash and debris litter the landscape. The few sources of natural water have been polluted or drained. In the summer of 2001, 21 undocumented migrants died from exposure after crossing the border at Organ Pipe Cactus National Monument.

Rangers interdicted over 30,000 pounds of drugs in 2002, up from 20,000 pounds in 2000. At Amistad National Recreation Area during 2002 over 5 tons of marijuana was seized with an estimated value of over $9 million. By contrast 1,300 pounds of marijuana was seized in 2000. In Big Bend National Park more than 6,000 pounds of marijuana was seized within the park in January 2003 - more than all total seizures in 2002. At Padre Island National Seashore smuggling in the park has increased since September 11 due to increased security at border crossings and checkpoints on primary highway routes. At Organ Pipe Cactus National Monument marijuana seized by park rangers has risen from less than 1,000 pounds in 1997 to over 14,000 pounds in 2002, and over 150 miles of illegal road has been created in the park, mostly in designated wilderness.

Currently, all the land management agencies in this part of Arizona have a reciprocal law enforcement agreement with the Department of Homeland Security's Bureau of Customs and Border Protection and routinely work together on special operations. Any training that is offered by one agency is made available to others, and the local managers meet regularly on all kinds of issues including natural and cultural resource management as well as law enforcement. For example, all agencies having any kind of responsibility for managing lands or managing the border have been participating fully in the preparation and planning for the proposed vehicle barrier at Organ Pipe National Monument and Coronado National Memorial.

The NPS has two special agents assigned to the Arizona Partnership of the southwest border High Intensity Drug Trafficking Area (HIDTA) office. HIDTA is a program that facilitates coordination, including information sharing, between Federal, state, and local law enforcement agencies on efforts to address illegal drug activity. HIDTA also develops initiatives to respond to drug threat assessments. The two NPS special agents, as well as a third agent assigned to the El Paso Intelligence Center, serve as critical liaisons between the NPS and the other state and Federal agencies involved in narcotics interdiction in the southwestern United States.

The National Park Service has responded to the threats along the Mexican border by significantly increasing the number of law enforcement rangers at border parks and reorganizing ranger activities. For example at Organ Pipe Cactus National Monument, NPS has added 9 new protection rangers, 3 maintenance workers dedicated to border-related efforts (maintaining ditches, barricades, gates, patrol roads) and one clerk to assist the protection staff, using $900,000 provided by Congress in FY03 for protection activities. Additionally, NPS is moving ahead with plans for a vehicle barrier along the entire 30-mile border of the Monument to halt illegal vehicle traffic using $7 million recently appropriated by Congress. Planning for that project is well underway and construction of the barrier is expected to begin by late 2003. The need for additional staffing at Amistad NRA will be accomplished through internal reprogramming of FY03 regional funds. The FY04 Intermountain Region border park law enforcement priorities reflect an additional 14 ranger positions. Big Bend National Park was authorized to begin the process of hiring seasonal ranger staff to work during the busy winter months.

The Intermountain Region has redirected an additional $100,000 in base funds for Organ Pipe

Cactus National Monument and Coronado National Memorial in FY04 to fund personnel and supplies necessary to maintain the vehicle barriers in both parks. The Regional Director provided $60,000 in FY03 to Organ Pipe Cactus National Monument to establish an extensive sensor program to detect intrusions. The region committed $35,000 for training for regional special event and incident management teams in FY03. These teams comprise the region's first response capability for tactical operations/staffing support and incident management.

Increased preparedness was provided through appropriations for operations in recent years. Base increases allowed for additional patrol of facilities, trained operators of security equipment, dispatch staff, and training at parks such as Mount Rushmore National Memorial, National Capital Parks, Independence National Historical Park, Jefferson National Expansion Memorial, Statue of Liberty National Monument, Boston National Historical Park and border parks such as Coronado National Memorial and Organ Pipe Cactus National Monument.

- Through a FY 2002 Supplemental Appropriation, the NPS received funding of $36.5 million for preparedness in the wake of the September 11, 2001 incident, with the majority of the funds provided to the U.S. Park Police for operations and security improvements in Washington D.C and New York City. Remaining funds went to operational security, physical facility and perimeter security and law enforcement equipment at selected icon parks such as Statue of Liberty National Monument and Jefferson National Expansion Memorial.

The serious nature of the issues will require constant re-evaluation of the situation so that all resources necessary are available to address the concerns members of the committee may have.

The NPS has proposed a new Law Enforcement Reform Implementation Strategy as a way to improve law enforcement effectiveness and safety. This strategy, as well as the plans and activities taking place on the border here in Arizona, is just one part of a broader initiative to improve law enforcement and security throughout the Department of the Interior.

The NPS has both the statutory and the moral responsibility to ensure that its 388 units are well managed, for this and future generations. National park rangers have always been seen as a critical element to that mission. Like many other agencies, the NPS will have to use available resources more efficiently to improve our law enforcement program. Even though the Service is proactive in identifying and solving problems, park staff should be able to expect that if help is needed, it will be available. Reviewing and managing our priorities—both human resources and natural and cultural resources—identifying problems and seeking out creative solutions that involve neighbors and partners will go a long way to protecting our parks.

Mr. Chairman, this concludes my statement. I would be happy to answer any questions you or other members of the committee may have.

Mr. SOUDER. Thank you very much. As I said at the beginning, the full statements will be in the record. I would also like to make sure that I put in the record at this point, after I hear testimony, a map that you gave me that shows the informal crossings and the patterns of how they go around the stations as well as a chart that documents some of the changes that you said. So I would like to have that after the National Park testimony.

We also have a similar map for the Wildlife Refuge to the west that we would like to have reduced down and put into the record as well, showing that the concept of traditional border crossings is nigh on to irrelevant when you are trying to deal with it. I mean you have to have a basic point for those who are following the law, but there are whole networks of passages through the resources. It is very difficult to protect resources when people are tromping through them illegally and thousands of numbers.

Next, Mr. Hugh Winderweedle, is that——

Mr. WINDERWEEDLE. Winderweedle [pronouncing], that is correct.

Mr. SOUDER [continuing]. The Port Director for the Lukeville Port of Entry for the U.S. Customs Service. Thank you for joining us and we look forward to your testimony.

Mr. WINDERWEEDLE. Thank you, Chairman Souder, for the opportunity to address this committee and for the opportunity to appear before you today.

My name is Hugh Winderweedle and I am currently assigned to the Port of Entry at Lukeville, AZ as the Port Director for the Bureau of Customs and Border Protection. I am accompanied today by Mr. Steve Minas, who is the Special Agent in Charge for the State of Arizona and Mr. Dennis Lindsay, who is the Special Agent in Charge for Air Operations for U.S. Customs and Border Protection for the State of Arizona.

I would like to discuss the efforts of the Bureau of Customs and Border Protection to address the impact of the drug trade on border security at the Port of Entry at Lukeville, AZ and the challenges that exist along the U.S./Mexican border in the Lukeville area.

The Port of Lukeville is located on the U.S./Mexican border between Lukeville, AZ and Sonoyta, Sonora. The Organ Pipe National Park lies adjacent to the port of entry on the west, north and northeast, separated only by an 80-acre tract of privately owned land with limited commercial development. Sells, AZ and the Tohono O'odham reservation are located 60 miles to the east. The Port of Lukeville is remote, and aside from a small commercial development at the border and Organ Pipe National Park, the area is mostly undeveloped and inaccessible within a 50-mile radius in all directions. The remoteness of the area and proximity to a State highway lead to the area's appeal to drug traffickers and undocumented entrants.

The Port of Entry at Lukeville services travelers from 6 a.m. to midnight via three traffic lanes. The port is situated on State Route 85 and is the gateway to the Mexican resort area of Puerto Penasco, also known as Rocky Point. The port services 442,00 vehicles arriving from Mexico each year, with a total of 1.5 million passengers or pedestrians arriving via the port of entry. Although the great majority of arriving persons are vacationers and compliant travelers, a startling number of extraordinary incidents occur at or near the Port of Entry at Lukeville. We in the Bureau of Customs and Border Protection and our colleagues in the Department of Interior and the Bureau of Immigration and Customs Enforcement, are working together with our Mexican counterparts not only to secure our Nation's borders, stop or prevent illegal activity, but also to serve and help the citizens and travelers of Mexico and the United States.

The Port of Lukeville intercepts large amounts of narcotics and a number of fugitives each year. For example, during calendar year 2002, the port intercepted over 5,000 pounds of marijuana. The interception of drugs and fugitives can often erupt into violence when desperate individuals resort to violent measures in an attempt to circumvent or evade authorities. In August 2002, a National Park Service ranger was shot by a Mexican national who had entered the Organ Pipe National Monument. On December 30, 2002, Mexican police were involved in a shootout with drug smugglers 50 yards south and 1 mile west of the port of the port of entry. On February 13, 2003, an inspector fatally shot a driver of a vehicle arriving from Mexico at the Lukeville Port of Entry. The subject fought with the officer, grabbing and dragging him with the vehicle in an attempt to run the officer over. As you can see, this violence sometimes ends in tragedy.

However, close working relationships and coordination among Federal, State, local and Mexican authorities have prevented many potentially violent incidents from escalating. The training and dedication to duty has allowed our officers to respond appropriately during crisis and contain situations that otherwise may have resulted in greater injury or loss. Our hearts weigh heavy for those officers lost in the line of duty, but we stand fast and ready to continue protecting the American people by securing our borders. The Bureau of Customs and Border Protection has addressed the situation at Lukeville on many fronts. We maintain a vigorous training program to prepare our officers for the increasing challenge of antiterrorism, the drug trade and border security. Technology also plays a key role in our efforts to secure the border. We currently use imaging systems, video surveillance, radio communications. Additionally, our officers are now wearing radiation detection devices to intercept sources of radiation that may be associated with weapons of mass destruction.

The Bureau of Customs and Border Protection and many law enforcement agencies at Lukeville and the surrounding southern border, have orchestrated many special operations through the coordination of the High Intensity Drug Trafficking Area Center. These intense operations are crafted to consolidate law enforcement resources to gather intelligence, disrupt smuggling organizations and displace the activities of drug trafficking operations. HIDTA operations conducted with Federal, State and local agencies have successfully intercepted and disrupted smuggling activities.

One striking aspect of these operations has been the displacement of smuggling activity. Increased law enforcement efforts and presence in one area, such as the Port of Entry at Lukeville, can redirect smuggling activities and cause an increase at another location, such as Organ Pipe Cactus National Monument. Increased drug smuggling and violence can present very challenging circumstances for all the officers in these locations.

One component of the new Bureau of Immigration and Customs Enforcement, the former U.S. Customs Office of Investigations, currently has offices located in Sells, Three-Points and Ajo, AZ. Additional resources from the five other offices in Arizona are deployed in this area when operational needs dictate. This integrated interdiction/investigative team has experienced tremendous success in the area surrounding the Lukeville Port of Entry, to include the Tohono O'odham Nation. During calendar year 2002, this team was responsible for interdicting 103,000 pounds of marijuana entering the United States from Mexico. The success is enhanced by our close working relationships with the Department of Interior law enforcement agencies, the U.S. Border Patrol, and our State, tribal and local law enforcement partners.

The increasing level of violence in the border region is of concern to us all. Officers involved in shootings and high-speed pursuits, which often involve law enforcement vehicles being purposely rammed by violators in their efforts to escape, are all too common. Because the surrounding area is remote, emergency services are not readily available. Frequently persons requiring emergency medical services are transported hundreds of miles from Puerto Penasco, Mexico to Phoenix through the Port of Entry at Lukeville. Helicopter Medivacs are not uncommon as the only means of reaching adequate medical care in time.

Mr. Chairman, members of the committee, I want to thank you for the opportunity to testify about the unique challenges of protecting this remote, yet important part of our Nation's border. I can assure you that staff, management and every employee of the Bureau of Customs and Border Protection is fully dedicated and fully qualified to continue to protect our Nation's borders and the 280 million residents of the United States.

I will be happy to answer any questions that you might have.

[The prepared statement of Mr. Winderweedle follows:]

STATEMENT OF HUGH WINDERWEEDLE, PORT DIRECTOR FOR THE BUREAU OF CUSTOMS AND BORDER PROTECTION, BEFORE THE HOUSE GOVERNMENT REFORM COMMITTEE, SUBCOMMITTEE ON CRIMINAL JUSTICE, DRUG POLICY, AND HUMAN RESOURCES.

MARCH 10, 2003

Chairman Souder, members of the committee, thank you for your invitation to address this committee and for the opportunity to appear before you today. My name is Hugh Winderweedle, and I am currently assigned to the Port of Entry at Lukeville, Arizona as the Port Director for the Bureau of Customs and Border Protection. I would like to discuss the efforts of the Bureau of Customs and Border Protection to address the impact of the drug trade on border security at the Port of Entry at Lukeville, Arizona, and the challenges that exist along the U.S. – Mexican border in the Lukeville area.

The challenges at the Port of Lukeville and the Southern Border

The Port of Lukeville is located on the U.S. Mexican border between Lukeville, Arizona, and Sonoyta, Sonora. The Organ Pipe National Park lies adjacent to the port of entry on the west, north, and northeast, separated only by an 80 acre tract of privately owned land with limited commercial development. Sells, Arizona and the Tohono O'odham reservation are located 60 miles to the east. The Port of Lukeville is remote, and aside from a small commercial development at the border and Organ Pipe National Park, the area is mostly undeveloped and inaccessible within a fifty-mile radius in all directions. The remoteness of the area and proximity to a state highway lead to the area's appeal to drug traffickers and undocumented entrants.

The Port of Entry at Lukeville services travelers from 6:00am to Midnight daily through three traffic lanes. The Port is situated on Arizona State Route 85 and is the gateway to the Mexican resort area of Puerto Penasco (Rocky Point). The port services 442,000 vehicles arriving from Mexico each year. A total of 1.5 million passengers and pedestrians enter the U.S. through the Port of Entry. Although the great majority of arriving persons are vacationers and compliant travelers, a startling number of extraordinary incidents occur at or near the Port of Entry at Lukeville. We in the Bureau of Customs and Border Protection, and our colleagues in the Department of Interior and the Bureau of Immigration and Customs Enforcement, are working together with our Mexican counterparts not only to secure our Nation's borders, stop or prevent, illegal activity, but also to serve and help the citizens and travelers of Mexico and the United States.

The port of Lukeville intercepts large amounts of narcotics and a number of fugitives every year. For example, during the calendar year 2002, the port intercepted over 5,000 pounds of marijuana. The interception of drugs and fugitives can often erupt into violence when desperate individuals resort to violent measures in an attempt to circumvent or evade authorities. In August 2002, a National Park Service Ranger was shot by a Mexican national who had entered Organ Pipe Cactus National Monument. On December 30, 2002, Mexican police were involved in a shootout with drug smugglers 50 yards south and one mile west of the Port of Entry. On February 13, 2003 an officer with the former Customs Service, fatally shot the driver of a vehicle arriving from Mexico at Lukeville. The subject fought with the officer, grabbing and dragging him with the vehicle in an attempt to run the officer over. As you can see, this violence sometimes ends in tragedy. However, close working relationships and coordination among federal, state, local, and Mexican authorities have prevented many potentially violent incidents from escalating. The training and dedication to duty has allowed our officers to respond appropriately during crisis and contain situations that otherwise may have resulted in greater injury or loss. Our hearts weigh heavy for those officers lost in the line of duty, but we stand fast and ready to continue protecting the American people by securing our borders.

The Bureau of Customs and Border Protection has addressed the situation at Lukeville on many fronts. We maintain a vigorous training program to prepare our officers for the increasing challenge of anti-terrorism, the drug trade and border security. Technology also plays a key role in our efforts to secure the border. We currently use imaging systems, video surveillance, and radio communications. Additionally, our officers are now wearing radiation detection devices to intercept sources of radiation that may be associated with Weapons of Mass Destruction.

The Bureau of Customs and Border Protection, and many Law Enforcement Agencies at Lukeville and the surrounding Southern Border, have orchestrated many special operations through the coordination of the High Intensity Drug Trafficking Area Center (HIDTA). These intense operations are crafted to consolidate law enforcement resources to gather intelligence, disrupt smuggling organizations, and displace the activities of drug trafficking operations. HIDTA operations conducted with federal, state, and local law enforcement agencies have successfully intercepted and disrupted smuggling activities.

One striking aspect of these operations has been the displacement of smuggling activity. Increased law enforcement efforts and presence in one area, for example, at the Port of Entry Lukeville, can redirect smuggling activities and cause an increase at another location, such as Organ Pipe Cactus National Monument. Increased drug smuggling and violence can present very challenging circumstances for officers in all of these locations.

One component of the new Bureau of Immigration and Customs Enforcement (BICE), the former U.S. Customs Office of Investigations, currently has offices located in Sells, Three-points and Ajo, Arizona. Additional resources from the five other offices in Arizona are deployed in this area when operational needs dictate. This integrated interdiction/investigative team has experienced tremendous success in the area surrounding the Lukeville Port of Entry, to include the Tohono O'odham nation. During calendar year 2002, this team was responsible for interdicting over 103,000 pounds of marijuana entering the U.S. from Mexico. This success is enhanced by our close working relationships with Department of Interior law enforcement agencies, the U.S. Border Patrol, and our state, tribal and local law enforcement partners.

The increasing level of violence in the border region is of concern to us all. Officers involved in shootings and high-speed pursuits, which often involve law enforcement vehicles being purposely rammed by violators in their efforts to escape, are all too common. Because the surrounding area is remote, emergency services are not readily available. Frequently, persons requiring emergency medical services are transported hundreds of miles from Puerto Penasco, Mexico to Phoenix, Arizona through the Port of Lukeville. Helicopter Medivacs are not uncommon as the only means of reaching adequate medical care in time.

Conclusion

Mr. Chairman, members of the committee, I want to thank you for this opportunity to testify about the unique challenges of protecting this remote yet important part of our nation's border. The Bureau of Customs and Border Protection will continue to make every effort possible, working with our fellow inspection agencies, with the Administration, with Congressional leaders, our Mexican counterparts, and the business community, to ensure the integrity of our border. We are committed to enhancing the safety and security of our neighbors and countrymen who depend on the rule of law in order to be able to live their lives as we would all hope to. I am happy to answer any questions you might have.

Mr. SOUDER. Thank you for your testimony. As you may know, John Stanton from Customs is currently serving as a fellow with our subcommittee and occasionally he acknowledges other agencies involved in these efforts. It is great to have a Customs expert on our staff helping us with these issues.

Our last witness on this panel is Mr. James Woolley, Assistant Special Agent in Charge of the Tucson Division Office, DEA.

Mr. WOOLLEY. Thank you and good morning, Chairman Souder, Congressman Shadegg. I am pleased to have this opportunity to appear before you today to discuss the role of the Drug Enforcement Administration [DEA] regarding the impact of the drug trade along the Arizona/Mexico border. My name is James Woolley, I am the Assistant Special Agent in Charge of the Tucson office of the DEA.

At the outset, Mr. Chairman, I would be remiss if I did not preface my remarks by thanking both you and the subcommittee for your unwavering support of the men and women of the DEA and our mission.

As a single mission component of the Department of Justice, the DEA is the world's premier drug law enforcement organization.

It is important to remember that we are an investigative law enforcement organization whose primary duty is to disrupt and dismantle the world's most sophisticated drug distribution networks. For us, the interdiction of drugs is often the beginning of an investigation, rather than the end.

Arizona has the unique role as both an importation and a transportation area out the southwest border and a metropolitan distribution center. Because of the substantial cooperation needed between the Federal, State and local law enforcement efforts, the collaboration of task forces help to define the responsibilities and improve the focus of the investigative efforts.

Mr. Chairman, the DEA has found that cartel leaders are combining their loads and working together to smuggle their narcotics. We see this in Arizona and we know about it in Texas and southern California as well. The Sonoran/Arizona border has no one cartel controlling the smuggling activity. However, numerous Mexican drug trafficking organizations, not looking to compete for specific cartel territories, consider Sonora as a prime smuggling route.

The unique character of the Sonoran/Arizona border creates an important tier of "Gatekeeper" organizations, with corridors through Yuma, Lukeville, Nogales, Naco and Douglas. These "Gatekeepers" are smuggling organizations that specialize in exploiting their areas for the sole purpose of getting drugs across the border and into the Tucson and Phoenix areas. The "Gatekeepers" can be characterized as well organized groups extended across the border communities that use their local ties to create a transportation infrastructure. They also maintain an intelligence apparatus along the border that targets the ports of entry as well as the areas in between.

Once the drugs are smuggled across the border, they are taken to "stash houses" for distribution throughout the metropolitan Tucson or Phoenix areas.

As I previously mentioned, DEA is primarily an investigative agency, not an interdiction agency. Our investigations allow us to share information with other law enforcement agencies, which is a vital responsibility of the DEA. It is the only way that we can effectively combat illegal narcotics. Mr. Chairman, I would like to highlight the collaboration of numerous partners at the Federal, State and local levels.

One of DEA's main functions is to coordinate drug investigations that take place along America's 2,000-mile border with the Republic of Mexico. This effort, known as the Southwest Border Initiative, involves thousands of Federal, State and local law enforcement officers. Our strategy is simple: attack major Mexican-based trafficking organizations on both sides of the border by simultaneously employing intelligence which is enhanced by enforcement initiatives and cooperative efforts with the Government of Mexico.

The El Paso Intelligence Center [EPIC], serves as the principal national tactical intelligence center for drug law enforcement. It has a research and analysis section as well as a tactical operations section to support foreign and domestic intelligence and operational needs in the field.

EPIC manages a highly effective Watch Program, to provide timely tactical intelligence to the field. This coordination brings together in one place the data bases of every one of the participating agencies. EPIC also has its own internal data bases which, combined with other agency information, provides the single most responsive, direct conduit available for the tactical intelligence center supporting every law enforcement agency in the Nation.

Another example of how DEA interrelates with the other agencies along the border is our participation in the High Intensity Drug Trafficking Area [HIDTA] program, whose goal is to reduce drug trafficking activities in the most critical areas of the country. The HIDTA program develops partnerships among Federal, State and local drug control agencies in designated regions by creating enforcement task forces and investigative support centers where they can synchronize their efforts. Arizona belongs to the Southwest Border HIDTA, along with southern California, New Mexico, west Texas and south Texas.

The DEA considers one of its greatest assets the State and local task forces with whom we work. Participating State and local agencies have a tremendous amount of input and are actually force multipliers, adding additional resources to DEA efforts. We participate in more than 210 task forces and have over 1,900 task force officers on board nationwide. These officers are able to access DEA's Narcotics and Dangerous Drugs Information System for data base checks. Those assigned to the task forces are deputized as Federal law enforcement officers, enabling them to follow leads and conduct investigations nationwide.

Drug trafficking organizations operating along the Arizona/Mexico border continue to be one of the greatest threats to communities across the Nation. The power and influence of these organizations is pervasive and continues to expand to new markets across the United States.

In conclusion the DEA is deeply committed to intensifying our efforts to arrest the leadership and dismantle these organizations that are trafficking.

Mr. Chairman, thank you for the opportunity to appear before you today and I would be happy to answer any questions that you may have. Thank you.

[The prepared statement of Mr. Woolley follows:]

Statement of

James A. Woolley
Assistant Special Agent in Charge
Tucson District Office
Drug Enforcement Administration
Before the
U.S. House of Representatives
Committee on Government Reform
Subcommittee on Criminal Justice, Drug Policy, and Human Resources
March 10, 2003

Good morning, Chairman Souder and distinguished members of Congress. I am pleased to have this opportunity to appear before you today to discuss the role of the Drug Enforcement Administration (DEA) regarding the impact of drug trade along the Arizona/Mexico border. First off, Mr. Chairman, I would be remiss if I didn't preface my remarks by thanking both you and the Subcommittee for your unwavering support of the men and women of the Drug Enforcement Administration and our mission. Your examination of drug trade on our borders contributes to this work.

As a single mission component of the Department of Justice, the DEA is the world's premier drug law enforcement agency. In addition to its domestic presence, the DEA maintains over 400 personnel in 56 countries to support global investigations and drug intelligence activities. DEA employees across the globe implement a policy of interagency teamwork, which is the bedrock of our longstanding tradition of cooperation.

It is important to remember that DEA is an investigative law enforcement agency whose primary duty is to disrupt and dismantle the world's most sophisticated drug distribution organizations. For us, the interdiction of drugs is often the beginning of an investigation rather than the end. DEA Phoenix Division is the lead Federal agency for enforcing the narcotics and controlled substance laws and regulations within the state of Arizona. Our mission here is to identify, target and dismantle major drug trafficking organizations operating within the state of Arizona and to support other DEA offices outside Arizona to further develop the investigations on their major targets. The Phoenix Division investigative priorities are cocaine, heroin, methamphetamine, marijuana, then other investigations.

Arizona has a unique role as both an importation and transportation area on the Southwest Border and a metropolitan distribution center. Arizona's various drug law enforcement efforts depend upon substantial cooperation between the Federal agencies and state and local jurisdictions to implement an effective overall enforcement program. The collaboration of State and Local Task Forces helps define responsibilities and improves the focus of investigative efforts in the law enforcement community.

Cartel leaders are combining their loads and working together to smuggle their narcotics. We see this on the Texas and Southern California borders with Mexico. The Sonoran/Arizona border has no distinct cartel that controls the smuggling activity. However, numerous

Mexican Drug Trafficking Organizations (MDTOs) not seeking to compete with specific cartel territories consider Sonora instead.

The unique character of the Sonoran/Arizona border creates an important tier of "Gatekeeper" organizations along this border with corridors through Yuma, Lukeville, Nogales, Naco and Douglas. These "Gatekeepers" are smuggling organizations that specialize in exploiting their areas for the sole purpose of getting drugs across the border and into the Tucson or Phoenix areas. The "Gatekeepers" are characterized as generational local families extended across the Sonoran/Arizona border communities. They have used these generational ties to leverage even more corruption, create a transportation infrastructure. They maintain an intelligence apparatus along the border specifically targeting the Ports of Entry. These "Gatekeepers" have constructed and maintained tunnel systems under the border, engineered increasingly sophisticated vehicle traps, and they have successfully co-oped (or simply stolen from) car rental companies to supply rental sport utility vehicles for smuggling purposes.

Once the drugs are smuggled across the border they are taken to "stash houses" for distribution through the metropolitan areas of Tucson or Phoenix. Over the last year, cases have included distribution destinations in Los Angeles, Chicago, and New York among other Midwest and East Coast markets.

COOPERATION WITH INTERDICTION AGENCIES

As I previously mentioned, DEA is primarily an investigative agency – not an interdiction agency. But we are not alone in our efforts. Sharing information with other law enforcement agencies is a vital responsibility of DEA. It is the only way that we can effectively combat illegal narcotics. The DEA looks forward to collaboration with the newly created Department of Homeland Security. In addition, I'd like to highlight the collaboration of numerous partners at the Federal, state and local levels.

SOUTHWEST BORDER INITIATIVE

One of DEA's main functions is to coordinate drug investigations that take place along America's 2,000-mile border with Mexico; this is an effort that involves thousands of federal, state, and local law enforcement officers. Mexican drug groups have become the world's preeminent drug traffickers, and they tend to be characterized by organizational complexity and a high propensity for violence. To counter this threat, federal drug law enforcement has aggressively pursued drug trafficking along the U.S./Mexico border. The DEA; Federal Bureau of Investigation (FBI); Department of Homeland Security's Bureau of Customs and Border Protection (BCBP), which includes the U.S. Border Patrol; United States Attorneys; and state and local law enforcement agencies continue to work together to reduce the amount of illicit drugs entering the United States through the U.S./Mexico Border. Our strategy is to attack major Mexican-based trafficking organizations on both sides of the border simultaneously by employing enhanced intelligence and enforcement initiatives and cooperative efforts with the Government of Mexico.

INTELLIGENCE OPERATIONS

Today, the El Paso Intelligence Center (EPIC) serves as the principal national tactical intelligence center for drug law enforcement. EPIC is multidimensional in its approach to intelligence sharing. It has a research and analysis section as well as a tactical operations section to support foreign and domestic intelligence and operational needs in the field. It is staffed by representatives from the DEA; FBI; U.S. Coast Guard; BCBP; the Bureau of Immigration and Customs Enforcement (BICE); U.S. Secret Service; Federal Aviation Administration; U.S. Marshals Service; National Security Agency; Bureau of Alcohol, Tobacco, Firearms and Explosives; Internal Revenue Service; and the Department of the Interior. Although the immigration and customs functions were recently incorporated into the Department of Homeland Security, representatives from BCBP and BICE will retain their participation in EPIC.

EPIC manages a highly effective Watch Program, manned by Special Agents, investigative assistants and intelligence analysts, to provide timely tactical intelligence to the field. The Watch Program is able to bring together in one place, the databases of every one of its participating agencies. EPIC also has its own internal database, which combined with the other agency databases, provides the single most responsive, direct conduit available for a tactical intelligence center supporting every law enforcement agency in the nation.

HIGH INTENSITY DRUG TRAFFICKING AREA (HIDTA) TASK FORCES

Another example of how DEA interrelates with other agencies along the border is through our participation in the High Intensity Drug Trafficking Area (HIDTA) program. HIDTAs are sponsored by the Office of National Drug Control Policy (ONDCP), and their goal is to reduce drug trafficking activities in the most critical areas of the country, thereby lessening the impact of these areas on other regions of the country. The HIDTA program develops partnerships between federal, state, and local drug control agencies in designated regions by creating enforcement task forces and investigative support centers with which they can synchronize their efforts.

The HIDTA we belong to in this area is the Southwest Border HIDTA, which is comprised of five partnerships along the U.S./Mexico Border. These HIDTA Southwest Border Partnerships are located in Southern California, Arizona, New Mexico, West Texas, and South Texas. They address important local issues such as methamphetamine trafficking, commercial interdiction, and intelligence collection.

OTHER TASK FORCE GROUPS

The DEA considers one of its greatest assets the state and local task force it works with. Participating state and local agencies have a tremendous amount of input and are actually force multipliers, adding additional resources to DEA efforts. DEA participates in more than 210 Task Force groups and has over 1,900 task force officers on board nationwide. State and local law enforcement officers are assigned to these groups on a permanent basis. DEA Supervisory Special Agents working alongside supervisory level officers from state and local organizations manage them. The Task Force groups facilitate information sharing through the interaction of task force officers and DEA agents. Task force officers also are able to access DEA's Narcotics and Dangerous Drugs Information System [NADDIS] for database checks. In the DEA Phoenix Field Division, we participate in state and local task forces in Phoenix, Tucson, Yuma, Nogales, Sierra Vista and Flagstaff. State and local officers assigned to these task forces are deputized as federal law enforcement officers, enabling them to follow leads and conduct investigations nationwide.

We also are maximizing the use of technology to combat drug trafficking organizations. The DEA's Special Operations Division (SOD) is a comprehensive enforcement operation designed specifically to coordinate multi-agency, multi-jurisdictional, and multi-national Title III investigations against the command and control elements of major drug trafficking organizations operating domestically and abroad. The investigative resources of SOD support a variety of multi-jurisdictional drug enforcement investigations associated with the Southwest Border, Latin America, the Caribbean, Europe, and Asia.

DEA participates at the federal level in Organized Crime Drug Enforcement Task Forces (OCDETF), which combine the resources of many agencies to provide a comprehensive approach against criminal organizations. Participating state and local agencies receive information from federal agencies that are involved in individual OCDETF investigations.

CONCLUSION

Drug trafficking organizations operating along the Arizona/Mexico Border continue to be one of the greatest threats to communities across this nation. The power and influence of these organizations is pervasive, and continues to expand to new markets across the United States.

The DEA is deeply committed to intensifying our efforts to identify, target, arrest, and dismantle the leadership of these criminal drug trafficking organizations. The combined investigations of the DEA and other federal, state, and local law enforcement agencies continue to result in the seizure of hundreds of tons of drugs, hundreds of millions of dollars in drug proceeds, the indictments of significant drug traffickers, and the dismantling of the command and control elements of their organizations. We will continue to give this important border area the attention it deserves.

Mr. Chairman, thank you for the opportunity to appear before the committee today. I would be happy to answer any questions that you or other members may have.

Mr. SOUDER. First, let me thank all of you for your long time efforts and make sure you extend that on behalf of the Congress to your employees.

Second, we are certainly going to go through multiple rounds of questions here because this is a tremendous opportunity for us. First off, we are not getting buzzed every 5 minutes to go vote and we can actually focus on the issues and having all of you in one place is a tremendous opportunity.

I am going to go through some of the different—each one of you—I am going to ask Mr. Lindsay some questions on the air after we kind of establish a little bit of a baseline.

So let me first start with the Border Patrol, Mr. Aguilar.

One thing for my own clarification, the Yuma sector starts where, is it west of the wildlife area where the range is—I do not know where that is.

Mr. AGUILAR. Yes, sir, it actually starts at the Yuma County line, which it takes in a part of the Barry Goldwater also.

Mr. SOUDER. Takes in part of what?

Mr. AGUILAR. The Barry Goldwater firing range.

Mr. SOUDER. OK, so your sector goes to the edge of the wildlife area?

Mr. AGUILAR. Yes.

Mr. SOUDER. Do you have any presence in the wildlife area at this point?

Mr. AGUILAR. In the Cabeza Prieta and the Organ Pipe; yes, sir, we patrol those areas on a daily basis.

Mr. SOUDER. Can you give your reaction to the concept of fencing in the Tohono O'odham and also a road along the border?

Mr. AGUILAR. First of all, Mr. Chairman, the accessibility and mobility along the immediate border is absolutely essential to our effective and efficient patrolling of the border out there. The fencing that we speak about today, I believe relates to border barrier that is being looked at by the Organ Pipe out there. And that of course, will stop the vehicular traffic, but it will not stop the pedestrian traffic. So I just wanted to make sure that I clarified that point.

Upon setting up that border barrier, we also, from an enforcement perspective, need to have a capability to access it and be mobile in and around the area, in order to attempt to address any kind of breaching that may still be attempted out there.

From an enforcement perspective, it would be of tremendous assistance wherever that is placed, as long as we have the capabilities to be able to be responsive to any continuing attempts to breach it, as I said.

The criminal element will in fact look to evade that border barrier. So it is important that we as an enforcement family take that into consideration and make the proper plans to address any resultant impacts of an immediate placement of either border barriers or fencing along our Nation's border.

Mr. SOUDER. If we put a fence in this area, we are going to put more pressure on this part of the aisle.

Mr. AGUILAR. Yes, sir.

Mr. SOUDER. And we have to be thinking a step ahead.

So you feel that—if I can make sure that I get it in the record and understand myself—when you get over 50, it gets a little harder sometimes—that if we did fencing beyond the Organ Pipe in either direction, there would need to be an access road along that as well or the fence would be irrelevant because somebody could cut it and you would not be able to get to it.

Mr. AGUILAR. Yes, an access road in order to patrol that area, to continue patrolling and continue that deterrence presence of not only the Border Patrol agent or the Customs officer that is going to be out there, but in addition to that, when our airplanes are flying over it and they spot something, they can vector our people into any kind of breaching that is occurring out there. In addition to that, of course, there is what we refer to as an enforcement model along our immediate border that takes in either border barrier, fencing, sensors, remote video systems—a combination of that type of infrastructure that will overall create that certainty of deterrence in order to maintain that deterrence posture along our Nation's border.

Mr. SOUDER. As a practical matter, what does it mean if we restrict vehicular traffic but not pedestrian traffic? Does that mean that they cannot penetrate as far in, so they have farther to walk, so is it a deterrent in that sense; not as many people can be transported?

Mr. AGUILAR. It depends on the area. In the area that we are referring to today, I think it would be a two-pronged result. One is that the vehicular traffic would not be able to drive in, but at the same time, pedestrian traffic would probably continue. And in those areas, as you have seen over the weekend and I believe you have gone over this area in the past, there are really remote areas, tremendously hot during the summer, so it would cause some other problems out there in the area of continued efforts to get through those areas.

What the smugglers of narcotics, smugglers of people, are looking for are a means of egress away from the border. What they are shooting for is in fact those highways leading away, leading to highway 10, leading to highway 8 into Phoenix or the staging areas that I think all of us have basically spoke about this morning.

Mr. SOUDER. Would you agree that most of the narcotics and people move at night?

Mr. AGUILAR. I do not have a percentage on that, sir. A large percentage of it would, but in this area out here, we have seen a lot of trafficking during the day also.

Mr. SOUDER. Let me then—this is an important assumption, let me throw in a couple of things. Would you agree that most that cross the border immediately are at night and then they are still moving in the desert areas during the day, or are you saying many even cross the border during the day?

Mr. AGUILAR. They cross the border during the day also and movement is continual.

Mr. SOUDER. Two-thirds at night, one-third in the day or 50?

Mr. AGUILAR. The best way I can probably answer that, sir, we split our resources for addressing the border, we have a 20/40/40 split, if you will—80 percent of our assets are deployed at night, the border patrollings, if you will, because that is when we see an upswing on the activity.

Mr. SOUDER. Do you sense that varies some depending on whether there is a fence—in other words, if we put a shield up at Organ Pipe and you have a road and you have agents patrolling, you are going to push it to where people can disguise themselves more. In the area like Tohono O'odham where it is unprotected, would it matter night or day other than the temperature?

Mr. AGUILAR. By placing up the fence barrier and the supporting infrastructure, by maintaining that presence, whether it be physical by way of high profile, high visibility or electronic surveillance capabilities, I think the impact out of this part of the country would be pretty much 24 hours a day, because of the remoteness and because of the hardship that it would be to get to the remainder of the United States. But again, this is including an entire enforcement package as close as possible to the border; yes, sir.

Mr. SOUDER. Now you have put together an impressive jerry-rigged system that was more mobile with cameras and other types of things over in the Douglas/Sierra Vista sector. Has that been picked up in other places, do you see that being able to give us more mobility to find people?

Mr. AGUILAR. Yes, sir, especially out of this part of the Tucson sector. The technology that you are referring to is part of that deterrence technology that I spoke about earlier. The skywatch is where we basically go up into the air, give us a hydraulic platform to have a lot more visibility and 24/7 visibility on the border, across the border, to see what's coming our way and things of this nature. From a deterrence posture, people have basically learned that when those platforms are up in the air, that in itself is a deterrent.

We are progressing beyond that in that we are working with the Nation for some of these border barriers that the chairman spoke about earlier, and things of that nature.

Mr. SOUDER. Thank you. Mr. Shadegg.

Mr. SHADEGG. Thank you, Mr. Chairman.

Mr. Aguilar, let me begin with you because I am curious. Your testimony before us today seems to suggest that the Tucson sector is a huge success and maybe it did not go quite this far, but it seems to report that you have had a great deal of success there, reduced the number of arrests and made progress there. And I have been aboard Operation Skywatch, I have been aboard a helicopter over the Nogales area, I have been in helicopters perhaps with you in the Sierra Vista area. It seems to me that the corridor here on the west side is just wide open. To me, it looks like we have got a dramatic amount of resources from perhaps Nogales east and nowhere near that level of resource from Nogales west. Is that accurate?

Mr. AGUILAR. That is accurate, sir. The achievements that I spoke to earlier during my testimony related to those areas in the Nogales, Sonora area of operation and the Douglas/Naco area. In this area, what we refer to as the West Desert area, is an area of about 120 miles and that is just Tucson sector, that is not——

Mr. SHADEGG. Let me stop you because I want to understand these terms. West sector area is from Nogales west, does it start in Nogales?

Mr. AGUILAR. The western corridor—the Border Patrol report refers to the west as a corridor, basically starts at the Sasabe area——

Mr. SHADEGG. OK, Sasabe.

Mr. AGUILAR [continuing]. Maybe a little bit east of there. And continues on out to the Yuma County line.

Mr. SHADEGG. All the way to the California line, or just the Yuma County line?

Mr. AGUILAR. Yuma County line. The Yuma sector of the Border Patrol takes in the remaining desert area of the desert out there.

Mr. SHADEGG. So from the Yuma County line west, that is not the area we are talking about, we are talking about from Sasabe to the Yuma County line.

Mr. AGUILAR. Yes, sir, and within that area, of course is the Tohono O'odham Nation with approximately 78 miles.

Mr. SHADEGG. Start at the west side of that, with regard to the Barry Goldwater range, are your operations restricted in the area with regard to the Barry Goldwater range?

Mr. AGUILAR. They are restricted in the sense that every time we go in there, sir, we call the range and advise them that we have a need to go in there. They work with us very closely. We get approval from them to go in there and work the situation that we need to work, whether it be an operation or something that we have intelligence on.

Mr. SHADEGG. Does that apply to both going in by ground vehicle and by helicopter?

Mr. AGUILAR. Yes, sir.

Mr. SHADEGG. You are allowed to go in by helicopter?

Mr. AGUILAR. Yes, sir.

Mr. SHADEGG. But only after you have obtained permission.

Mr. AGUILAR. After we notify them that we have need to go in there and they will give us certain limitations. If their aircraft are flying at a certain level, we have to stay below or we have complete access if it's not an active range day.

Mr. SHADEGG. At the pace we are continuing to improve your resources, how long will it take with the same level of intensity of enforcement to the area from Sasabe to the Yuma line that we have from Sasabe east?

Mr. AGUILAR. I would hesitate to give you an answer on a time line for that, sir, because of course, that's dependent on when we got the resources that we have gotten on some of the other corridors. Out here in the West Desert corridor, one of the things that is going to be critical is going to be infrastructure such as border barriers, the fencing, the technology that we referred to. And of course, all that depends on the procurement and things of that nature.

Mr. SHADEGG. Safe to say it does not look good right now for obtaining the resources to do to the west what you are doing to the east. We are way short of resources to do that, are we not?

Mr. AGUILAR. We are short of resources, sir, but as with the other corridors, we continue to get built up in the area of technology and infrastructure; yes, sir.

Mr. SHADEGG. As I mentioned a few minutes ago, I was at the Lukeville Port of Entry a few weeks ago and saw the fencing in that area. I also noticed the roads in that area. On the southern side of border, where we were, and we were east of Lukeville, on the Mexican side of the border, there is a very good road, well-maintained, you can drive it—it was a dirt road, but you could drive it at 30 or 35, maybe even 40 miles an hour, access it pretty easy. On the Arizona or U.S. side of the border, where the fence was built, there is a pathetic road that you could perhaps do 2 or 3 miles per hour on. And the same is true of the road west of where we were, west of Lukeville, and not far west of Lukeville, you have of course, Mexican Highway 2 with very high speed traffic.

I am curious, my friends in Congress talk about fencing. I think they are clueless about the degree of lack of fencing that we have, and for example, the information we gathered down there about fencing being stolen and moved south and how actually the fencing that has moved south does more good than the fencing that is right on the border, because the fencing that is on the border gets cut so quickly. Would we be better off, speaking of your point about infrastructure, to simply build a high-quality gravel road all along the U.S. side of the border in this west sector so that we could move agents up and down that border and we could watch footprints and simply have access where we do not have that access now.

Mr. AGUILAR. Yes, sir, that would certainly help quite a bit, but I feel like I need to clarify also that immediate accessibility to the immediate border is not only critical, it is absolutely essential. In addition to that, there is supporting infrastructure that is required with that border road. For example, one of the challenges that you spoke to indirectly there are the environmental concerns that we deal with in a lot of this area out here. A smuggler will go through the desert, will go through the Organ Pipe, will go through the Barry Goldwater range. We are restricted in actually following these people out there unless it is an emergency situation. In a tragic situation like when Ranger Eggle got shot out there, of course, we disregard all that. But at all other situations, we have to follow the statutes and regulations and policy that impact our ability to patrol the border out there.

So that immediate border road, absolutely. But that is the reason I used the terminology a little bit ago about the need for an enforcement model. We have a need also for what we refer to as a sign cutting capability, which basically gives the ability to track anything that may have breached that primary road, in order to access anything that has breached that first road or that first deterrent posture on the line. That can and should be very compressed to the border, so that immediate deterrence impact is as close as possible on the border as is required in order to maintain the security of our borders.

Mr. SHADEGG. Mr. Chairman, I would probably have a followup question along the lines of what you asked to the chairman of the Tribe, as to whether you believe you need exemption from certain environmental requirements in a zone along the border. I think I heard the answer to that question as yes. I think I also heard that you may need clarified authority with regard to environmental protection to track individuals who are further in the United States than that; is that right?

Mr. AGUILAR. Yes, sir.

Mr. SHADEGG. I yield, Mr. Chairman.

Mr. SOUDER. And the fencing that we are talking about for Mr. Wellman is not like the fencing that is there currently. I believe there is a terminology difference between a barrier and a fence, is that correct?

Mr. WELLMAN. Yes, we are strictly looking at a vehicle barrier and it will not be able to stop pedestrians.

Mr. SHADEGG. Mr. Chairman, maybe I could ask a followup. I would like each of the witnesses to testify on the question that I asked and that is would a road—given limited resources, would a high-speed access road that would let you access the border be, in the short run, a more valuable tool than yet another fence or vehicle barrier.

Mr. AGUILAR. Is that for me, sir?

Mr. SHADEGG. I think you answered it, you said the road would be very helpful. I was interested in what the other witnesses have to say.

Mr. CICCONE. From Fish and Wildlife Service perspective, I see how the road would help. I would be concerned about creating a road like that without some type of barrier or fence with that road.

Mr. WELLMAN. Actually as part of the vehicle barrier, the road that you saw will be improved somewhat. It will not be a high-speed road, but it will be improved considerably over its current condition.

Mr. SHADEGG. I do not think you could build that fence that I saw designed without building a better road.

Mr. WELLMAN. You are absolutely right.

Mr. SOUDER. Did you not say they are going to have to fly in parts of it though?

Mr. WELLMAN. There are some parts on the steeper slopes where we will not build a road and would like to fly the barrier in and place it on the surface.

Mr. SOUDER. Because we are not talking about a flat area. When we look at that whole border, some parts are amenable to roads and some parts are not.

Mr. WELLMAN. And some parts are not. In the area that is not, there will be a road that will go around so that you can control the whole border in Organ Pipe.

Mr. SOUDER. Is that true in the Wildlife areas too?

Mr. CICCONE. There are definitely some very rugged areas, yes.

Mr. SHADEGG. Mr. Wellman.

Mr. WELLMAN. To finish answering your question, improving the road will help, but given the limited numbers of people, I would agree with the Chief, we need the barriers as well. A barrier will work 24 hours a day and it is unlikely in the near future we are going to be able to have that entire section of border manned 24 hours a day.

Mr. WINDERWEEDLE. Congressman, as to the road, of course the road and barrier has no direct impact or influence over the port of entry. But I would offer the comment that you are talking about two what should be concurrent infrastructure developments and one is merely of no value without the other.

Mr. WOOLLEY. From the DEA perspective, I would say that anything that would facilitate a law enforcement presence in the area certainly would help, but it would have to be combined with the barrier and additional resources to do the patrolling.

Mr. SOUDER. Thank you. Mr. Ciccone, I wanted to try to figure out a little bit more about your challenges.

Currently, is there any presence of Federal agencies along the border other than the refuge—in your refuge?

Mr. CICCONE. Other Federal law enforcement officials?

Mr. SOUDER. Yes.

Mr. CICCONE. Well, yes, we do have cooperation with Border Patrol, with Customs, with other State and local authorities that help, that we work with, and who assist us on the refuge.

Mr. SOUDER. You do not have any official crossing in your refuge?

Mr. CICCONE. Border crossings?

Mr. SOUDER. Yes.

Mr. CICCONE. No official ports of entry.

Mr. SOUDER. And there is no road along the border currently that you are allowed to go on, as opposed to illegally go on?

Mr. CICCONE. There is no road right along the border that is open to the public and the roads that are along the border are very rough.

I should clarify, we do have on our Buenos Aires Refuge, we are adjacent to the Sasabe Port of Entry, but nothing that is right within the refuge.

Mr. SOUDER. And does the Border Patrol have a presence along the not very passable road?

Mr. CICCONE. The Border Patrol does use those roads, as do our refuge officers and I am sure other law enforcement agencies.

Mr. SOUDER. And you testified that you had significant drug seizures, you had lots of illegal—in fact, was it in your testimony that you said it was predominantly in 3 months, that you thought that the biggest months were February, March, April?

Mr. CICCONE. There was a period of time of I believe April, May and June where the indications from the Border Patrol sensors on I believe the Cabeza Prieta Refuge that between 4,000 and 6,000 undocumented alien crossings per month during the months of April, May and June. I cannot say for sure if those are the busiest months, but those were——

Mr. SOUDER. Let me ask a couple of general questions and then when I come back, I have very specific questions for the Wildlife Refuge. Is it true, because often what we hear in Congress are numbers extrapolated based off the highest month, that there are periods of the year where this is more intense on the Arizona border or is it uniform across the year? Do you know, Mr. Aguilar?

Mr. AGUILAR. Specific to illegal aliens?

Mr. SOUDER. Yes.

Mr. AGUILAR. Or narcotics smuggling?

Mr. SOUDER. I was going to ask narcotics smuggling as a separate part of the question.

Mr. AGUILAR. Basically it varies throughout the year. At the beginning of the calendar year and on through about the month of April or May, is when we typically see an increase in illegal alien activity crossing the border. And then what we refer to as harvest season, unfortunately, for the marijuana crop where during certain times of the year, we see an increase because the smugglers attempt to bring it in as it is being harvested.

So there is a little bit of a cyclical activity, if you will, throughout the year.

Mr. SOUDER. And is there also a cyclical—you know, for the individuals who may be coming back and forth a couple times of the year for certain jobs, which is a different type of threat to the system, do they get counted multiple times, are they in and out one time illegals who are coming to the United States and leaving their family back in the country—should they be taken out of that system of guest worker numbers? I get these phenomenal numbers and the numbers do not gibe with the practical numbers that we hear from each subsection.

Mr. AGUILAR. Yes, sir, what you are referring to there is what we refer to as recidivists—speaking to the illegal immigrants now—recidivists, we do have a recidivism rate that varies along the southwest border. I do not have the most immediate figures for my sector, but the last time I looked at them was about a couple of months ago and at that point it was varying anywhere from 18 to 20 percent, depending on what month of the year we are looking at, things of this nature. We have, as an example, individuals that we will catch, we will apprehend 10, 12 times, they will be crossing. There are certain thresholds that will be met in situations like that. And then we have intelligence sources south of the border that tell us that people are turning around, going back home because after 15, 20, 30 times they have tried, they have either been apprehended, turned back, deterred; so again, we have an ident system, I believe you are familiar with that system, that captures every—I should not say every—close to every arrest that we make, we capture biometric information in order to try and track that recidivist rate.

Mr. SOUDER. Mr. Woolley, is the drug pattern at all cyclical—two part question. Is the drug pattern cyclical depending on the marijuana harvest season or does it tend to stay kind of uniform through the year, whereas immigration may be somewhat in flux. And then, the second thing is, what is your estimate of—just rough—and Mr. Aguilar and others, if you have any input into this—what percent of the illegal immigrants are carrying at least small doses, if not large doses. Clearly the largest quantity of drugs come in the big interception of a huge load. But you have all sorts of things, like we saw yesterday, a painted jug, which was comparatively a small amount. But what percentage of the illegals, 10, 20, 30, does it vary by time of year; if there are more coming in the spring, do a lower percentage have narcotics because narcotics are going to move other than the harvest season. Some insight if you have it.

Mr. WOOLLEY. Yes, sir, thank you. I would agree historically with what the Chief Patrol Agent said about the marijuana trafficking, it was a harvest season type trafficking pattern. But in the last several years, we have seen that there is really no slowdown in the amount of at least marijuana coming through the borders. The only time we see kind of a dip is around Easter time, for whatever reason. But our intelligence indicates that not only is the harvest fully functional, but that there are stockpiles and they are able to stockpile the marijuana and then if there is a slowdown through the harvest completion, that they go into the warehouses and bring it across there.

When you talk about methamphetamine or cocaine, there is no shelf life, so that can come across at any time and it is coming across in increasing numbers.

To answer your question about percentage on illegals carrying narcotics, I would not venture a guess on that, but what I would say is if they are coming up here looking for employment, that I know there is an increased monetary incentive for those folks to backpack across. And seeing the seizures and the weights of some of the backpacks, several hundred pound loads. I am very impressed that these folks can walk extended miles carrying these types of loads. So I know there is a monetary incentive, but I would not venture a guess on the number of illegals that are actually employed in that capacity.

Mr. SOUDER. In your arrests at the border, Mr. Aguilar, do you have a rough percentage how many have narcotics on them?

Mr. AGUILAR. No.

Mr. SOUDER. They can dump that. Is it different in the east sector of Arizona from the west?

Mr. AGUILAR. Probably the best way for me to answer that, sir, is the following—from the beginning of the fiscal year through yesterday, the 9th, there were 741 Border Patrol incidents of interdiction—741. Now within each one of those, we have had 10, 12, 15 people involved in each incident, accounting for 188,000 pounds of marijuana. The total apprehensions year to date right now in this sector is 122,000. So I am giving you those numbers, it is a small percentage of the people we encounter being involved with narcotics. Of the people that we do encounter involved in narcotics, I would have to say that the vast majority of them are in fact illegal in the country, employed, as Mr. Woolley said, backpacking, muling the stuff into the United States, getting it across and into the United States.

Mr. SOUDER. Basically the data on the percent that have narcotics on them at the time they are apprehended is less than 1 percent?

Mr. AGUILAR. Yes, sir, I would say that is about correct.

Mr. SOUDER. I will come back to Fish and Wildlife.

Mr. SHADEGG. I would like—Mr. Ciccone, I would like to give you or Mr. DiRosa an opportunity, since this map is now in the record of this hearing, to describe what it depicts and to give the committee, in terms of testimony, some information on what these lines mean, what the blue symbols mean and the degree of environmental damage that is being done by what they depict. Do you want Mr. DiRosa to do that?

Mr. CICCONE. Yes, sir, I would like to defer to Mr. DiRosa.

Mr. SHADEGG. Mr. DiRosa, you will need to come forward and we will need to swear you in.

Mr. SOUDER. Would you raise your right hand?

[Witness sworn.]

Mr. SOUDER. The witness responded affirmatively.

Mr. SHADEGG. If you could just put into the record some of the information describing this and what it tells the committee.

Mr. DIROSA. If you will look in the left hand corner, you will see a legend which depicts the various symbols and color designations which you see on the map.

The red north and south lines are clandestine roads created by smugglers—both people and drug smugglers.

Mr. SHADEGG. If I could interrupt, those roads are all illegal?

Mr. DIROSA. They are all illegal. The only legal roads for public use is a corridor that runs east and west and then one part of it goes north about—further to the west, a little more. Those are public use roads. There are some other roads called administrative roads that can be used by law enforcement and that we can use, but this is a designated wilderness area and we have to do what is called work with minimum tools. We ourselves do not have the capability to use those administrative roads whenever we want, because of the wilderness designation. Illegals coming through the refuge, of course, are paying no respect to any regulations of any sort. The amount of damage caused by these roads is extreme.

You will notice the little blue symbols, vehicles, little blue vehicles, they indicate abandoned vehicles, those vehicles that have been abandoned by mostly drug dealers, they have gotten stuck, they have broken down, sometimes they will stash their loads in the area and we will find it. We have to get those vehicles out of the wilderness area which causes additional damage as well.

Other symbols that you will see there are points where there have been a number of deaths, there are points where much of our border fencing has been stolen and now we are getting ingress from Mexican domestic stock. There are points showing drug apprehensions.

This is a drop in the bucket really, this is only what we can gather. There are additional data that are coming that we will put on the map. The map is a living document.

Mr. SOUDER. I wanted at the same time to have Mr. Wellman to give matching testimony, similar roads in the park. You told me yesterday that one of the things you had done on one of the roads is put some trenches to the side and that you have disabled quite a few vehicles. Could you describe that, and how many roughly?

Mr. WELLMAN. Well, as you saw yesterday, this is typically very open country, so it is difficult to stop vehicles. We have had success two places, one along South Puerto Blanca Drive, but we made the ditches considerably deeper, approximately 3 feet deep. In the first year after we did that, we trapped over 20 illegal vehicles in the ditches.

On one of the illegal roads that you see that goes to a very tight wash, we were able to take Jersey barricades, the type you see on the side of the highway, and put them in the narrow point of the wash and have actually stopped use on that route. That is probably the only 100 percent effective thing we have done and it is probably the only one that will be 100 percent effective until they can figure out some way to go around it.

Mr. SOUDER. You also use some strips?

Mr. WELLMAN. We do use tire replacement devices on a fairly regular basis, usually when vehicles are fleeing back to Mexico at high rates of speed.

Mr. SOUDER. And how many cars have you found through the use of that.

Mr. WELLMAN. Year before last, we successfully spiked 17.

Mr. SHADEGG. Mr. DiRosa, I just wanted to point out, immediately north of the entire refuge is the Barry Goldwater Range, is that correct?

Mr. DIROSA. That is correct, and to the west side as well.

Mr. SHADEGG. So anybody transitting the refuge would either have to enter the Range, dangerous territory, or a second concern that I believe I understood to be expressed was that they transit the wildlife refuge and then once they are further north, go back over into the park and do damage in the park, is that correct?

Mr. DIROSA. That is correct. We are really not the area of choice that smugglers like to use because we are so remote and then when smugglers get through us, they have to negotiate a gunnery range. They tend to try and move back to the east to access the highway. The reason they are now using the refuge is because of the greater enforcement that Border Patrol has been showing to our east and also with Park Service beefing up, we are going to get much more activity in that respect.

Mr. SHADEGG. When you say they are not the area of choice and they like to get back into the national monument, that would explain the reason for all of these roads over here on the eastern end?

Mr. DIROSA. That is correct.

Mr. SHADEGG. Thank you very much.

Mr. SOUDER. Let me followup with some additional questions on this refuge. The refuge was created for bighorn sheep? What was the original—and what are your predominant featured species?

Mr. DIROSA. The refuge, if you will look at the enabling legislation for the refuge, it did not specifically mention bighorn sheep, however, if you follow the information, legislation that led up to that point, it spoke very heavily about bighorn sheep. So that really was one of the reasons the refuge was created. And then it goes on to say for the resources of that time, it mentions grazing resources, which is a moot point now. That is not part of our mission any more, we are not jointly managed with the BLM, we are a full national wildlife refuge.

So species of concern for us regarding the illegal traffic, that will probably have the most impact is the endangered Sonoran pronghorn, also called antelope; the long-nosed bat, we have already documented maternity nests that have been abandoned directly because of smuggling activity. And just the overall natural resources of the refuge. It is very hard to quantify.

Mr. SOUDER. Is there something unique in this area, where the species are at, have they tried to move to the west?

Mr. DIROSA. Many of the species cannot flee. The Sonoran pronghorn are a very mobile animal, however they do tend to congregate in the eastern portion because that is where the resources are. we get approximately 8 to 9 inches of rain on the eastern portion, only 3 inches to the west. And these animals will follow the forage and the water resources.

Interesting comments are received from the public that the illegals or smugglers have much more access to the refuge than the citizens of the United States do, because we have to shut down some of these areas because of the endangered nature of the pronghorn, say for instance in the fawning season this year, we will prohibit people from recreating in the refuge, yet the illegal traffic is continuing to escalate and both the traffic and the law enforcement activity damage the resources.

Mr. SOUDER. My understanding is that in the park, while there has been damage to cactus, it is not substantial, is that because it is not endangering the Saguaro or the Organ Pipe, although theoretically because of the fewer Organ Pipe, it could. And if you could also elaborate on—I am floundering for the term, but whether it be cactus, flowers, other things, habitat that supports both in the monument and in the refuge, the impact of increasing traffic, both human and narcotic and if there is a narcotics nexus, clearly there are random incidents with narcotics, but I am not sure narcotics is the primary threat to the resources.

Mr. WELLMAN. The Organ Pipe Cactus is not endangered. We do lose cactus to illegal activities, particular vehicles coming into the park running over cactus. When sleeping sites are cleared under trees, they clear out cactus seedlings. So we are losing a substantial amount of resources, but not to the point that it is endangering the existence of the cactus.

Probably a bigger impact on our wildlife, and I suspect it is the same in Cabeza, in Organ Pipe, there are only two permanent water sources and one happens to be right on the border, one is about in the middle of the park. Beyond those two springs, all of the water available for wildlife in Organ Pipe is found in tanahas, in catchment basins.

Our legal visitors are not allowed to use that water. As rare as water is in the desert, we want all of that for our wildlife. We know that several of the tanahas, and actually even one of the springs was completely drained by illegal traffic. Probably most of that was illegal aliens rather than drug smugglers, but they both take water that our wildlife needs.

The other thing, particularly the Sonoran pronghorn, pygmy owls, some of the shier wildlife, there is a tremendous disturbance factor because the traffic in the park is pervasive now. Typically we have visitors in the winter, the pronghorn are usually west of the park in the winter and move into the park in the summer. Traditionally when they would come back to the park, they would pretty much have the whole place to themselves. We do not get a lot of visitors, a few German visitors, in the heat of the summer. But now we have the illegal traffic going through, so there is a disturbance to the wildlife year-round, which is a new phenomenon and something they are not very well adapted to.

Mr. SOUDER. Do the traffickers, the illegals move toward water resources? Is it stressing your water resources that are limited already?

Mr. DIROSA. Many of the people coming through do not know where the water resources are. Those that are providing guide service in some cases do know where the water resources are, but they do not tell the people that they are guiding because they want to maintain full control. That is why we have a number of deaths on the refuge.

I would like to emphasize that the people that are trying to negotiate the refuge in that regard are not border citizens, they are coming from very far south Mexico, central Mexico, South America, etc. They get up this far, they are pretty well committed and we are going to put signs to warn people, the Border Patrol does not expect those signs to help much, because they are committed and once they get into the refuge, if they do not find the water, they are in real big trouble. Most of our water is very difficult to find unless you know it is there.

Mr. SOUDER. One of the things we talked about yesterday was one of the two trails that both of you mentioned that illegals have more access to the resources than the citizens who paid for the resources have. But one of the biggest attractions of Organ Pipe is occasionally endangered merely because it may not be as safe or as open, and one of the goals of the National Park Service in this new border protection is to try to secure areas where visitors come to Arizona who want to see these tremendous resources, is that not correct, and could you explain that?

Mr. WELLMAN. Yes. The Sweetwater Pass area is a peak area of Organ Pipe and has been listed as one of the best hikes in Arizona. Right now, because of the tremendous amount of illegal traffic through Sweetwater Pass, we do not recommend visitors use that area, particularly overnight. Keno Valley, Keno Peak, which is almost the center of the park, is one of the most spectacular places in the Sonoran Desert, if you decide to backpack into Keno Valley and spend the night, there is almost a 100 percent probability you will have people walking through your campsite that night. We have had visitors go in, set up their tents, get up in the middle of the night and leave because of the amount of traffic coming through.

Mr. SOUDER. It is a frustrating process here, and part of the reason to have this discussion is obviously with the deaths related to narcotics. People dying at the border areas and concern about homeland security are huge issues. But we have had past cases inside the National Park Service, I am sure to some degree in Fish and Wildlife as well, where the government sets aside an area to be protected and for one reason or another, either people went and stole the artifacts, degraded, whether it be through grazing or other things, resources such that the thing we went to preserve gets destroyed. And we are seeing this not just here, but our drug habits in the United States are wrecking the Amazon Basin. When you fly above, you see whole areas where the Amazon River Basin has cocaine chemical going down through the river, wildlife is gone, cutting down trees so they can put the stuff in. The drug problems are becoming an environmental disaster as well as a human disaster and it is important for us to understand also the need to balance.

Now let me ask another question about the fish and wildlife in the park area. Because this is, obviously as you all know, an explosive question whenever you deal with wilderness or other environmental protections. If we had a 2-mile waiver for homeland security for land and a 5-mile for air surveillance, do you believe that would enable us to get better control along the borders over time? Say we are looking at this in a 5-year or longer term period, and protect the resource more than the way we are currently doing it and trying to have people go through and not much intercept and potentially pushing more. In other words, we do not have a lot of options here, we can put up a perimeter, but then everybody is moving through and it is a wider zone. We can try to put more pressure in the middle or we can really concentrate heavily on the border, or we can just say hey, we do not care, we are going to cover the rest of the United States but if terrorists come through this border or drugs come through this particular area, we are not going to patrol it. This is a tough dilemma and a conflict between legislation that Congress has to deal with and I wonder how you feel about what kind of slots would give us the flexibility, and I want to ask the patrol agencies the same question.

Mr. WELLMAN. I will go first. In Organ Pipe, we do not have the military airspace of the park, so we do not have the problem that the basin has. The problem we have is there are no aircraft to patrol. And yes, having air surveillance along the border would be a great benefit.

The second question is tougher. Along the international border, and probably 2 miles is a pretty good distance, a lot of the more violent crimes tend to happen within that first 2 miles. We need some different rules of engagement, if nothing else for the protection of our rangers and other law enforcement officers along the border.

Mr. SOUDER. How do the Wildlife people feel about it?

Mr. DIROSA. I think it sounds good in theory. It is certainly preferable to stop all the activity at the border and if I were going to be asked where would I do it and invest my resources, it would certainly be at the border. I think it would be problematic, it would be very expensive, we have 56 miles of very remote border that is very difficult to access. It would be easier if we could access it from Mexico on Highway 2 and obviously that is not practical.

To give what might be carte blanche for a 2 mile segment that is currently wilderness would be difficult for me to accept without sitting down and perhaps going through negotiations, etc. So it is a difficult question to answer. There would be any number of non-governmental organizations that would weigh in on this as well, as I am sure you suspect.

But again, I think the border is the place.

Mr. SOUDER. There are variations you could have: You could theoretically have a road and a fence or border barrier and then a hot pursuit rule up to 2 miles unless there is endangerment to go more, you could have some exceptions in that area if it was a particular endangered species that would be extra, although what you are going to do, wherever you put these exceptions, you are going to drive the traffic to that exception, which is what happened on the California border. They had a nesting area and also one type of snail and they just trampled it because if you say you cannot go through here and the Border Patrol had orange cones that said you cannot go through here, there became a run to that area and in one area alone, I saw 900 people massed to go over the fence in 1 night, which is standard, around 1,000 a night, heading for the endangered species areas. Because when you mark them specifically, hey, if we cannot go there, then that is where they go. This is a huge dilemma to try to address it without actually endangering the zones more.

But I do not think the American people assume right now in the terrorism angle, that the greatest threat are Arab nationals, but that is not going to remain the case. As soon as they figure out that we stopped that group, just like any other type of thing, you go to a different profile and contract with other people and it is clear we cannot have borders where thousands of people are coming through a night, it is just not going to be tolerated. And so we have to figure out what is the best way to do it.

Since you have suggestions and work with it—I am not trying to put you on the spot today, but these have to be addressed and I would like to hear Border Patrol, DEA, Customs responses also. And let me ask one other question. What about the 5 miles for air surveillance?

Mr. DiRosa. Would you repeat that?

Mr. Souder. Let me have—at this point before I go to the next—Dennis, what is your last name?

Mr. Lindsay. Lindsay.

Mr. Souder. Yes, could you come forward? One of the things that I understood from John on our staff is that there was a proposal to have like a tunnel where air patrols could go through. The range is blocking this because some of this is very rugged. If you cannot get a road to the barrier, theoretically the air patrols would be able to help to some degree.

Could you elaborate a little bit on what the discussions are on that and how we could do air patrol on the border?

Mr. Lindsay. Yes. Currently right now, we have had some limited success when we have an officer call for assistance, bringing a helicopter in. But that does not allow us to do routine patrol and use some of the sophisticated technologies they have aboard those aircraft to combat the number of vehicles that are coming across. That is what we want to do.

So in essence, what we want to create is a road in the air that is 5 miles wide up to 9,000 feet where we can put some of this technology to look for aircraft and vehicles that are coming across. We currently do not have that. We have been in negotiation with the Air Force since September of last year and so far, we have been denied that corridor to actually put aircraft in there.

Mr. Souder. Are airplanes actually ever down in that zone, and if so, how would they know where the border is?

Mr. Lindsay. To answer your question, they should not be down in that zone, I do not know how they would know where the border is.

One of the things that came out of this discussion with the Air Force was they wanted to be sure that we could provide aircraft separation. Currently they did not have a clear radar picture of the aircraft that were working the bombing ranges. Our radar facility that belongs to Customs in Riverside, CA can provide them that data, so we can assure them aircraft separation which should alleviate that obstacle that they brought up to us.

Mr. SOUDER. And is it something that would have any impact on the resources in the refuge if there were regular——

Mr. LINDSAY. I would think that any time you have some jets flying over the refuge, the noise would be a problem, especially at a low level.

Mr. SOUDER. So a Customs plane would be nothing compared to that problem?

Mr. LINDSAY. No. Now one of the problems is that their low level deck we think is about 20,000 feet at the border. They should not be below 14,000 feet, so we provided an adequate buffer from 9,000 to 14,000, we thought.

Mr. SOUDER. Any other comments or anybody see any reason why that would not be helpful?

[No response.]

Mr. SOUDER. Thank you. Is there anything else you want to add with that? I felt it was really important to get that into the record, that there are proposals in how we run into and counter conflicts sometimes among the agencies in trying to address it.

Mr. LINDSAY. I have a map of the corridor we propose that I would like to enter into the record.

Mr. SOUDER. Yes, thank you very much.

Mr. Aguilar.

Mr. AGUILAR. Yes, Mr. Chairman, if you are asking if we have any more input into what you just brought forward, I would like to say that hearing from an enforcement perspective and homeland security concern, I appreciate you asking that question because my answer to that zone, as you call it, would be a resounding yes, it would help tremendously, in order to give us something that would allow us to work efficiently out there, effectively to create the deterrence posture that we are looking for. I firmly believe that if we deploy the corridor in as efficient a way as we can, as effective a way as we can, it is going to ultimately protect that environmental concern that we have throughout those entire areas out there.

A further clarification—earlier Congressman Shadegg spoke about the successes we have had in the sector. I very quickly came back and talked about the achievements that we have had, because I want to make sure that there is an understanding that yes, we have made some dramatic achievements in Douglas/Naco and Nogales, but we are still in a gain mode out there, we are not finished yet in those areas of operation. One of the things that is very impacting in those areas of operation where we are still very assertive and very aggressively expanding our operation from an enforcement perspective, relates exactly to what you are pointing out here, that we are deploying in such a way as to work around these parameters, statutes, policies and regulations that have an impact on our capability to deploy them on the immediate border.

So again, in citing that, it is important that it would be—my answer would be a resounding yes, it would help tremendously, fully recognizing that we need to be very careful with some of the environmental and cultural treasures that are out there. But from an enforcement perspective, yes, it would help tremendously.

Mr. SOUDER. Any other comments on that?

[No response.]

Mr. SHADEGG. Thank you, Mr. Chairman. Mr. Winderweedle, you have had experience across the whole Arizona border, I think you have been stationed in several different locations.

Mr. WINDERWEEDLE. Yes, sir, I have, with the exception of Nogales.

Mr. SHADEGG. I am curious as to just your comments about the conditions that you face or that you faced when you were in the eastern sector versus the conditions that you faced in the western sector. I also want to ask a followup question. The chairman of the Tohono O'odham Nation testified about the three crossings that they have where members of the Nation go back and forth across the border. As a Customs official responsible for cross border traffic, are you concerned about those three crossings and about the fact that they are functional but not monitored by your department. So if you could address those two questions.

Mr. WINDERWEEDLE. OK, just a point of clarification, Congressman, you say what conditions that we face. Conditions as they pertain to where?

Mr. SHADEGG. The degree of cross border activity you see, either drugs or individuals or goods that you were able to seize and maybe even the level of cooperation that you have across the border in the two different areas, and just contrasting the two different areas.

Mr. WINDERWEEDLE. Well, I think what you are going to find with Bureau of Customs and Border Protection, at least as far as the ports of entry are concerned, that there is consistency. Certainly there is consistency at Lukeville. And certainly the levels of cooperation at Lukeville and it has been my experience, in Arizona as well that the cooperation inter-agency is absolutely excellent.

Mr. SHADEGG. What about cross border cooperation?

Mr. WINDERWEEDLE. I have not always worked in a position to be involved in cross border cooperation, I can say that cross border cooperation at the port of entry at Lukeville at this particular point in time is quite good. My counterpart and I probably speak every week or 10 days on some topic of mutual concern. And that relationship seems to be building and solidifying.

Mr. SHADEGG. And the other part of the question, what about the three crossings on the Tohono O'odham Nation. Is there commercial traffic going across there?

Mr. WINDERWEEDLE. No, sir, there has been no commercial traffic, any legitimate commercial traffic. There may have been attempts, but I think that Mr. Aguilar has had some of his staff involved in that and those attempts have been directed to the port of entry.

I know there are issues with the Tohono O'odham Nation that the legalities of all this are in front of the Congress right now in legislation that was proposed by Congressman Grijalva.

Do we have an immediate binding concern on that? Since it is outside of the port of entry, it would be appropriate for me to defer to Mr. Minas on that topic.

Mr. SOUDER. I would like to ask a couple more of this panel, and I appreciate your tolerance and those who are planning things after this, but this is why we are here.

Mr. Woolley, a couple of things. You mentioned that we are going to be doing a hearing in El Paso next month and working some on the Texas border, we tend to have in the U.S. Government, things pretty organized by usually Arizona area, here is the New Mexico area, here is the Texas area, here is the California area. In the cartels and those who are trying to smuggle the large volume of narcotics over, do they tend to work—I know they are not set up on our State system, but does the eastern side of Arizona tend to flow more toward New Mexico and El Paso; the Yuma side more toward California, or in fact is there a corridor that comes up through Arizona? What are the networks of how the cartels are distributed?

Mr. WOOLLEY. As you point out, they are very well organized and there is a focus in the southern Texas and western Texas area, the Juarez cartel has that pretty well taken care of and their narcotics flow into and up to Chicago and the midwest. We see some of the San Diego based Tijuana traffickers that have established a very good route there through Tijuana, coming further east. And we have very well established cartel members from central Mexico coming up through Nogales.

But like the panel pointed out, if you exert influence in one area, it is like squeezing a balloon and if you squeeze in one area, it has a tendency to pop out elsewhere, so law enforcement initiatives both south of the border and here have a tendency to influence the trafficking patterns. Competition being as it is, there are a number of transportation cells and smuggling cells here in southern Arizona that will sell their services to the highest bidder, so competition will be something that will influence what organization gets used.

Mr. SOUDER. Do they have earmarked zones where they—in other words, how flexible are they in fact to move across borders, if you are a cartel? And can you go into another guy's zone, can your transportation guy go into another guy's zone? Or in fact is it kind of marked and does our structure reflect their structure or does our structure affect our political structure?

Mr. WOOLLEY. Well, you would not go into somebody else's established neighborhood without some concern by that particular group. But if there is some influence, say one of the members get assassinated or the families break down or whatever, there would be probably incentives to try to get in and take over that very lucrative trafficking pattern.

Mr. SOUDER. What are the predominant patterns you see in trafficking changes, is a high percentage of what is intercepted in your sector, taking Phoenix and Arizona as a whole, is it moving more and more toward large quantities or is it breaking up into smaller where they consolidate into truckloads farther up into the State?

Mr. WOOLLEY. Both of those things, sir. As you pointed out earlier, the estimate is between 60 and 65 percent of the drugs coming into the United States is crossing through the southwest border. I would say Arizona has certainly their predominant share of that, 25 to 30 percent. They will shotgun the border with various vehicles, the cottage industry with secret compartments in cars and trucks can contain significant amounts of narcotics—cocaine, methamphetamine and marijuana. Trucking business as it is and the border being open to trade, that is certainly a concern of ours. So they shotgun, they use small loads, they use larger loads. It comes in across the border, is staged in southern Arizona, Tucson, gets up to Phoenix and then it is distributed to the various cities in the United States.

Mr. SOUDER. I was flabbergasted yesterday—and you can explain what in the world that area is across the border at Lukeville, where you have all those trucks and cars on the Mexican side that are impounded, most of which are relatively new, which would suggest there is—if they are in fact saying those were illegal, was it licensing, was it drugs, was it—what in the world is going on there? I mean why are they not being sold in auto salvage—I mean, it goes for an extensive area and there are tons of trucks in there.

Mr. WINDERWEEDLE. It is my understanding that those vehicles have been seized and confiscated by Mexican law enforcement agencies. As far as what their ultimate and final disposition is, I do not know, I have no knowledge of how they get rid of them or if they ever get rid of them, but those are all from Mexican law enforcement agency seizures and confiscations, apparently for violations of laws that were committed in the Republic of Mexico.

Mr. SOUDER. There was one fire there where people had been sleeping and it almost looked like it could be a low-rent motel zone. Do you see that much along there?

Mr. WINDERWEEDLE. We do not have a good view of that through the Port, but that area is transitted literally over, under, around and through. Our counterparts on the other side have made some efforts as far as securing that area. They recognize and understand their responsibility toward that property that is contained in there, but it is a difficult task.

Mr. SOUDER. Do you have very many legitimate use trucks coming through, is it a major trucking port? Do you see an increase when they put pressure on at Nogales or Yuma?

Mr. WINDERWEEDLE. As it stands currently, we are very limited use as far as commercial importation and exportation activity. Our predominant use is with the north and south-bound legitimate compliant travelers—tourist, trade, people transitting through the area on their way south and north.

Mr. SOUDER. Mr. Woolley, do you see much coming in by air, small planes landing, clearing the whole border area?

Mr. WOOLLEY. Yes, sir, we have intelligence information that in fact is happening. Again, my colleagues would probably have better information on that. Up in Tucson, we do not see that too much.

Mr. SOUDER. Do you sense that if we put more pressure on the border as far as other things, that if you were taking narcotics or weapons of mass destruction, you might go that route as opposed to people?

Mr. WOOLLEY. Absolutely.

Mr. SOUDER. Any other comments that anybody would like to put into the record before we move to the third panel?

Mr. SHADEGG. Mr. Woolley, I am a little bit surprised by your last answer on cross border flights. When I was in the Arizona Attorney General's Office, we were aware there was a great deal of cross border flying and random dirt airstrips all over the State. I recall being aware of a number of incidents involving airstrips in

Mojave County. Do you know—that was obviously a number of years ago, say 10–13 years ago. Is it your belief that there is ongoing drug trafficking across the border in small airplanes and landing strips further north in Arizona?

Mr. WOOLLEY. I do not think particularly, sir, that is happening now with the increased diligence that we have since September 11th, that everybody is very attentive to that and from your experience, I am sure you know about the spotters that used to be out there and we have seen a decrease in that, although we do know that there are places down at the border area, there are still some strips that are at least up in the other areas in Arizona, but I do not have any information that those are being used for smuggling.

Mr. SHADEGG. No information that planes are coming across at low altitudes, we have essentially deterred that activity?

Mr. WOOLLEY. I have no information along those lines, but I would be happy to check and get back to you.

Mr. SOUDER. I am confused. You do not have it farther up in Arizona, but you do along the border?

Mr. WOOLLEY. Yes.

Mr. SOUDER. Thank you very much.

Will the members of the third panel please come forward—Ms. Fern Salcido, Mr. Augustine Toro, Colonel Ben Anderson, Ms. Jennifer Allen and Reverend Robin Hoover. And will you remain standing so I can administer the oath?

[Witnesses sworn.]

Mr. SOUDER. Let the record show that each of the witnesses responded in the affirmative.

I would appreciate it if those who have conversations would take them outside and show respect for the witnesses who are here.

Ms. Salcido, we will start with you.

STATEMENTS OF FERN SALCIDO, TOHONO O'ODHAM NATION LEGISLATIVE COUNCIL MEMBER; AUGUSTINE TORO, CHAIRMAN, CHUKUT KUK BOUNDARY COMMITTEE, TOHONO O'ODHAM NATION; COLONEL BEN ANDERSON, U.S. ARMY (RETIRED); JENNIFER ALLEN, BORDER ACTION NETWORK; AND REVEREND ROBIN HOOVER, PRESIDENT, HUMANE BORDERS, INCONSISTENT

Ms. SALCIDO. Good afternoon, Members of Congress and welcome to Tohono O'odham Nation. My name is Fern Salcido.

I am very honored to speak before your subcommittee today. The issue of cross-border narcotics smuggling is one that I am very concerned about. I am a member of the Tohono O'odham Legislative Council elected by Gu Vo District. I live in the community of Meneger's Dam about a quarter of a mile from the border and just a few miles east of the Port of Entry at Lukeville. I have lived in Meneger's Dam all of my life and I am a mother and a grandmother and I care very deeply about my family, my community and my Nation.

Drug smugglers travel through our village day and night. They are very open about their business; they recruit our children, 8 and 9 year olds, to watch for approaching law enforcement agents. They pay our children in drugs. It is common that when a law enforcement officer comes across these smugglers, they chase them at high rates of speed through our villages and communities. It is truly a miracle that none of our children or elders have been run over by either the smugglers or the law enforcement agents. Many years ago, we asked the Bureau of Indian Affairs to install speed bumps in our villages and communities. We were told there were not enough funds for speed bumps.

I want to share with you two incidents that happened to me and perhaps you will better understand my concerns.

Late in 1999, at about 7 p.m., well after dark, someone knocked at my door. I opened the door and found a man dressed in a Mexican military uniform carrying a machine gun. A Humvee vehicle was parked in my front yard and four other uniformed and heavily armed men stood next to the vehicle. The man at the door asked for a man I did not know. It was obvious to me that the men at the door were looking for a lost drug load. My children were in the house and I was very scared for our safety.

Last summer, Federal agents and the Tohono O'odham Police Department surrounded my neighbor's house about 200 yards from my house. As the law enforcement officers moved in on the house, a drug runner tried to escape driving out of the property at a high rate of speed. The man was shot by Custom agents and crashed his vehicle into my shed. Several shots were fired in the direction of my home. Again, I was very fearful for the safety of my children, my grandchildren, myself and my community. Unfortunately, incidents like these two occur regularly in our community and they put us all at grave risk.

The Gu Vo District is bounded on the west by the Organ Pipe Cactus National Monument. I am deeply troubled by the plan to put a vehicle barrier fence along the Organ Pipe border. This will most surely result in even more drug smuggling traffic into my community and in the Gu Vo District. If any of the Organ Pipe border area is fenced, then my community is of the opinion that the vehicle barrier fence should continue east the length of Gu Vo District. I understand our neighboring District, Chukut Kuk, is current discussing their position on the vehicle barrier fence. The Gu Vo District is committed to working in partnership with our neighbors and the United States to deal with cross-border drug smuggling, but we need help and we need it now.

I support Chairman Manuel's proposal that the United States build and maintain a road immediately adjacent to the border and that the Federal law enforcement officials be stationed on the border. Our elders and our children and our families and our communities need protection.

Thank you and I will be pleased to answer any questions you may have.

Mr. SOUDER. Thank you for your willingness to come forward and testify today. Mr. Toro.

[The prepared statement of Ms. Salcido follows:]

Testimony on the Effects of Cross Border Drug Smuggling

Presented by
Tohono O'odham Nation Legislative Council Member
Fern Salcido

Before the Criminal Justice, Drug Policy and Human Resources Subcommittee
Of the House Committee on Government Reform

March 10, 2003

Sells, Arizona

Good Morning Members of Congress and welcome to the Tohono O'odham Nation.

I am very honored to speak before your Subcommittee today. The issue of cross-border narcotics smuggling is one that I am very concerned about. I am a member of the Tohono O'odham Legislative Council elected by the Gu Vo District. I live in the community of Meneger's Dam about a quarter of a mile from the border and just a few miles east of the Port of Entry at Lukeville. I have lived in Meneger's Dam all of my life. I am a mother and a grandmother and I care very deeply about my family, my community and my Nation.

Drug smugglers travel through our village day and night. They are very open about their business. They recruit our children, eight (8) and nine (9) year olds; to watch for approaching law enforcement agents. They pay our children in drugs. It is common that when law enforcement officials come across these smugglers they chase them at high rates of speed through our villages and communities. It is truly a miracle that none of our children or Elders have been run over by either the smugglers or the law enforcement agents. Many years ago we asked the Bureau of Indian Affairs to install speed bumps in our villages and communities and were told there were no funds for speed bumps.

I want to share with you two incidents that happened to me and perhaps you will better understand my concerns.

Late in 1999, at about 7:00 in the evening, well after dark, someone knocked at my door. I opened the door to find a man dressed in a Mexican military uniform carrying a machine gun. A Humvee vehicle was parked in my front yard and four (4) other uniformed and heavily armed men stood next to the vehicle. The man at my door asked for a man I did not know. It was obvious to me that the man at my door was looking for a lost drug load. My children were in the house and I was very, very scared for our safety.

Last summer, federal agents and the Tohono O'odham Police Department surrounded my neighbor's house, about 200 yards from my house. As the law enforcement officials moved in on the house, a drug runner tried to escape driving out of the property at a high rate of speed. The man was shot by Customs agents and crashed his vehicle into my shed. Several shots were fired in the direction of my house. Again, I was very fearful for the safety of my children, myself and our community. Unfortunately, incidents like these two occur regularly in our community and they put us all at grave risk.

The Gu Vo District is bounded on the west by the Organ Pipe Cactus National Monument. I am deeply troubled by the plan to put a vehicle barrier fence along the Organ Pipe border. This will most surely result in even more drug smuggling traffic into my community and the Gu Vo District. If any of the Organ Pipe border area is fenced then my community is of the opinion that the vehicle barrier fence should continue east the length of the Gu Vo District. I understand our neighboring District, Chukut Kuk, is currently discussing their position on the vehicle barrier fence. The Gu Vo District is committed to working in partnership with our neighbors and the United States to deal with cross-border drug smuggling but we need help and we need it now. I support Chairman Manuel's proposal that the United States build and maintain a road immediately adjacent to the border and that federal law enforcement officials be stationed on the border. Our elders, our children, our families and our communities need protection.

Thank you. I am please to answer any questions you might have.

Mr. TORO. Good morning, Members of Congress, welcome to the Tohono O'odham Nation.

I am very honored to speak before your subcommittee today. I live and work on our family ranch which is located 12 miles north of the international boundary in the Chukut Kuk District on the Tohono O'odham Nation. My family has lived on this land since the late 1800's.

I serve my community as a representative on the Chukut Kuk District Council and serve as the chairman of the Boundary Committee for the District. The Boundary Committee is comprised of five representatives from the Council who work closely with Border Patrol and other law enforcement agencies to address many issues; for example, to make sure that the Chukut Kuk District fencing remains secure along the international boundary. This is important to ensure that our cattle and horses remain in our District boundaries. And also to protect our environment and our sacred sites from unwanted intrusions. Fifty miles of the Chukut Kuk District is contiguous to the international boundary.

Not so long ago, many ranchers from both sides of the border worked together to resolve our common problems. Today, our fences are regularly cut by drug smugglers and our cattle strays south of the border. Our sacred environment is desecrated by vehicles driving over our pristine desert.

Our family ranch is located in a very remote area at least 1 hour from the nearest law enforcement officials. Sometimes people come to our ranch asking for food and water. We see they are carrying large bundles and know that they are transporting drugs.

I am very concerned about the safety of my family and other community members that reside in the Chukut Kuk District. Recently, the Chukut Kuk District and Tohono O'odham Nation entered into an agreement with the Border Patrol to build a joint use facility in our District close to the border. I believe this unique collaboration to be the first of its kind anywhere in the United States.

We must act together with our neighbors and the United States to effectively address the issues of border crossing for importation of drugs.

Thank you again and I am pleased to answer any questions you might have.

Mr. SOUDER. Thank you for coming forth with your testimony as well.

Now, Colonel Anderson.

[The prepared statement of Mr. Toro follows:]

Testimony on the Effects of Cross Border Drug Smuggling

Presented by
Augustine Toro
Chairman Chukut Kuk Boundary Committee

Before the Criminal Justice, Drug Policy and Human Resources Subcommittee
Of the House Committee on Government Reform

March 10, 2003

Sells, Arizona

Good morning Members of Congress. Welcome to the Tohono O'odham Nation

I am very honored to speak before your Subcommittee today. I live on our family ranch twelve miles (12) miles north of the International Boundary in the district of Chukuk Kuk on the Tohono O'odham Nation. My family has lived on this land since the early 1900s.

I serve my community on the Chukut Kuk Boundary Committee. The Boundary Committee is comprised of ranchers and others who work to make sure that Chukut Kuk District fencing remains secure. This is important to insure that our cattle and horses remain within our District boundaries and also to protect our environment and our sacred sites from unwanted intrusions. Fifty (50) miles of the Chukut Kuk District is contiguous to the International Boundary.

Not so long ago, ranchers from both sides of the border worked together to resolve our common problems. Today our fences are regularly cut by drug smugglers and our cattle get out. Our sacred environment is desecrated by vehicles driving over pristine desert.

Our family ranch is in a very remote area at least one hour from the nearest law enforcement officials. Sometimes people come to our ranch asking for food and water. We see they are packing large bundles and know they are transporting drugs.

I am very concerned about the safety of my family and my community. Recently, the Chukut Kuk District and the Tohono O'odham Nation entered into an agreement with the U. S. Border Patrol to build a joint use facility in our District close to the border. I believe this unique collaboration to be the first of as its kind anywhere in the United States.

We must act together with our neighbors and the United States to effectively address the issue of cross-border importation of drugs.

Thank you and I am pleased to answer any questions you may have.

Colonel ANDERSON. I am Ben Anderson, a retired U.S. Army Colonel. I am a resident of Cochise County and for almost 30 years as a soldier and officer in the Army. I spent a significant portion of my career planning and executing the defense of other people's borders. We are the world's experts at border security.

So far today, it would appear that we have heard a litany of all the problems we have and why things are not going right, and maybe we are going in the wrong direction and that given the funding that might be considered, it will take far too long to get the problem solved. I do not see this as a means to a solution.

I wish to make three points immediately.

First, your letter that you issued to us stating that "Substantial progress on these issues has been made since the attacks of September 11."

We in Cochise County see no basis for such a positive statement. Cochise County does not even have any Border Patrol checkpoints in operation. Illegal aliens of whatever ilk who get past the initial porous line of sparse Border Patrol presence are free to drive direct to anywhere in the United States. This unique tactic surely does cut down on the number of apprehensions or arrests and improves statistical numbers for bureaucratic reporting, but surely does not solve the problem.

Second, it is difficult to separate people smuggling from drug smuggling to terrorist smuggling. All are intertwined and mutually supportive.

Third, there is far too little attention being paid to the danger of exotic human and animal diseases resulting from the ingress of large masses of medically unscreened illegal aliens—illegal aliens—from the Third World's under-developed countries.

The situation in Cochise County is out of control. Briefings by Border Patrol authorities do not reflect reality. The measure of success is now how many illegal aliens are caught, but how many illegal aliens successfully get through. The arrest/apprehension rate has decreased from 1 in 5 to 1 in 10, it could be zero out of 200. There is no known measurement standard that calls 10 percent or less a passing grade.

There continue to be a series of gambits to assuage the concerns of the border citizens. The standard ploy is to ask for more funding to offset the costs of medical care or prison incarceration costs or whatever. It is not the money that is needed, it is the military. We do not want other taxpayers' money, we want the problem stopped. Attempts to regularize—which is amnesty—or institute some guest worker programs, so as to appease those who profit from cheap slave labor, are mere political gambits.

Recently we had two Border Patrol or official government agents murdered, one south of Naco and Kris Eggle. I mean if Border Patrol agents or National Park agents can be murdered, what message does that send to drug traffickers, smugglers, the Mexican Government and what message does it send to the ranchers in the area—they are terrified. What measure of safety does a lone rancher or property owner feel?

The general mantra at all levels is the lack of funding. Caught in the middle are the ranchers, property owners and the families who live along the border and who must escort their children to the local bus stop to catch a school bus because illegal aliens are hiding in the undergrowth awaiting their rides to the north. Families find drug stashes on their property awaiting pickup by drug traffickers. They fear being charged as drug traffickers themselves.

It is wrong that American high school boys and girls must go about their ranch chores armed at all times. Children have been threatened and attacked by illegals over 30 miles from the border. Others have been co-opted into being drivers and suppliers for coyotes and drug traffickers. The lure of enormous amounts of cash for little effort is overwhelming. They become high school dropouts and may never be recovered to a proper way of life.

The environmental and economic costs to the ranching communities have been overwhelming. Ranching families have been forced into bankruptcy, others are on the verge of bankruptcy. Land values have plummeted.

As a result, citizen groups have been formed to take the matter into their own hands. Three groups are already formed and operating, a fourth out-of-state group, is forming now. Gun dealers in Cochise County are unable to keep up with the surge in demand for both guns and ammunition. Citizens are arming themselves. They feel that bloodshed is on the horizon. All fear it will take a major bloodletting to get relief or to get the ball rolling.

Last week, Fort Huachuca apprehended 90 illegal aliens on the military reservation, 180 previously. The full total is unknown. Fort Huachuca is the U.S. Army's Intelligence Center, is a closed military installation.

No amount of funding or manpower increases or realignment can fix the Border Patrol in a timely manner. It cannot be grown to the task in time.

However, our military is structured, manned, funded, trained and capable of quickly accomplishing the mission. It has decades of experience in border security missions all over the world. The American military is the world's expert at protecting other nation's borders. Safeguarding ours is a snap given interior lines of communication.

There is no need for large military units or heavy equipment or tracked vehicles such as tanks, artillery or armored personnel carriers; or heavy weapons or any equipment that might be ecologically destructive. Light forces with rapid helicopter mobility can cover large remote areas with minimal assets while freeing up the limited Border Patrol assets to concentrate on congested urban areas or where their particular expertise is needed.

In southeast Arizona, where the main concentration of illegal alien and drug traffic exists—upwards of 1.5 million illegal aliens per year successfully cross into Cochise County—the stationing structure already exists. Fort Huachuca provides a perfect location for border operations of any needed military units.

Military engineer units from the active and reserve can rapidly emplace requisite fencing. Units can be rotated to maintain the operational temp of DOD. The task is simple and requires very limited training. Standard rules of engagement suffice.

Concurrently, INS and Border Patrol forces can take on their mandated task of searching out illegal aliens and drug traffickers within the country and repatriating them to their country of origin or prosecuting them.

I strongly urge consideration of a military option in Arizona, if not across the entirety of the U.S./Mexico international border.

Attempts to deny——

Mr. SOUDER. Sir, you are over your time. Can you submit the rest for the record?

Colonel ANDERSON. I surely can, a much larger version was already submitted.

Mr. SOUDER. OK, can you summarize then?

Colonel ANDERSON. I would state that the attempt to use the posse comitatus argument as we are using why not to, is invalid because it is a matter of national security, not law enforcement.

I thank you.

Mr. SOUDER. Thank you very much.

Mr. SHADEGG. Mr. Chairman, point of order.

Mr. SOUDER. Yes?

Mr. SHADEGG. The gentleman's testimony was I think very helpful and useful for this hearing. He indicated it had already been submitted. We do not have a copy. Can you be sure—I just checked with the committee staff and they say they do not have a copy.

Colonel ANDERSON. There is the electronically submitted copy and I have about 50 copies here. I have 10 more to give to you.

Mr. SHADEGG. We want to make sure we have one in the record.

Colonel ANDERSON. I will do that.

Mr. SHADEGG. Thank you.

Mr. SOUDER. The staff came to Arizona sooner to do the backup, so anything that came in, we would not have seen it yet.

Ms. Allen.

[The prepared statement of Colonel Anderson follows:]

The Cochise County View of the Border

Testimony of Ben L. Anderson Jr., Col US Army Retired, submitted to U.S. Subcommittee on Criminal Justice, Drug Policy and Human Resources, Representative Mark Souder, Chairman.

March 10, 2003

Sirs:

My name is Ben L. Anderson Jr.; I am a retired U.S. Army Infantry Colonel. I am a resident of Cochise County, Arizona. I served my country for almost 3 decades as a soldier and officer in the U.S. Army. A significant portion of my career was spent planning for defense of and defending other nation's borders. We did quite well. We won the cold war and we are the only standing superpower. We are the world's experts at border security.

I have no personal interest in illegal immigration or in U.S. drug policy except as a patriotic citizen of the United States. I am not being paid or influenced by any entity whatsoever for my testimony submitted to you this day.

I wish to make three points immediately.

Firstly, your letter regarding this hearing states: *Substantial progress on these issues has been made since the attacks on September 11, 2001…"* I can assure you that we in Cochise County see no basis for such a positive statement. In fact, Cochise County does not even have any Border Patrol checkpoints in operation. Illegal aliens of whatever ilk who get past the initial porous line of sparse Border Patrol presence are free to drive direct to Phoenix or Omaha or anywhere else in the continental U.S. Admittedly, this unique tactic surely does cut down on the number of apprehensions and improve the statistical numbers for bureaucratic reporting, but does little to solve the problem.

Secondly, it is difficult to separate people smuggling from drug smuggling from terrorist smuggling. They all are intertwined and mutually supportive.

Thirdly, far too little attention has been paid to the danger of exotic human and animal diseases resulting from the ingress of large masses of medically unscreened illegal aliens from most of the 3rd world's undeveloped countries.

The US/Mexico border situation in Cochise County, Arizona has been and remains out of control. Briefings by US Border Patrol senior authorities do not reflect reality and the Border Patrol's credibility in this regard has been in question by the local citizenry for years. The measure of success is not how many illegal aliens the border patrol catches and re-catches. The measure is how many they missed and how many illegal aliens successfully penetrated into the interior of the United States. Currently, ranchers and other knowledgeable citizens estimate the apprehension rate has decreased from 1 in 5 to 1 in 10. On occasion is can be 0 out of 200. Thus, any apprehension statistic quoted by Border Patrol executives must be multiplied ten-fold or more to ascertain the failure rate. There is no known measurement standard that calls 10% or less a passing grade.

Documentation by various US government agencies to include the GAO; numerous civilian organizations; the media - print, radio and TV; American citizens along the border and congress itself have proven without any doubt that the current and programmed INS/Border Patrol structure will not be able to contain the illegal alien invasion from Mexico. Doing a name change or a line diagram adjustment under the Department of Home Security or placing this motley crew under the Pope will not effect changes soon enough.

There continue to be a series of gambits to assuage the concerns of the border citizens. The standard ploy is to ask again and again for more funding and/or new funding to offset the costs of medical care or prison incarceration costs or whatever. These quests for more money are akin to throwing oats at a dead horse. The current policy horse is dead.

I shall not waste the committee's time discussing whether or not we should protect or defend our sovereign borders or whether illegal aliens have any standing or justification for invading our sovereign nation. I shall not waste my time debating the parsing of their illegal status.

34 EUPHEMISMS FOR ILLEGAL ALIENS:

"undocumented," "undocumented workers," "undocumented immigrants," "undocumented Mexicans," "immigrants," "illegal immigrants," "illegal residents," "foreign-born," "foreign-born workers," "foreign-born inmate," "foreign-born newcomers," "lower-wage illegal workers," "migrant workers," "alien absconders," "guest workers," "border crossers," "foreign nationals," "Mexicans," "Mexican nationals," "Mexican-born expatriates," "Hispanic immigrants," "Spanish speakers," "Hispanics," "under-banked, under-served population," "newcomers," "illegal newcomers," "poor immigrants," "entrants," "Hispanic Community citizens," "border jumpers," "visitor," "Latinos," "people without papers", "people."

More euphemisms are invented daily. They are legally defined as "illegal aliens".

It is not money that is needed to fight this synergistic and symbiotic business of crime and corruption; it is the military. Only the military can close the border to the illegal entry of those who would do our nation and its economy harm. Trying to buy off the problem with other taxpayer's money is rather insulting to all of us who live in Cochise County. We don't want other taxpayer's money - we want the problem stopped. We want the military. Further, any attempts to "regularize" (code for amnesty) or institute some guestworker program, so as to appease those who profit from cheap slave labor, are mere political gambits.

It is most disturbing that a young U.S. Border Patrol Agent, stationed in Naco can have been murdered south of the border and yet hear no cry of outrage from any of our elected officials at any level. It is as if the young 23 year old agent, married and a father had been run over by a truck or some other innocuous accident. He was murdered by a known drug trafficker – recently released by our authorities in a business as usual fashion.

Equally, disturbing was the murder of Kris Eggle of the National Park Service by similar thugs from Mexico.

If a U.S Border Patrol Agent and a U.S. Park Service Ranger can be murdered with such a muted uproar – what message has been sent to the illegal alien smugglers and drug traffickers and to the Mexican government? And what measure of safety does any lone rancher or property owner feel?

Both incidents bring to question – Just what does Congress think is going on here on the border? And what does it take to make an impact? This is admittedly the seventh field hearing held by the Subcommittee along the nation's borders to address the situation. How many more will it take? And does this all not sound like the United Nations contemplating its navel with regard to Saddam Hussein and Iraq?

There have already been six of these hearings, yet no progress in the eyes the American citizens who live along the border in Cochise County. In fact, matters worsen daily. Since the last such session that I am aware of back on February 22, 2002 in Sierra Vista, not only has there been absolutely no progress, but now various citizen groups have formed to take the matter into their own hands to defend the border and deter the invasion of illegal aliens, drug traffickers and potential terrorists. Three that come to mind are The Ranch Rescue group out of Texas, the American Border Patrol formed in Hereford, (just south of Sierra Vista) and the Citizen Homeland Defense Corps formed in Tombstone. I have received correspondence that another out of state group also wishes for form up for the same purpose. Each group operates independently according to its own agenda and methodology.

These citizen groups have been assailed by various open-borders activist groups as being vigilantes and as militias for doing what they feel they must do to fill the void left by the inaction of government at all levels charged with protecting the general public. We can expect that there will be more groups. I also expect that given the continued failure of agencies at all levels to properly address the problem, the situation will devolve into even more tragic events.

The general mantra by agencies at all levels is the lack of funding and much finger pointing. Everyone wants more funding and all blame the federal government. No one takes any responsibility at any level. Caught in the middle is are the ranchers, property owners and families who live along the border. The bureaucratic non-action is of little solace to American parents who must escort their children to the local rural bus stop or mail box a catch a school bus because illegal aliens are hiding in the undergrowth while they await their "rides" to Phoenix and other distant destinations. Ranchers and property owners continue to find drug stashes on their property awaiting pickup by drug traffickers. They fear that they can be charged as drug traffickers themselves.

The people and drug smuggling is not just limited to Cochise County. Two Peoria elementary schools in Phoenix were placed in lockdown recently as police searched a home suspected of being a haven for dozens of illegal immigrants. Officers later surrounded a house, and at least 45 people stepped outside and surrendered to federal immigration officials. An estimated 20 others remained inside, refusing to surrender, as the operation continued into the evening. At least six of the 45 were suspected "coyotes," or immigrant smugglers. During the initial stages of the probe, Santa Fe Elementary and Ira A. Murphy Elementary schools were placed in lockdown as officers targeted a home, later identified as the "safe house," across the street from the school playground. SWAT teams were employed. Illegals reported that as many as 100 illegal aliens were kept in the safe houses. Peoria is in Phoenix.

Ranching families are sick and tired of having to have their high school boys and girls go about their ranch chores armed and carrying radios at all times. I stress again that American high school children are forced to carry weapons to be safe on their own ranches in the United States. Some of these children have already been threatened and attacked by illegals over 30 miles north of the border.

Communities are sick and tired of having their youth co-opted into being drivers and suppliers for coyotes and drug traffickers. The lure of enormous amounts of cash for little effort is overwhelming. These youths become high school dropouts and may never be recovered to a proper way of life.

The environmental and economic costs to the ranching communities have been overwhelming, yet have never been addressed. As a result, many Arizona ranching families have been forced into bankruptcy; many others are on the verge of bankruptcy. Land values have plummeted. The cause is the lack of border security. Currently, gun dealers in Cochise County report that they are unable to keep up with the surge in demand for both guns and ammunition. Citizens are arming themselves. They feel that bloodshed is on the horizon.

Just last week Ft. Huachuca reports that nearly 90 illegal aliens were apprehended on the military reservation. Some were apprehended walking in the housing areas of the senior officers. Ft. Huachuca is the U.S. Army's Intelligence Center. Over 180 have been apprehended on the post from Oct thru December. The total is unknown from January to now. Ft. Huachuca is a closed military installation. When I drive on to post I must show a picture military ID card.

Environmental concerns to include the valuation of wildlife freedom of movement that compromises border security or safety is simply unethical and immoral. To suggest any form of fencing that compromises the war on drugs or illegal aliens or potential terrorists for environmental concerns is similarly repugnant.

While nature abhors a vacuum, so too does the lack of border security and general lawlessness. We all fear that it will take a major bloodletting to get Congress off the dime.

It is not business as usual solved by simple funding increases. We have a border war going on under the radar. Neither the U.S. Border Patrol, nor surely the U.S. Park Service was ever expected to face this type of situation.

We simply are not taking this invasion of our nation seriously; certainly, not seriously enough.

No amount of funding or manpower increases can fix the Border Patrol structure, organization or operational shortfalls in a timely manner. The Border Patrol was simply never envisioned to face such a daunting threat. It cannot be "grown" to the task in any reasonable timeframe.

However, the mission of protecting US national border sovereignty remains and the mission cannot be compromised given the threat to the national security, the economy and America's culture and values. The chaotic border situation reflects a significant weak link in national security at a time in history when uncontrolled access to the American Homeland by terrorists, illegal aliens and drug traffickers can have demonstrated horrific repercussions as witnessed in the WTC and Pentagon attacks.

Our nation remains on constant terrorist alert, yet a multi-thousand mile border with Mexico -- a 3rd world country noted for corruption at all levels in most of its agencies, drug trafficking, general lawlessness and mistreatment of its own underclass -- remains like a sieve. It is a moral imperative that appropriate measures are taken to seal the border and contain this invasion. It must be repeatedly stressed that the mission is one of national security and not law enforcement.

The United States Military is well structured, manned, funded, trained and capable of quickly accomplishing the mission. There is no need to tell our nation's superb military how to do anything. The command structure, when given the task, will quickly be able to task organize its assets in an efficient and cost-effective manner. The US Military has accepted many a new, difficult, distant and often non-traditional task with alacrity and succeeded. Desert Storm and the Afghanistan mission are but examples. The mission in Iraq will be another. There will be more.

It is not the military that needs instruction on how to do any of its tasks. It is the congress that needs to educate itself as to the feasibility of the mission. Regrettably there are members of congress who are not versed in border denial operations or basic military matters, and who, in their ignorance, do a disservice to the nation by refusing to consider the military option.

Our military has decades of experience in border security missions - from 1945 till the collapse of the Soviet Union in Europe, from the end of open hostilities in Korea and continuing in to this day, and Bosnia and Kosovo, etc. In fact, the American military is the world's expert at protecting other nation's borders. It is time that unique experience is used at home where it is sorely needed.

There is no need for large military units, or heavy equipment or tracked vehicles such as tanks, artillery or armored personnel carriers; or heavy weapons or any equipment that might be ecologically destructive. Light forces with rapid airmobile (helicopter) mobility can cover large remote border areas with minimal assets while freeing up limited Border Patrol assets to concentrate on congested urban areas or where their particular expertise is needed.

In southeastern Arizona, where the main concentration of illegal alien and drug traffic exists, (upwards of 1.5 million illegal aliens per year successfully cross into the United States through Cochise County alone), the stationing structure already exists for rapid deployment. Ft. Huachuca provides a perfect location for border operations of any needed military units.

Military engineer units from the active and reserve components can rapidly emplace requisite fencing in areas where needed. Units (active and reserve) can be rotated to maintain the operational tempo of other Department of Defense missions. The task is simple and requires very limited training, if any at all. Standard "rules of engagement" suffice.

Concurrently, INS and Border Patrol forces can take on their mandated task of searching out illegal aliens within the county and repatriating them to their country of origin.

Finally, the military would be genuinely welcomed by the local citizenry who are frustrated at the unsatisfactory state and national response to the problem.

It is a wining situation for the military, for the local citizenry, the state and the nation.

Frankly, the refusal to defend our borders with our own well trained military seems very similar to the games being played out by the United Nations in refusing to face up to the reality of Sadam Hussein. The difference is that the UN asks for more time; whereas with regard to the assault on our borders there remain those politicos who would ask always for more funding to appease the monster hoping to buy their way out of the problem with taxpayer's money. Yet, all indications support the undeniable fact that matters are getting worse, far worse.

In light of the current and programmed INS/Border Patrol structure's inability to contain the illegal alien invasion from Mexico - I urge strong consideration of a military option in southeastern Arizona, if not across the entirety of the US/Mexico international border.

Any attempts to deny protection of the United States sovereign borders on the basis of any *Posse Comitatus* nonsense is trumped by Article IV, Section 4 of the U.S. Constitution. – "*The United States shall guarantee to every state in this union a republican form of government, and shall protect each of them against invasion;….*". Again, it must be stressed that the mission is one of national security and not law enforcement.

I also stress that the solution is not more taxpayer funding, but rather military presence.

Respectfully,

Ben L. Anderson Jr.
Colonel, USA (Infantry) (Retired)

947 Calle Camellia
Sierra Vista, AZ 85635
(520) 439-4627
Email: blajr@c2i2.com; Website: www.azanderson.org

Military on the border:

The solution is doable –

1. Put the military on the border to release the INS and Border Patrol to go apprehend the illegal aliens current running amok in the United States and return them to their countries of origin.
2. The fix of the INS and Border Patrol will be a major undertaking that will take many years - at least a decade. A review of U.S. Military structure, career patterns, schooling and training is highly recommended.
3. Back off the military from the border when the INS and Border Patrol have grown into their jobs. This will take several years.

Basic suggested concepts include, but are not limited to -

The security of the U.S. border should be accomplished with a combination of Border Patrol, selected regular Military, National Guard & Reserve and a little innovation.

The Border Patrol should apprehend, process and repatriate illegal aliens in accordance with their mission.

The National Guard & Reserves assume those logistic and maintenance functions (transportation – truck and bus driving, vehicle maintenance, communications and administrative tasks, house keeping tasks, etc.) to free up Border Patrol personnel to concentrate on their basic mission.

The regular military provides high tech reconnaissance, surveillance & scouting with manned aircraft and UAVs, monitoring of remote areas, air-lift, and selected units to secure remote areas of the border. The border mission will provide an excellent training opportunity. Most importantly, the border mission is a national security mission.

Some more innovative concepts include -

1. Ultra-light aircraft. Ultra-light aircraft would be appropriate for daytime missions. Ultra-lights are inexpensive (cost less than current Border Patrol SUVs), low maintenance, require only limited training (do not require an FAA pilots license), and fly low & slow allowing for excellent tracking of illegal activity. They can be either single or double occupant and would allow for a dedicated pilot and tracker. They are available for purchase in Arizona.

2. Unmanned Aerial Vehicles (UAVs). UAVs that are in the current inventory provide the nighttime continuation of the daytime mission, yet with advanced high-tech all-weather and limited visibility sensors to acquire and track infiltrating illegal movement.

Both ultra-lights and UAVs can complement each other with reverse cycle maintenance: Ultra-light maintenance at night and UAV maintenance during the day. All UAVs would be stationed and operate from Ft. Huachuca. Ultra-lights would be ground transported to the area of use. State of the art light-weight high-tech communications and position locating systems can be easily installed in proposed ultra-light.

2. Native American Border Patrol Augmentation. A dedicated Native American Border Patrol augmentation would be an excellent way of capitalizing the unique and honored traditional skills of our Native American citizens. Their time honored skills at tracking and outdoor skills can be tapped to the nation's advantage. They should be employed as trackers working in conjunction with US military, Border Patrol, ultra-lights and UAVs. A military occupation specialty (MOS) type training program could provide structure to the concept. Entrusting them with our national borders would be a compliment to their heritage along the line of the *"Code Talkers"* of WW II. A name for consideration would be *"Border Stalkers"*. It might be that this new opportunity would provide a needed and well-deserved niche for the Native American community beyond what is currently available. Currently such a concept is in place with the *"Shadow Wolves"* of the U.S. Customs Service on the Tohono O'Odham Reservation in southern Arizona. The Shadow Wolves unit is composed solely of Native Americans of Blackfoot, Cheyenne and Pima tribes who are known for their uncanny ability to track aliens and the drugs they may carry.
(See: http://www.tucsonweekly.com/tw/2001-09-27/feat.html and http://www.foxnews.com/story/0,2933,70147,00.html)

Ms. ALLEN. Thank you for the opportunity to speak with you all today. It is a great honor. My name is Jennifer Allen, I am the director of the Border Action Network. We were founded in 1999 and we are a grassroots organization that works with Arizona/Mexico border communities to protect our human rights, civil rights and the Sonoran Desert.

On a Federal level, there has been no distinction between drug enforcement, immigration enforcement and border enforcement. Drug war funds and resources have blended almost seamlessly into border enforcement and immigration efforts. As a result, immigrants looking to improve their lives or unite with family, U.S. citizens and legal residents that live on the border are subjected to what has become an essentially lawless and de-Constitutionalized zone where our rights and civil liberties have been undermined. Adding insult to injury, these same enforcement strategies are clearly failing.

Last summer's 130-plus deaths of men, women and children who were looking for work, joining their families or coming to better their lives in the United States is the clearest and most devastating consequence of current U.S. border policies and strategies. The militarization of the border has essentially turned this region into a war zone with solid steel walls, stadium-style lights, 30-foot surveillance towers, underground surveillance, armed military troops, military equipment and tactics, and inter-agency task forces that are not trained to operate on domestic soil.

History should have taught us that building walls to divide countries and people has consistently failed and subsequently been torn down. Nevertheless, we have proceeded with a militarization strategy that has now backfired. The goal of deterrence has failed. In fact, this approach has served to further sophisticate and professionalize the same smuggling networks. For this reason alone, the government's approach to border enforcement should be drastically changed.

A lesser discussed issue in the region, but of equal importance, are the civil rights and human rights consequences of current border policies. From our work and discussions with immigrants and border communities, we want to draw your attention to: The impact of Border Patrol buildup in border communities; the lack of oversight or investigation into the Border Patrol; the growing anti-immigrant movement in Arizona; and the increasing criminalization of immigrants and its devastating impacts on their lives and families.

Border enforcement efforts along the southwest border account for over 70 percent of the INS' budget and over 90 percent of their staffing power. According to the General Accounting Office, the Border Patrol has had enormous employee turnover rates. The result is over 1,200 agents in the Tucson sector alone who show great disregard for the rights and dignity of the people that live on the border—citizens, legal residents and undocumented immigrants alike.

Examples include: In May 1999, Arizona Border Patrol agents Matthew Hemmer separated a 21 year old Salvadoran woman from her friend and drove her to a remote location where he tied her hands together, forced her to kneel on the ground and raped her.

Agent Hemmer was arrested in August 2000, charged with kidnapping, sexual assault and sexual abuse. He pled guilty to merely aggravated assault and for transporting the woman without her consent. If he completes 36 months probation, his record will only show a misdemeanor.

A mother that lives in Pirtleville, a small community outside Douglas, tells of Border Patrol agents driving 80 miles an hour over narrow dirt neighborhood streets chasing suspected immigrants. The dust plume from the speeding vehicles aggravates her children's asthma and the parents fear to let their children play outside.

Another woman from Sasabe described how a Border Patrol agent interrogated her young niece and drove her to tears as she was on her bicycle on her way to the grocery store.

As of February 2002, Agent Matthew Sheffler, the prime suspect in the murder of his girlfriend and fellow agent in 2000, continued to work at a Border Patrol checkpoint near Douglas.

Other stories include incidents similar to this of agents shooting the people and in some cases killing people, running people over with their vehicles and sexually assaulting women. Our sources are from people that live in the communities as well as investigative reports and government reports.

Adding insult to injury, most people in border communities report that they do not know how to file a complaint against an agent. And those that do, express doubt that anything would result other than retaliation against them. The Office of the Inspector General is responsible for investigating criminal complaints; however, the office's seven investigators monitor more than 1,200 Border Patrol agents in the Tucson sector alone, plus thousands of other INS, U.S. Marshals and Bureau of Prison employees in Arizona and Nevada.

Clearly the system that exists for monitoring the Border Patrol and ensuring fair and expeditious review of cases and complaints is not working. As the budgets of what was the INS and the Department of Defense, who is playing a greater physical role on the border, budgets that reach nearly $20 billion, it is critical that the impacts of these activities on communities be addressed.

Another key area of concern is the growth of anti-immigrant, white supremacist groups along the border. These groups, like human rights and community groups also see the failure of U.S. border enforcement efforts. They, however, are exacerbating the violence and fear that U.S. strategies have created. In December 2002 we released a report entitled Hat or Heroism: Vigilantism on the Arizona-Mexico Border, that we have submitted as evidence, and we would appreciate if you could take time to look at it.

These are neither individual acts nor isolated events, the activities of the border vigilante groups; they are organized, unlawful and are receiving significant media attention. Nonetheless, they continue. What is equally disturbing is that local law enforcement and the Border Patrol tout their support for these groups even in the face of national INS concern about these groups and their activities.

The State and Federal Government's inaction and failure to stop these groups and rights violations is a tacit approval, a green-light for violent, anti-immigrant groups to continue harassing, kidnapping and holding immigrants at gun point.

These are just snapshots of the many, many lives who have been lost, destroyed and threatened by the current U.S. border policies and enforcement strategies. The Federal Government is responsible for protecting the rights of all people that call this country home. Our border policies are in fact undermining the principles and values that we espouse.

I thank the subcommittee for taking the time to hear from us today and hope that you all will take up the responsibility of carrying our voices and stories to Washington and converting them into safe and just policies that neither waste our money nor our lives.

Thank you.

Mr. SOUDER. Thank you and we will put your full statement in the record; thank you for abbreviating.

Ms. ALLEN. Thank you.

Mr. SOUDER. Reverend Hoover.

[NOTE.—The Border Action Network report entitled, "Hate or Heroism, Vigilantes on the Arizona-Mexico Border, December 2002," may be found in subcommittee files.]

[The prepared statement of Ms. Allen follows:]

Border Action Network

PO Box 384, Tucson, AZ 85702
Ph 520.623.4944 Fax 520.792.2097
ban@borderaction.org www.borderaction.org

Testimony for the Government Reform Committee's Subcommittee on Criminal Justice, Drug Policy and Human Resources

From: Jennifer Allen, Director of the Border Action Network
Date: March 8, 2003

Thank you for the opportunity to speak with you all today. It is a great honor. I am pleased that the subcommittee came to Sells to better understand the implications of border enforcement policies and strategies on our communities.

My name is Jennifer Allen. I am the director of the Border Action Network. We were founded in 1999 and are a membership-based organization that works with Arizona-Mexico border communities to protect our human rights, civil rights and the Sonoran desert.

On a federal level there has been no distinction between drug enforcement, immigration enforcement and border enforcement—drug war funds and resources have blended almost seamlessly into border enforcement and immigration efforts. As a result, immigrants looking to improve their lives or unite with family, U.S. citizens and legal residents that live on the border are subjected to what has become an essentially 'lawless' and de-Constitutionalized zone where our rights and civil liberties have been undermined. Adding insult to injury, these enforcement strategies are clearly failing.

Last summer's 130-plus deaths of men, women and children who were looking for work, joining their families or coming to better their lives in the U.S. is the clearest and most devastating consequence of current US border policies and strategies. The *militarization* of the border has essentially turned the region into a war zone with solid steel walls, stadium-style lights, 30' surveillance towers, underground surveillance, armed military troops, military equipment and tactics, and inter-agency task forces that are not trained for operating on domestic soil.

History should have taught us that building walls to divide countries and peoples has consistently failed and have subsequently been torn down. Nonetheless, we have proceeded with a militarization strategy that has now back-fired. The INS' Southwest Strategy (which relies on building up first urban areas on the border with walls and agents, then moving to the rural areas) has resulted in nothing more than funneling trafficking of humans and drugs from one part of the region to another and more recently, into the most deadly and remote areas along the border. The goal of deterrence has failed. In fact, this approach has served to further sophisticate and professionalize smuggling networks. For this reason alone, the government's approach to border enforcement should be drastically changed.

A lesser discussed issue in the region, but of equal importance are the civil rights and human rights consequences of current border policies. From our work and discussions with immigrants and border communities, we want to draw your attention to:

- The impacts of Border Patrol buildup in border communities
- The lack of oversight or investigation into the Border Patrol
- The growing anti-immigrant movement in Arizona
- The increasing criminalization of immigrants and its devastating impacts on their lives and families

Border enforcement efforts along the southwest border account for over 70% of the INS' budget and over 90% of their staffing power. As the General Accounting Office has noted, the Border Patrol has had enormous employee turnover rates. The result is over 1,200 agents in the Tucson Sector alone who show great disregard for the rights and dignity of the people that live on the border—citizens, legal residents and undocumented immigrants alike.

Examples include:

- In May 1999, Arizona Border Patrol agent Matthew Hemmer separated a 21 year old Salvadoran woman from her friend and drove her to a remote location where he tied her hands together, forced her to kneel naked on the ground, and raped her. Agent Hemmer was arrested in August 2000 and charged with kidnapping, sexual assault and sexual abuse. He pled guilty for aggravated assault and for transporting the woman without telling her where she was going. If he completes his 36-month probation, his record will only show a misdemeanor.

- A mother that lives in Pirtleville, a small community outside Douglas, tells of Border Patrol agents driving 80mph over narrow dirt neighborhood streets chasing suspected immigrants. The dust plume from the speeding vehicles aggravates their children's asthma and the parents fear to let their children play outside.

- A mother tells how agents stopped almost her daily because she drives a Suburban with tinted windows.

- Another woman from Sasabe described how a Border Patrol agent interrogated her young niece and drove her to tears as she rode her bike to the store to buy her mom milk.

- Border Patrol agent Jason Wood, based in Nogales was put on paid administrative leave. He was the lead suspect for the murder of his uncle. He was hired in spite of his long history of run-ins with law enforcement including a 1997 memo from Nogales police sergeant after a number of run-ins with Agents Wood trying to draw the border patrol's attention to the agents "potentially explosive situation". In 1998 Woods was arrested for aggravated assault, intimidation, stalking and domestic violence for which two children were treated in a hospital.

- As of February 2002, BP agent Matthew Scheffler, the prime suspect in the murder of his girlfriend and fellow agent in 2000, continued to work at a Border Patrol checkpoint near Douglas.

Other stories include incidences of agents shooting at people and in some case killing people, running people over with their vehicles, and sexually assaulting women. Our sources are from people living in Border towns, investigative reports from the Tucson Citizen and Arizona Daily Star and reports from the Office of the Inspector General.

Adding insult to injury, most people in border communities report that they don't know how to file a complaint against an agent. And those that do, express doubt that anything would result other than retaliation against them. The Office of the Inspector General is responsible for investigating criminal complaints; however, the office's seven investigators monitor more than 1,200 Border Patrol agents in the Tucson sector alone, plus thousands of other INS, US Marshals, and the Bureau of Prisons employees in Arizona and Nevada.

Clearly, the system that exists for monitoring the Border Patrol and ensuring fair and expeditious review of cases and complaints is not working. As the budgets of the INS and Department of Defense (who is also playing a greater physical role on the border) border enforcement efforts reach nearly $20 billion, it is critical that the impacts of these activities on communities be addressed.

Another area of concern is the growth of anti-immigrant, white supremacist groups along the border. These groups, like human rights and community groups, also see the failure of U.S. border enforcement efforts. They, however, are exacerbating the violence and fear that U.S. strategies have created. In December 2002 we released a report entitled *Hate or Heroism: Vigilantism on the Arizona-Mexico Border* which lays out clear and concrete policy recommendations. Please take the time to read this document.

These groups include American Border Patrol, Ranch Rescue, Civilian Homeland Defense, the Barnett brothers, Arizonans for Immigration Reform, and others. Clad in camouflage fatigues or uniforms similar to Border Patrol or the National Guard, using high-tech equipment and operating out of secret headquarters, these groups are taking the law into their own hands. Heavily armed, they are rounding up people suspected to be undocumented immigrants, holding them at gunpoint, with dogs at bay, and turning them over to Border Patrol. In several cases, immigrants have been beaten, abused or bit by their dogs.

These are neither individual acts nor isolated events; they are organized, unlawful and are receiving significant media attention. Nonetheless, they continue. What is equally disturbing is that local law enforcement and the Border Patrol tout their support for these groups, even in the face of national INS concern about these groups and their activities. David Aguilar stated "I know these groups. And I know many of the people in these groups.

Some of my friends are in these groups. These people are not anti-immigrant, and (these) are not hate groups." (see *Hate or Heroism*, page 22).

The state and federal government's inaction and failure to stop these groups and rights violations is a tacit approval, a green-light for violent, anti-immigrant groups to continue harassing, kidnapping and holding immigrants at gun-point.

My last point is one that I believe you have heard from immigrant advocates from across the country, so I will focus on the civil rights issues we face in the southwest. With passage of the Illegal Immigrant Reform and Immigrant Responsibility Act, Anti-terrorism and Effective Death Penalty Act, the USA Patriot Act and the many changes and over-rides of immigration policy by Attorney General Ashcroft, we are seeing immigrants increasingly being pulled into the criminal justice system.

In March 2002, we were involved in a campaign to prevent the construction of up to four new, privately-run federal prisons that would house immigrants convicted of crimes. That proposal was cancelled in March 2002. Now, we have heard rumor that the INS will be looking for a series of new, privately-run detention centers at the same locations with the same companies. It appears that the immigrants are being doled out to boost the profits of struggling private prison companies who themselves are renown for brutality, lack of oversight, poor management, escapes and terrible working conditions.

Furthermore, with the current sentencing structure, we are talking with immigrants—undocumented, asylum seekers and legal residents—who spend years in detention centers and prisons for petty, non-violent crimes. Sitting in a Nogales shelter was a young man, a legal permanent resident, who moved to North Dakota with his family when he was 4yrs. old. He had an unpaid traffic violation from several years ago, and then got stopped again on a traffic violation. For these crimes, he spent almost a year in prison and then was deported to Mexico, a country that he barely knows. Shortly after being sentenced, his wife gave birth to their baby who he has only seen once through a plexy glass window at the prison.

These are just snapshots of the many, many lives who have been lost, destroyed and threatened by the current US border policies and enforcement strategies. The federal government is responsible for protecting the rights of all people that call this country home. Our border policies are in fact, undermining the principals and values that we espouse, particularly in the international forum.

I thank the subcommittee for taking the time to hear from us today and hope that you all will take up the responsibility of carrying our voices and stories to Washington and converting them into safe and just policies that neither waste our money nor our lives.

Recommendations:
Current reliance on enforcement strategies ignores the root causes drug trafficking and immigration. We make the following recommendations that will affect underlying issues:
To decrease illegal border crossing:

- Approve the legalization of undocumented immigrants already in the country so that people do not have to smuggle family members into the country. This would also allow people to enter and leave the country through ports of entry.
- Approve a guest worker program that affords immigrant workers the right to organize, health care, job mobility, a U.S.-standard living wage and other rights afforded to resident workers.

To decrease drug trafficking:

- Reallocate drug enforcement resources to treat the demand for drugs as human health issue in the US, including support for treatment of drug addiction and drug use.
- Reallocate drug enforcement resources into the socio-economic issues behind drug use, including allocation of resources for living wage jobs and improved education.

Rev. HOOVER. Congressman Souder and Congressman Shadegg, thank you for the opportunity to testify. My verbal remarks are slightly different from my written testimony at the request of the committee and I will provide copies of my spoken words.

I began working in the area of migration policy during the Salvadoran exodus to the United States in the 1980's and I hold a 1998 Ph.D. narrowly focused in political science of the area of migration.

To begin, Humane Borders, Inc. and its member organizations wish to acknowledge that we support the underlying premise of law enforcement of all the agencies all along the border. That is, that the government has the absolute sovereign right to determine who crosses the U.S./Mexico border, when, where, what, with what and under what circumstances. The member organizations of Humane Borders support the presence of law enforcement efforts to reduce the scourge of cross-border smuggling. I and volunteers on two occasions have been in the desert during operations when smugglers were apprehended with fully automatic weapons and we were asked to leave the area.

The violence related to this traffic is escalating and it has already claimed far too many lives of persons on both sides of the U.S./Mexico border. Additionally, drug smuggling contributes to environmental degradation in many ways each and every day, particularly with vehicular traffic, as you have heard.

While law enforcement officers and various public administrators, particularly the land managers, etc., focus primarily on questions of efficiency and effectiveness of policy, we are a faith-based organization, particularly concerned with equitable questions. We do not find though that these differences place us at odds with those that are trying to implement current policies.

However, all that said, U.S. border policies are collectively very fatally flawed. They result in totally unacceptable annual death tolls. Social scientists, both in the academy and in public service confirm that the buildup of personnel and technologies has continued to intentionally move the migration and consequently the drug smuggling into more and more inhospitable, precious pristine areas of the desert, resulting in more deaths. In southern Arizona alone, the death toll in the desert is now 25 times as high as it was just 6 years ago.

In our judgment, two things need to be addressed. Of course, in the long term, the inexorable flow of humanity from south to north needs to be moved back to the ports of entry where migrants are documented, inspected and cleared for security and otherwise processed in order to contribute to the security of citizens of the United States.

Moving the migration back to the ports of entry would radically change the ratio of law enforcement officers to the number of persons seeking to enter the United States without inspection and change their assumptions about those that they encounter in the desert. BCBP personnel between the ports would be more justified in assuming that they were encountering a felon rather than a person merely in administrative violation. In our judgment, the long-term political solution to the migration is actually more relevant today than prior to September 11th.

In the short term, law enforcement in southern Arizona should continue to work with various land managers and with non-governmental organizations like Humane Borders, Inc. to reduce the number of deaths in the desert. Fortunately, there are a number of low-cost, low-environmental impact technologies, including those proposed currently by law enforcement yet to be employed.

Simply count the staff time and count the dollars. Time and money spent on search and rescue operations, provision of medical transportation and services, supervision, media relations, community relations, other activities could be significantly reduced if death were substantially taken out of the immigration equation. Failure to do so will continue to demoralize BCBP personnel and further increase concern within a significant segment of the resident population.

Additionally in the short term, absent a comprehensive change in border policies and absent a border law enforcement buildup of several times as many personnel, border crossing enforcement through deterrence and apprehensions can only be improved incrementally, as we have heard. In fact, we may reach the time when dollars spent on this side of the line would be more effectively spent on the other side.

In June 2001, more than 20 people gathered, representing Humane Borders and various Federal, State, county and tribal authorities on two occasions in Ajo, AZ. A consensus was articulated that land managers should not act unilaterally through deterrence and other measures, because to do so would only push cross-border traffic onto adjacent property, increasing environmental degradation there and potentially contributing to the further loss of life.

In conclusion, we acknowledge the depth and the breadth of this border problem. Absent a complete overhaul of the U.S. border policies, incremental changes in enforcement practices will only shift the migration around, contribute to more deaths and further degrade the environment.

Thank you for the opportunity to share this analysis and I would welcome your questions.

[The prepared statement of Rev. Hoover follows:]

Humane Borders
740 E. Speedway Blvd.
Tucson AZ 85719
520-628-7753

Submitted March 10, 2003

TESTIMONY OF REV. ROBIN HOOVER, Ph.D., PRESIDENT OF HUMANE BORDERS, INC. BEFORE THE GOVERNMENT REFORM COMMITTEE'S SUBCOMMITTEE ON CRIMINAL JUSTICE, DRUG POLICY, AND HUMAN RESOURCES INVESTIGATIVE HEARING ENTITLED, "THE IMPACT OF THE DRUG TRADE ON BORDER SECURITY AND NATIONAL PARKS" MEETING IN SELLS, ARIZONA MARCH 10, 2003, AT THE TOHONO O'ODHAM NATION LEGISLATIVE COUNCIL CHAMBERS AT 10A.M.

Subcommittee chairman Souder and Congressional Representatives, thank you for being in Arizona, and thank you for the opportunity to present this brief testimony.

Humane Borders, Inc. is a faith-based organization that places water in the deserts of the states of Arizona and California. We operate under federal and county permits and on private lands to reduce the number of deaths in the desert and to reduce costs to local governments. In 2001, we received a $25,000 contract from Pima County Government for these purposes. We advocate on both sides of the US-Mexico border for a political solution to the continuous human tragedy of death in the desert.

We also provide public education on border issues. I have included copies of our February 2003 "Report From the Border" for your files as well as 2002 maps indicating migrant death locations and location of our water stations. In limited ways, water stations are now part of the strategy of land managers to reduce the deleterious effects of the migration on public lands.

US Border Policies are fatally flawed, and no matter how unintended, law enforcement strategies including INS operations continue to contribute to the death toll. Migrants are not crossing at Ports of Entry and urban areas, but choosing to run the gauntlet through the desert, or being led there by smugglers. In Southern Arizona last year over 200 men, women, and children died, the youngest known being 11 years in age. Unfortunately, no changes in border policies since 9-11 can rationally be predicted to lower the expected record number of deaths in the desert this year. Water must be placed in the desert and policies must change.

We work with federal law enforcement to remove death from the immigration equation. Our water stations give agents and officers more time to achieve their objectives of deterrence and apprehension, instead of spending time on search and rescue. We provide extra eyes and ears, and we frequently call US Border Patrol to effect rescues of migrants. Additionally, strategically placed water stations and frequent organized efforts to pick up migrant trash contribute to the protection of precious natural resources on federal lands. Our organization picked up over 300 cubic yards of trash last season alone.

Specifically addressing the goals of this hearing, I wish to comment on both macro and micro policies. First, in order to improve the law enforcement function concerning both drug traffic and national security, the inexorable migration of workers from Mexico to the US must be moved from the deserts back to the Ports of Entry. This can only be accomplished with substantive policy changes. Neither further militarization of the border or significantly augmented law enforcement resources will accomplish this task. Such efforts only re-locate crossing points. It's like placing rocks in a stream. The water goes around the rocks. Well over 98% of the people federal law enforcement officers encounter in the deserts are workers whom employers reward with jobs, often arranged before they cross the line. These same employers successfully pressured Congress to eviscerate employer sanctions. Even if further militarization or enhanced law enforcement were successful, further employer dissatisfaction and policy resistance should be anticipated.

Second, on a micro level, current federal law enforcement practices routinely elicit complaints from US Citizens fearing life lived in this militarized zone. Regularly rotating Border Patrol agents from one station to another reduces cultural sensitivities of agents to resident populations. High-speed pursuits result in deadly auto accidents and additional costs. Agents and officers apprehend only healthy migrants to avoid paying local health care providers for services rendered in compliance with federal laws.

Moving the migration back through the Ports of Entry with necessary investigations, inspections and safeguards, informs us of who is here, where they are going, and what they are bringing. It is also the only responsible way to exercise national sovereignty. Moving the migration back to the ports of entry frees law enforcement resources to perform traditional policing functions in the desert and to change their assumptions about who is in the desert and what they are doing.

Anecdotally, one agent in this sector has also worked in San Diego Sector. He has been present at the recovery of more than 175 dead migrants. The first thing that goes through this man's mind when he gets a call on the radio is not to look for a terrorist.

So again, moving the migration back to the ports would dramatically reduce the impacts of the migration on natural resources, the impact of law enforcement deterrence practices on the lands, as well as search and rescue damage to the desert.

In Sum, the shift of roles and missions of federal law enforcement can be predicted to push the migration into even more difficult terrain resulting in more deaths. This shift can also be predicted to increase violence between US officers and both migrants and drug smugglers.

In our judgment, it is immoral to use the desert as part of a policy of deterrence. We believe that the US government has a moral responsibility to reduce the number of deaths in the desert by erecting and maintaining water stations, by strengthening law enforcement, by maintaining search and rescue capacities, and by moving toward what our President has called "regularization" of the migration.

Mr. SOUDER. Thank you all for your testimony. As you can see all day we have heard from a wide range of opinions.

Let me start with Mr. Hoover. Do you favor any limitations on the number of immigrants?

Rev. HOOVER. Limitations on?

Mr. SOUDER. The number of immigrants. In other words, you define different ways—guest workers, illegal aliens and so on. Do you favor any limitations?

Rev. HOOVER. That is our right to choose to do that and I think that we would be better served to exempt Mexico from the worldwide quota of visas, precisely because empirically they are already here, we already have the cross-border traffic. Our current enforcement practice is attracting the huge number of people here.

Mr. SOUDER. A large percentage of that people coming through the south border are in fact not Mexican, as we have heard, they are Salvadoran, Honduran and Central American. Would you limit them?

Rev. HOOVER. Yes, I would. About 98 percent are Mexican national right now crossing.

Mr. SOUDER. That is disputed, but I agree it is the overwhelming majority. Of course, the policy that we have seen in other places like Canada on the north, is that system would depend on Mexico having it. Even if I granted that premise, that you were not going to limit Mexico, that depends on their citizenship criteria because all that would mean is you would have to move into Mexico if it was 6 months 1 year in 5 years. Libya is doing this and the Caribbean Islands, establishing European citizenship when their European islanders are coming in under European common market rules for immigration, and that is one of our big focuses on terrorism right now.

How would you not have absolute chaos on the south border if there were not limitations and that was seen as a carte blanche once you made it into Mexico?

Rev. HOOVER. We have absolute chaos on the border. And if you were to inspect folks and check them out and so forth, give them documentation, make an opportunity to come here legally, you would have more port of entry entrants that you would know was here.

Mr. SOUDER. I am not necessarily disagreeing with the guest worker or changes in numbers, what I am trying to establish is that we will never have, nor will we ever agree to completely open borders.

Rev. HOOVER. Sir, a border exists, our question before us, even when we named our organization is we have a border, the question is how do we make it humane.

Mr. SOUDER. Would you support then if someone had a guest worker privilege and they overstayed it, immediate deportation, tough penalties if they came back?

Rev. HOOVER. I fully believe that someone needs to probably have a little grace period, but yes, you go home. A tremendous number of the folks who are here are folks who have overstayed and from other places other than Mexico.

Mr. SOUDER. My point being is that would that person then not go through the port of entry the next time?

Rev. HOOVER. It all depends. There are so many variables in that scenario.

Mr. SOUDER. I believe with modifications of immigration strategy, we can have some percentage, higher percentage moving through the port of entry, but I do not think it is realistic to think that only drug felons or others would be moving in the illegal zones. We are always going to have to have a Border Patrol presence that is fairly substantial.

Rev. HOOVER. Yes, sir, I just think this changes the ratio and changes the assumptions of what is happening in the desert, if we could get a lot of the migration back to the ports of entry.

Mr. SOUDER. One last question. When you put water or other outposts in land, do you check with the landowner whether that—do you just do this unilaterally?

Rev. HOOVER. We operate under Federal permits in Cabeza Prieta National Wildlife Refuge, Organ Pipe Cactus National Monument, Bureau of Land Management, U.S. Fish and Wildlife operated Buenos Aires National Wildlife Refuge, we do so under permits. We provide insurance for these activities, it is at no cost to the organization. In fact, the land managers are interested in our presence there because in their absence to control the migration, they can at least manage some of the effects on their property. So we are here at the invitation.

Mr. SOUDER. So you are permitted.

Rev. HOOVER. Yes, sir.

Mr. SOUDER. And similarly on Tohono O'odham?

Rev. HOOVER. We have no water stations on this Nation's land.

Mr. SOUDER. What about on anybody's private land?

Rev. HOOVER. [Shakes head.]

Mr. SOUDER. So the only places you do this are where you are permitted?

Rev. HOOVER. We are on Federal property, we are on one county's property and we are on about 11 private locations. They are all very strategic and remote—strategically located, very remote situations.

Mr. SOUDER. In the Border Action Network, Ms. Allen, do you support any limitations on immigration?

Ms. ALLEN. We support immigration policies that incorporate root causes of immigration, which then reflect the economic needs within this country and also reflect the economic push factors within Mexico. So in that sense—that is what we believe should be the basis of immigration flow. And right now, they are devoid of understanding the economic push.

Mr. SOUDER. So you do not believe immigration standards should be based on U.S. needs or requirements, you believe they ought to be international?

Ms. ALLEN. Within the U.S. economy, we believe that immigration policy should be much more formed around the recognition of the dependency on immigration, of immigrant labor and that there is also——

Mr. SOUDER. Well, I understand that, my question was more precise. Let us say if our unemployment rate is low and there is a big push back for coming to the United States, that is one thing, but what if our unemployment has stayed stable for 5 years and Mexico's economy has a problem. Are you saying we should adjust our immigration strategy based on their economy too, because I heard you say it should be on the whole push and pull.

Ms. ALLEN. I think part of our concern is that we close off the border or say that we do not want X number of Mexicans or only—set some limits, but those limits are outside, they do not fit within the context of the impacts of globalization, that part of the push of other immigrants from Mexico and Central America is a direct result of our policies. So we are pushing people out of their lands, but then sealing our border and not providing people anywhere to go.

Mr. SOUDER. Thank you. Mr. Shadegg.

Mr. SHADEGG. I want to begin, Mr. Hoover, with you. You responded to the chairman's question by saying that you operate under Federal permits and you cited a number of them. Could you provide the committee with copies of those Federal permits?

Rev. HOOVER. Yes, we can do that.

Mr. SHADEGG. That would be greatly appreciated.

Rev. HOOVER. May I respond to one thing. They changed over time, the location. For instance, at Ironwood now, that particular permit was negotiated with BLM, Department of Justice, Department of Interior and has $10 million worth of liability insurance—complex.

Mr. SHADEGG. Is it safe to assume that each of these permits specifically authorizes you to go out and place water in these locations?

Rev. HOOVER. That is correct.

Mr. SHADEGG. Under a grant of authority and permission from the Federal Government.

Rev. HOOVER. The one exception is Cabeza Prieta National Wildlife Refuge, that has some water on the land, and in those locations, rather than us servicing those in the environmentally sensitive areas, they have some existing wildlife water locations that are marked with our 30 foot poles and blue flags, equipment that we supply to them.

Mr. SHADEGG. And it would be your testimony that you do not go into any Federal lands, either in violation of Federal environmental laws or without permit to go in and put the water there.

Rev. HOOVER. That is absolutely correct. In addition to that, I would point out, since we have been looking at the impacts on the land, volunteers from our organization have probably removed over 200 cubic yards of trash this year.

Mr. SHADEGG. I actually read in your written testimony it was over 300 cubic yards of trash.

Rev. HOOVER. I am from Texas.

Mr. SHADEGG. And I compliment you—[laughter]—I hope you remove as much as you can, it is a serious problem.

Some people would argue, and representatives of the Tribe came to me when I was at Organ Pipe and said they are concerned about the presence of water as a magnet drawing people and the trash that is brought. So to the extent that you remove trash as a complement to bringing water, I am certain that is an appreciated factor.

With regard to your work on private land, your organization does no work on private land without first obtaining permission?

Rev. HOOVER. Oh, absolutely. We have permission slips from everybody.

Mr. SHADEGG. OK. Could you provide the committee with a copy of those as well, a copy of those permission slips?

Rev. HOOVER. [Nods head.]

Mr. SHADEGG. And the last one, you mention in your testimony, at least—I know you modified your testimony, but in your original submitted testimony, you mentioned a $25,000 contract from Pima County.

Rev. HOOVER. Yes.

Mr. SHADEGG. Can you tell me what that contract calls upon your organization to do?

Rev. HOOVER. During the time of that contract, it was to identify sites, erect and maintain water stations in Pima County. Actually it was not limited to Pima County, but practically it was. They never specified that.

Mr. SHADEGG. Well, they do not have the authority to grant you permission——

Rev. HOOVER. The whole justification there is to reduce to very significant amount of cost to rehydrate people in the University Medical Center, etc.

Mr. SHADEGG. I understand that the ongoing activity of your organization is to put water out for humane reasons so people do not die.

Rev. HOOVER. Yes.

Mr. SHADEGG. At the same time, the rest of your testimony was that we need to revise our policy to get people back to ports of entry.

Rev. HOOVER. We will support anything that will get people out of the desert, so that there will be a lot less death out here and less damage to our desert.

Mr. SHADEGG. One question I wanted to ask, I think getting people to go back to ports of entry and come into the country under some sort of a legal framework is certainly a strategy that, quite frankly, to me makes more sense than driving them into remote area where they do environmental damage and die. But to that point, has your organization taken any efforts to deal with organized labor's opposition to any kind of a structured process by which non-U.S. citizens can come into the country and work?

Rev. HOOVER. We have no systematic contacts with organized labor. Of course, they have been in a change since January 2 years ago, of now choosing, wishing to represent undocumented folks, etc. But we do not have any recent conversations with labor.

Mr. SHADEGG. Ms. Allen, I would like to ask you the same question. One of the problems that those of us who believe the guest worker program may be an appropriate way to address some of these problems, is opposition by organized labor across the country to any program that would allow guest workers in. As you know, Governor Cole advocated the guest worker programs to legalize or regularize the process by which people cross the border.

Has your organization done anything to deal with that issue or have you stayed away with that political opposition?

Ms. ALLEN. It is similar to Mr. Hoover, we have not had structured conversations with labor groups around the issue.

Mr. SHADEGG. So neither one of you has dealt with that aspect of those problems?

Ms. ALLEN. No.

Rev. HOOVER. Congressman Shadegg, let me mention one other thing that is not evident anywhere else. Humane Borders and U.S. Border Patrol are working significantly with officials in Mexico to try to achieve consensus or efforts on their part to reduce the number of people that are dying in our desert as well; information programs, etc.

Mr. SHADEGG. Colonel Anderson, let me turn to you. As I indicated, I appreciate your testimony, it is helpful to me. You heard—you were present and heard Mr. Aguilar testify, basically a glowing picture about everything that is happening east of Nogales. You have been retired and on the border for a number of years. Can you give me information on whether you see the problem getting better or getting worse?

Colonel ANDERSON. It is getting worse. I have right here, this same committee back in 1999, April 27th, had a hearing I believe it was—April 27th. And the person from Cochise County at that time was a Gail Griffin, who was a legislator in the House of Representatives in Arizona.

Mr. SHADEGG. I know her.

Colonel ANDERSON. OK. And this was her testimony here. Last night, she said, "Will you please take this and give this to the committee and say nothing has changed. I cannot change it, it has just gotten worse." And in my briefcase are papers and documents and everything else, some of it from the Border Patrol, indicating that it is getting much worse.

Mr. SHADEGG. Mr. Chairman, I would like to put that testimony into the record. I would also like the Colonel to at least summarize it briefly.

Colonel ANDERSON. Basically it is everything I have said but 4 years old. I have submitted testimony several times, I merely had to update mine, and it has just gotten worse. It is getting worse every day. Now these groups that are forming for civil defense or protection of the border that some people allege may be vigilantes or militia types, they are merely reacting to the vacuum. They see nothing going their way and they are very frustrated.

We are hopeful that someone will step in and make them not necessary.

Mr. SHADEGG. Is it your opinion that in reacting to the vacuum, they are trying, nonetheless, to abide by existing laws or is it your belief that they are operating outside the law?

Colonel ANDERSON. No, they are attempting in every way to abide by existing laws. I have personally helped write the concept paper for the Tombstone one that is called Civil Homeland Defense Corps. What we did was we made sure that everyone has to go, who volunteers to be a participant, must go through a concealed weapons course, not to get weapons training, but to be forced to go through an FBI background check. Their purpose is to deter, not to arrest, not to apprehend. That is not the purpose of that particular group.

Another group seems merely to document, to provide you information, problem the American public information of what is going on that may not be reported properly.

Another group is from Texas called Ranch Rescue, that is a different group, they have been a little more aggressive. Now we do not affiliate with them whatsoever.

But there is a fourth group, I received message traffic, a fourth group is asking to startup also in a similar vein.

Now this is getting worse and worse and worse, it is not getting better.

I would like to add, if I could, one thing—you mentioned the guest worker program, in reviewing the data, many of us down there tried to figure out what to do in that regard and what we have done is talk to those American business people or citizens who for some reason uniquely work in Mexico. They are guest workers in Mexico. A typical case would be a veterinarian who takes care of the cattle problem on one side or the other. We asked him to bring his stuff and there are programs called FM–2 and FM–3 sanctioned by the Mexican government, that they use for American citizens or others to go to be guest workers in Mexico. I would submit that the committee might want to pull this data, review those documents and those procedures and methodologies and that would be a very good turnaround as a fair play way to do business, because the documentation is rather severe, but it does work and that might be the way to go about things.

Mr. SHADEGG. Ms. Salcido and Mr. Toro, I want to thank you for your testimony, it is precisely what I hoped to get into the record to document the deep concern of the people of the Tohono O'odham Nation with regard to drug problems. It seems to me that is a grave concern and a legitimate concern and an obligation of the Federal Government to participate in that.

Do you see—when you say that—Ms. Salcido, in your testimony, children as young as 8 and 9 years old that are recruited to watch for law enforcement agents and then paid in drugs, do you see those children then using the drugs or is it that those drugs are in quantities that they become sellers of the drugs? And is this a growing problem or is it sort of an episodic thing that is not as significant?

Ms. SALCIDO. It is steadily growing. They are users, but they also become sellers. And it has hit our schools, which affect the other children, who would have to say no. We are trying very hard with our children to say no to drugs.

But it is getting worse, and I just feel that most likely what happens when you put the fence in the Organ Pipe, it is going to filter through. Again, Meneger's is right there, we are going to get hit first. The same thing as on the other side of Organ Pipe, they are going to get hit also, because—you indicated you had toured the area, well we are on the other side, east of there. And we are just in harm's way, and as I say, it is a hop, skip and jump from where we are at.

It is a corridor and it is an area where we just, as of last night, 500 immigration people, IAs came through. Well, we do not know how many of those 500 were carrying guns, we are not aware of what is happening in the desert area, we are 15 miles from Gu Vo

District's border and the Mexican border and that 15 miles is saying that we are the ones that are going to get hit first, along with the other district.

We are one of three the chairman referred to that we wanted the gates open so we can have members go in and out for ceremony purposes. But we have now come to say no, we do not want it no more. Why? Because it is damaging not only the land, not only the desert land, it is damaging our lives by our children being utilized to be able to be scouts basically for them, not knowing any better. They use the concept of threatening your family, threatening your life. Again, to an 8 or 9 year old, when $100 is given to them, that is a lot of money.

And we are very concerned, if you are going to put a fence up, put it all the way. If you are going to help us to do anything, with all these things that are happening, you know, put some funding in the area that we need it. We can talk about all the things that are coming up, well the safety of the United States and inner America, you know, we are the first ones to get hit and it makes us feel like we are second class citizens and it makes us feel like we are expendable. And that is not right, because we are citizens of these United States, even though we were here first, but we try to cooperate, we try to utilize all the laws that would benefit not only our people but also the rest of the United States.

Mr. SHADEGG. My last question, you may have heard me relate earlier that when I was at Cactus Pipe—Organ Pipe National Monument, I was told a story about a woman whose daughter I gathered was in her teen years, late teen, early 20's, had a friend who, for no explicable reason, had acquired a very expensive automobile and her mother cautioned her that she suspected that was as a result of her involvement in drug activity. Have you heard of other incidents, does that sound familiar, is that a believable story, is that a recurring theme that you see here?

Ms. SALCIDO. Yes, it is. There are a lot more stories out there that you have not even heard. Five minutes of testimony just does not do it justice, to give information that you need to know.

Mr. SHADEGG. No.

Ms. SALCIDO. There are a lot of things like people who come through, who use sophisticated—the drug cartels use sophisticated communications equipment. And I would use myself as an example. I was home before I got this job, staying home, close to the border and all the runners coming through, I would report suspicious vehicles coming through or heavy looking suspicious vehicles.

When they finally determined that it was me, they came to me and said we know you are the one that is telling. Why do they know that? Because a load came in with no lights, no nothing and it was dark, a dark vehicle, no moonlight, no nothing. It passed by, I happened to have gone outside at that time and saw this. I called. Well, they found out—they had that sophisticated communications equipment and said we heard you. Well, how did you hear me, it was a telephone call, it was in my house and my house is a traditional home which is about a foot of mud, you know. It is not concrete or whatever. But you cannot hear that. The only way you can do that is scanning. They have all these things that they utilize.

One of things that we are really scared about, another thing, was the drug war—not the drug war, but horses coming in with hoof and mouth disease and all these other—chemical warfare, I should say, that are coming through too. That is scary because of our animals. We live by—some of our ranchers live by their cattle. Those are some of the things that we are afraid of that is going to happen. And we are the last ones to be able to receive any kind of funding to ensure that it would close off any activity that comes through.

The Police Department has testified to you concerning things that they are encountering in that area. We have done the same thing just outside of Meneger's, which is about a quarter of a mile from there, a large ditch that the water runs through. If you go any time throughout the day into that area, you will see backpacks, beds, anything that the IAs bring across for sleeping or to eat or whatever. They kind of set up places there and the trash that they accumulate there.

Those are some of the things that we have to deal with. The vehicles that they come in and abandon in the different areas, the bikes, the all terrain vehicles, you name it, it is there.

We also have had airplane incursions that have come across and also with the situation I indicated in my testimony, it is in the military. And it is very scary when things like that happen to people who just live there. The children are not playing out there, the mothers cannot allow their children out in their front yard. We have to be worried to do that, because of all the gunfires that happen.

Meneger's is a paved road, it is not in very good condition now, but it is paved so you can drive it. It is the closest to the border, it is accessible where there is no—they are available, the police officers or even the drug people, the narcs we call them, are stationed all over the place, but it is like they have to be stationed in a mountain area to see the valley area and also it takes awhile to come down. It is not something—you can see from it far away, but it takes awhile to come down, when we talk about the roads there at the border. They climb the mountain and they sit there and they watch. But we do not have the surveillance everywhere that everyone else has.

Fencing the area you talked about, they are open, they come right through. There are a lot of things that I could tell you.

Mr. SHADEGG. You are an eloquent spokesman and you have done a fine job of adding to that 5 minutes. We very, very much appreciate the information.

Mr. SOUDER. Mr. Anderson, I had a question about these different groups and certainly—I mean I understand the frustration that people have. One of the things that—and certainly there are neighborhood watches all over America to protect neighborhoods. The question is it is a fine line and it is legal to own a gun and it is in an organized effort where it is public, you are able to do these kind of watches.

But what we have seen—most of the Democratic members of this committee represent major metro areas. Elijah Cummings, who is the ranking Democrat represents inner-city Baltimore where drug dealers torched the home of the Dawson family burning the mom and the five kids inside, who were—I guess she had reported the drug dealers. It happens multiple times. Danny Davis, who is on this committee, represents the south side of Chicago. One of the things that has happened there is gangs have grown up to provide protection and has run into additional problems.

We have also seen, and we are dealing with this right now on the Columbia. Understanding the motivation, but how do you not have this slide into chaos?

Colonel ANDERSON. Well, I cannot answer that question, no one can. What we can say is that given the vacuum, given the failure of agencies at all levels, from Federal to local, to step in the breach and solve the problem, the citizenry on its own has deemed it necessary for their own safety and well-being, to do something. Now so far—and I anticipate—I would like to say I would anticipate that in the future there will not be a problem and there has not been. They have not shot anybody, have not done anything and I do not believe that is going to happen. But it does allow for an accident, an unintended consequence. All of those things can happen.

Recently, we had a representative, House Majority Leader Randy Graff, has introduced into the House a proposal, it will probably come again next year, to have a volunteer type of group like that under the auspices of the Arizona DPS, Department of Public Safety, Highway Patrol, to bring all these groups together and give them "some adult leadership" and I strongly recommend that is the way to go. There are those that do not want to have that because they do not want to have anything to do with these things, but if you do nothing, the vacuum will attract something and you may not like what it attracts.

So you spoke earlier, 5 years, things will get better. We do not have 5 years, we really do not. It is getting worse and worse. And these groups are an outgrowth of that. We can fix it or we can stand around and wait for it to happen. We prefer of course that we do not do that.

Each one of these groups right now has no intention whatsoever of doing anything illegal. That is my view of the ones that I know of. I cannot speak for other States or anything else. But we watch it very carefully. I am not a member of one of the groups, but I do watch them because I have seen this coming, I spent all my life overseas mostly be it South America or the Far East or the Middle East, Egypt or any place else, and these things can get out of control if the government does not do its job. And that is what we have here.

Mr. SOUDER. Rev. Hoover, I am just kind of curious, I know that you view as part of your religious calling to help those who are potentially in distress. Do you also do things to encourage them to follow the law?

Rev. HOOVER. Well, we——

Mr. SOUDER. Or do you believe in effect it is an unjust law, therefore, it does not need to be followed?

Rev. HOOVER. I do not think that is the issue. The issue right here is to rescue, which means to remove from imminent peril, and the people are in peril in our desert precisely because we have incrementally moved the migration farther and farther. The assumption from INS was that they would not make the desert trek, I was told it is an unintended consequence. I said yes, it is deadly, we are going to try to do something about it in our neighborhood.

Mr. SOUDER. Will you also speak out for enforcement of the laws?

Rev. HOOVER. I think that was in my opening remarks, that we are also speaking out clearly for Mexico to accept responsibility for allowing these—you know, you go over here and you interview a 15 year old Mayan beauty queen who thinks she is going to be in Las Vegas in 2 hours and that is wrong. And the country of Mexico has a moral obligation to inform its people what they are about to encounter.

Mr. SOUDER. Have you ever done anything at the border to help warn people coming across, do you have people posted who would say look, do not come?

Rev. HOOVER. Sir, I have met with six Cabinet officers of the government in Mexico City, I meet with officials down here, spoke with the Under Secretary of Foreign Relations who was in Tucson Thursday night, with the Ambassador, who is over all the consulates. I am working feverishly to try to reduce—to produce migrant safety.

Mr. SOUDER. I also want to thank the witnesses from the Tohono O'odham because it was very specific information. Do you believe, Mr. Toro, that if you had protection and more Border Patrol, that you in fact would have a reduction in people going through your ranch and immediate area?

Mr. TORO. Definitely. The concern right now is that there is not enough Border Patrol agents out there to cover the whole Nation. On our outfit there, in the past, illegal immigrants have come walking through our ranch area requesting food and water and for the most part, we have not denied them any food or water, but it becomes tedious at times when they get word back to other immigrants on the southside saying we know a place north of the border that will give you food and what-not, but then it also burdens our family with the budget, because we are not a rich farm, we are not there to feed—we will definitely give them water.

Just last Sunday before I left the ranch, I left about 3 p.m., and my sister had told me that shortly after I left there was 17 vehicles came up behind me carrying immigrants also. So yes, more agents would probably deter the immigrant issue coming north of the boundary.

Mr. SOUDER. Well, I thank each of you for your testimony.

Mr. SHADEGG. Based on your questioning of Mr. Hoover, I just wanted to—with regard to enforcement of the law, Mr. Hoover, do you occasionally come upon undocumented aliens crossing the desert when you are putting out your water?

Rev. HOOVER. Yes, sir.

Mr. SHADEGG. And when you do, do you advise the Border Patrol?

Rev. HOOVER. Not every time. Most of the time it turns out that way. If we encounter someone that has come out to the road, they are actually looking for help usually. Now there have been occasions when we have found folks and said do you know what you are doing, do you know where you are, etc. Yes, we do. Well, OK, be careful because they may kill you. But Border Patrol agents will confirm that we have called in dozens of times and effected a number of rescues, including medical rescues from the desert. It is not our job to enforce——

Mr. SHADEGG. Right. But as I understand your question, if they are looking to be rescued, you advise the Border Patrol.

Rev. HOOVER. Absolutely.

Mr. SHADEGG. If they are not looking to be rescued, they are looking to get on in——

Rev. HOOVER. On in is a relative concept out here, so we ask them do you have water, do you need some food, do you have any clue where you are. I have talked to people that were rescued, oh well, we are going this way 3 hours and we will be in Phoenix. No, sir, you will not. I will get the map out and say you are right here, you are only—how long you been walking, so forth. So we call Border Patrol.

But that is a negotiated kind of a thing. I want to make sure that they have some concept of who they are, where they are, what is going on. We will not make any phone calls, we will not transport anyone, we have never done that. But we do not notify every contact that we have. Most of the time when we encounter somebody on the road though, they are looking for help.

Mr. SHADEGG. I appreciate your candor.

Mr. SOUDER. Thank you. And there are no easy answers to the border questions and the numbers are in dispute. I do feel it is important to state on the record that it is indisputable that as a whole, we have made progress on the border and we have made progress on the narcotics question. That does not account for specific zones. It is clear when we address some progress in some zones, it moves to other zones and our responsibility as the Federal Government is then to back up. If we switch more pressure in some zones, it is also our responsibility to have a responsible enforcement legal system. At the same time, it is our obligation to enforce the law.

We have seen a reduction nationwide in drug use, it is fairly significant and it is becoming consistent, that means less is coming in. We have seen crime rates drop in some areas and when you look at the border as a whole, we have made progress.

We have, probably due to rising unemployment in the United States, seen some drop in the—do not assume that everything you have just seen is the only way we have to count people who are coming across. Sometimes, bluntly put, the word of mouth is less accurate than the counters when you move through like WalMarts or others and some of those are mobile. I believe we have made some progress but I believe there are huge gaping holes, many of those gaping holes are in Arizona.

If you are in a home that is being overrun with bullets going around, I can understand you are tremendously unhappy. Same thing with the ranchers and we will continue to try to address it in as fair a way as possible. But there are tens of thousands of people in other parts of the United States who also are endangered nightly because of the drug traffic, because of the crime in their neighborhoods and it is a balance that we have to do as far as resources. People want roads, people want prescription drugs, people want to make sure we are secure of terrorism and we are doing the best we can.

I came down here today to hear first-hand the pressures. There are obviously intense disagreements on how to handle this in Arizona inside the different areas themselves, difficult policy questions on wilderness areas, non-wilderness areas. The unions in my district, I have a very heavily unionized district, hate the concept of visa or work permits. It drives down the wage rates for the union groups, there is no question. On the other hand, the manufacturers in my district are desperate to have the labor, if they need the labor, in order to keep the companies competitive in the United States. That puts tremendous pressure on your homes and your families in the midwest and we have to come up with equitable ways.

And one of the ways to do that is to listen to each other, try to talk it through and come to as fair and just solutions as we can and spare as many lives as possible. And today, your testimony is helping us do that.

And with that, we appreciate everyone who has been in attendance as well. The hearing stands adjourned.

[Whereupon, at 2:15 p.m., the hearing was adjourned.]

[Additional information submitted for the hearing record follows:]

HUMANE BORDERS
FRONTERAS COMPASIVAS

740 E Speedway Blvd
Tucson, AZ 85719
Office: 520-628-7753
Fax: 520-624-0890
www.humaneborders.org

Mr. Nick Coleman
Subcommittee on Criminal Justice, Drug Policy and Human Resources
Government Reform Committee
U.S. House of Representatives
B-373 Rayburn Building
Washington, DC 20515

June 25, 2003

Dear Mr. Coleman,

My positive response concerning appropriate permits, etc. to Congressman Shadegg was intended to convey the fact that we do not enter any private lands without the consent of owners or land managers. I continue to affirm that declaration. In support of that claim, please find enclosed special use permits for our water station operations at the following locations:

Organ Pipe Cactus National Monument
National Park Service, Department of Interior

Buenos Aires National Wildlife Refuge
US Fish and Wildlife Service, Department of Interior

Ajo Block
Bureau of Land Management, Department of Interior

Ironwood Forest National Monument
Bureau of Land Management, Department of Interior

Pima County Solid Waste Transfer Station
Pima County Government

Rio Rico Properties
Rio Rico, AZ

Seven of our flag poles and flags fly over existing wildlife water locations in the Cabeza Prieta National Wildlife Refuge, US Fish and Wildlife, Department of Interior. The only supporting documentation for these stations is in the hands of

Cabeza staff. Cabeza staff assisted us in erecting these stations following the minimum tool requirements approved by the Albuquerque, New Mexico regional office of US Fish and Wildlife in September of 2001. I assume that the documentation can be obtained from one office or the other.

One of our member organizations, American Beginnings of Yuma, Arizona contributes labor in support of Water Station, Inc. in California which operates on Bureau of Land Management lands in southeast California. These stations are funded, in part, and supported by the personal labor of Congressman Shaddegg's colleague Duncan Hunter.

No water stations exist on the Tohono O'odham Nation lands or upon lands in the Arizona State Trust. Additional water stations do exist on private properties. As soon as a water station is erected, the exact location is communicated to the US Border Patrol of the Bureau of Customs and Border Protection, Department of Homeland Security using Global Positioning Satellite data.

A few water stations exist on private property. Out of concerns for privacy, we choose not disclose agreements between Humane Borders, Inc. and private citizens.

Sincerely,

Robin Hoover

Rev. Robin Hoover, Ph.D.

03/25/03 08:35 ☎520 387 7144 ORGAN PIPE CNM 002

Form 10-114
Rev. DEC. 99

Page 1 of 2

UNITED STATES DEPARTMENT OF THE INTERIOR
National Park Service

Special Use Permit

Name of Use Incidental Business Permit

Date Permit Reviewed 3/1/03
Expires 3/1/04

Long Term ___

Short Term X

Permit # IRM ORPI 9500 005
Region Park Type No. #

Organ Pipe Cactus National Monument
Name of Area

Humane Borders Inc. 740 East Speedway Tucson, AZ 85719 520-360-7818

is hereby authorized during the period from **March 1, 2003** through **March 1, 2004** to use the following described land or facilities in the above named area:

APS Powerline Right of Way; 2 locations at approximately milepost 60 and 73

For the purpose(s) of:

Providing water and water stations for Undocumented Aliens

Authorizing legislation or other authority (RE - DO-53): 16USC 4601 Outdoor Recreation Coordination, 36 CFR 5.5

NEPA Compliance: CATEGORICALLY EXCLUDED X EA/FONSI ___ EIS ___ OTHER APPROVED PLANS ___

PERFORMANCE BOND: Required ___ Not Required X Amount $___

LIABILITY INSURANCE: Required X Not Required ___ Amount $ 300,000 minimum

ISSUANCE of this permit is subject to the conditions on the reverse hereof and appended pages and when appropriate to the payment to the U.S. Dept. of the Interior, National Park Service of the sum of **WAIVED**.

The undersigned hereby accepts this permit subject to the terms, covenants, obligations, and reservations, expressed or implied herein.

PERMITTEE Rev. Robin Hoover, Ph.D. 3-28-03
Signature Date

Authorizing Official ___
Signature Superintendent Date

CONDITIONS OF THIS PERMIT

1. The permittee shall exercise this privilege subject to the supervision of the Superintendent, and shall comply with all applicable laws and regulations of the area.

2. Damages - The permittee shall pay the United States for any damage resulting from this use which would not reasonably be inherent in the use which the permittee is authorized to make of the land described in this permit.

3. Benefit - Neither Members of, nor Delegates to Congress, or Resident Commissioners shall be admitted to any share or part of this permit or derive, either directly or indirectly, any pecuniary benefits to arise therefrom: Provided, however, that nothing herein contained shall be construed to extend to any incorporated company, if the permit be for the benefit of such corporation.

4. Assignment - This permit may not be transferred or assigned without the consent of the Superintendent, in writing.

5. Revocation - This permit may be terminated upon breach of any of the conditions herein or at the discretion of the Superintendent.

6. The permittee is prohibited from giving false information; to do so will be considered a breach of conditions and be grounds for revocation [Re: 36 CFR 2.32(a)(4)].

7. Permittee will comply with applicable public health and sanitation standards and codes.

8. NPS will provide garbage can and bags for collection and removal of trash by permittee.

9. Permittee will place flags (NPS approval only) on the power poles to mark the water station locations.

10. Permittee will schedule maintenance of stations to prevent depletion of water supply.

11. Permitte will provide a public information program in Spanish on the Mexican side of the border describing the program

UNITED STATES DEPARTMENT OF THE INTERIOR
FISH AND WILDLIFE SERVICE

Buenos Aires National Wildlife Refuge

SPECIAL USE PERMIT

Station No. to be Credited	Permit Number
22530	2003-7
Date	
12-11-2	
Period of Use (inclusive)	
From 1/1/03	
To 12/31/03	

Permittee Name	Permittee Address
Humane Borders, Inc.	740 E. Speedway Tucson, AZ 85719 (520)624-8695

Purpose (specify in detail privilege requested, or units of products involved)
Construct, maintain and monitor humane water sources throughout Refuge. Stations will be attended to on a weekly basis and use date will be collected.

escription (specify unit numbers; metes and bounds, or other recognizable designations)
Three water stations on Refuge near roads (286 and Arivaca Road)

Amount of fee ________ if not a fixed payment, specify rate and unit of charge: ________

☒ Payment Exempt -Justification:
☐ Full Payment
☐ Partial Payment -Balance of payments to be made as follows:

Record of Payments

Special Conditions
Permittee or those working under this permit must carry a copy of this form while on the refuge
Provide Refuge with summary of activities
Permit renewed annually(Calendar Year)

This permit is issued by the U.S. Fish and Wildlife Service and accepted by the undersigned, subject to the terms, covenants, obligations, and reservations, expressed or implied herein, and to the conditions and requirements appearing on the reverse side.

Permittee Signature	Issuing Officer Signature and Title
Rev. Robin Hoover, PhD	Sally Gall, Asst Mgr

Form 3-1383 (Rev. 6/85)

This form was electronically produced by Elite Federal Forms Inc.

General Conditions

1. Payments

All payments shall be made on or before the due date to the local representative of the U.S. Fish and Wildlife Service by a postal money order or check made payable to the U.S. Fish and Wildlife Service.

2. Use limitations

The permittee's use of the described premises is limited to the purposes herein specified; does not unless provided for in this permit allow him/her to restrict other authorized entry on to his/her area; and permits to the Service to carry on whatever activities are necessary for (1) protection and maintenance of the premises and adjacent lands administered by the Service and (2) the management of wildlife and fish using the premises and other

3. Damages

The United States shall not be responsible for any loss or damages to property including but not limited to growing crops, animals, and machinery; or injury to the permittee, or his/her relatives, or to the officers, agents, employees, or any others who are on the premises from instructions or by the sufferance of the permittee or his/her associates; or for damages or interference caused by wildlife or employees or representatives of the Government carrying out their official responsibilities. The permittee agrees to save the United States or any of its agencies harmless from any and all claims for damages or losses that may arise or be incident to the flooding of the premises resulting from any associated Government river and harbor, flood control, reclamation, or Tennessee Valley Authority activity.

4. Operating Rules and Laws

The permittee shall keep the premises in a neat and orderly condition at all times, and shall comply with all municipal, county, and State laws applicable to the operations under the permit as well as all Federal laws, rules, and regulations governing National Wildlife Refuges and the area described in this permit. The permittee shall comply with all instructions applicable to this permit issued by the refuge officer in charge. The permittee shall take all reasonable precautions to prevent the escape of fires and to suppress fires and shall render all reasonable assistance in the suppression of refuge fires.

5. Responsibility of Permittee

The permittee, by operating on the premises, shall be considered to have accepted these premises with all the facilities, fixtures, or improvements in their existing condition as of the date of this permit. At the end of the period specified or upon earlier termination, the permittee shall give up the premises in as good order and condition as when received except for reasonable wear, tear, or damage occurring without fault or negligence. The permittee will fully repay the Service for any and all damage directly or indirectly resulting from negligence or failure on his/her part, or the part of anyone of his/her associates, to use reasonable care.

6. Revocation Policy

This permit may be revoked by the Regional Director of the Service without notice for noncompliance with the terms hereof or for violation of general and/or specific laws or regulations governing National Wildlife Refuges or for nonuse. It is at all times subject to discretionary revocation by the Director of the Service. Upon such revocation the Service, by and through any authorized representative, may take possession of the said premises for its own and sole use, or may enter and possess the premises as the agent of the permittee and for his/her account.

7. Compliance

Failure of the Service to insist upon a strict compliance with any of this permit's terms, conditions, and requirements shall not constitute a waiver be considered as a giving up of the Service's right to thereafter enforce any of the permit's terms, conditions, or requirements.

8. Termination Policy

At the termination of this permit, the permittee shall immediately give up possession to the Service representative, reserving, however, the rights specified in paragraph 9. If he/she fails to do so, he/she will pay the Government, as liquidated damages, an amount double the rate specified in this permit for the entire time possession is withheld. Upon yielding possession, the permittee will still be allowed the reenter as needed to remove his/her property as stated in paragraph 9. The acceptance of any fee for liquidated damages or any other act of administration relating to the continued tenancy is not to be considered as an affirmance of the permittees action nor shall it operate as a waiver of the Government's rights to terminate or cancel the permit for the breach of any specified condition or requirement.

9. Removal of Permittee's Property

Upon the expiration or termination of this permit, if all rental charges and/or damage claims due to the Government have been paid, the permittee may within a reasonable period as stated in the permit or as determined by the refuge officer in charge but not to exceed 60 days, remove all structures, machinery, and/or other equipment, etc., from the premises for which he/she is responsible. Within the period the permittee must also remove any other of his/her property including his/her acknowledged share of products or crops grown, cut, harvested, stored, or stacked on the premises. Upon failure to remove any of the above items within the aforesaid period, they shall become the property of the United States.

10. Transfer of Privileges

This permit is not transferable, and no privileges herein mentioned may be sublet or made available to any person or interest not mentioned in this permit. No interest hereunder may accrue though lien or be transferred to a third party without the approval of the Regional Director of the U.S. Fish and Wildlife Service and the permit shall not be used for speculative purposes.

11. Conditions of Permit not Fulfilled

If the permittee fails to fulfill any of the conditions and requirements set forth herein, all money paid under this permit shall be retained by the Government to be used to satisfy as much of the permittee's obligation as possible.

12. Official Barred from Participating

No Member of Congress or Residential Commissioner shall participate in any part of this contract or to any benefit that may arise from it, but this provision shall not pertain to this contract if made with a corporation for its general benefit.

13. Nondiscrimination in Employment

The permittee agrees to be bound by the equal opportunity clause of Executive Order 11246, as amended.

Privacy Act Statement--Special Use Permit

NOTICE: In accordance with the Privacy Act of 1974, 5 U.S.C. 552a, please be advised that:

1. The issuance of a permit and collection of fees on lands of the National Wildlife Refuge System is authorized by the National Wildlife Refuge System Administration Act (16 U.S.C. 668dd - 668ee), and the Refuge Recreation Act, (16 U.S.C. 460k-3); implemented by regulations in 50 CFR 25-36.
2. Information collected in issuing a permit may be used to evaluate and conclude the eligibility of, or merely document, permit applicants.
3. Routine use disclosures may also be made (1) to the U.S. Department of Justice when related to litigation or anticipated litigation; (2) of information indicating a violation or potential violation of a statute, regulation, rule, order or license, to appropriate Federal, State, local or foreign agencies responsible for investigating or prosecuting the violation or for enforcing or implementing the statute, rule, regulation, order or license; (3) from the record of the individual in response to an inquiry from a Congressional office made at the request of that individual; (4) to provide addresses obtained from the Internal Revenue Service to debt collection agencies for purposes of locating a debtor to collect or compromise a Federal claim against the debtor, or to consumer reporting agencies to prepare a commercial credit report for use by the Department (48FR 54716; December 6, 1983).
4. Any information requested is required to receive this permit. Failure to answer questions may jeopardize the eligibility of individuals to receive permits.

Form 2920-1
uary 1999)

UNITED STATES
DEPARTMENT OF THE INTERIOR
BUREAU OF LAND MANAGEMENT
LAND USE APPLICATION AND PERMIT
(Sec. 302(b) of P.L. 94-579, October 21, 1976, 43 U.S.C. 1732

APPLICATION

FORM APPROVED
OMB NO. 1004-0009
Expires: October 31, 2001

FOR BLM USE ONLY
Application Number
AZA-32147

1. Name *(first, middle initial, and last)*
Humane Borders

Address *(include zip code)*
740 E. Speedway Blvd
Tucson, Arizona 85719

Phone *(include area code)*
520-628-7753
520-624-0890 (Fax)

2. Attach map or sketch showing public lands for which you are applying

3. Proposed date(s) of use: from to

4. Give legal basis for holding interest in lands in the State of Arizona
(Check appropriate box at right and explain.)

- ☐ Resident
- ☐ Partnership
- ☐ Corporation
- ☐ County
- ☐ Local Government
- ☐ State Government
- ☒ Other Non Profit Organization

5. Are the lands now improved, occupied, or used? ☐ Yes ☐ No *(If "yes," describe improvements and purposes, identify users and occupants.)*
No

. Do you need access to the land? ☐ Yes ☒ No *(Describe needed or existing access)*
Sites are adjacent to exiting roads.

7a. What do you propose to use the lands for?
Water Stations

b. What improvements and/or land development do you propose? *(To complete application processing, engineering and construction drawings may b required.)*

SEE ATTACHED STATEMENT

c. What is the estimated capital cost?
$ ____________

d. What is the source of water for the proposed use?
Brought to site by water service vehicle

I CERTIFY That the information given by me in this application is true, complete, and correct to the best of my knowledge and belief and is given in good faith.

Rev. Robin Hoover, Ph.D
(Signature of Applicant)

8-1-02
(Date)

Title 18 U.S.C. Section 1001, makes it a crime for any person knowingly and willfully to make to any department or agency of the United States any fals fictitious, or fraudulent statements or representations as to any matter within its jurisdiction.

(Continued on reverse)

PERMIT

Permission is hereby granted to **HUMANE BORDERS, INC.**
of 740 E. SPEEDWAY BLVD, TUCSON, ARIZONA 85719
to use the following-described lands:

Permit Number: AZA-32147

WNSHIP	RANGE	SECTION	SUBDIVISION
T. 14 S.,	R. 5 W.,	Sec 4,	SW¼SE¼
T. 13 S.,	R. 6 W.,	Sec 15,	SW¼NE¼
T. 14 S.,	R. 6 W.,	Sec 17,	SW¼SE¼

Meridian	State	County	Acres (*number*)
Gila & Salt River	Arizona	Pima	1.0

for the purpose of

Water Stations consisting of two 60-gallon blue polyethylene tanks.

and subject to the following conditions:

1. This permit is issued for the period specified below. It is revocable at the discretion of the authorized officer of the Bureau of Land Management, at any time upon notice. This permit is subject to valid adverse claims heretofore or hereafter acquired.
2. This permit is subject to all applicable provisions of the regulations (43 CFR 2920) which are made a part hereof.
3. This permit may not be assigned without prior approval of the authorized officer of the Bureau of Land Management.
4. Permittee shall not enclose roads or trails commonly in public use.
5. Authorized representatives of the Department of the Interior, other Federal agencies, and State and local law officials shall at all times have the right to enter the premises on official business.
6. Permittee shall pay the United States for any damage to its property resulting from the use.

   Permittee shall notify the authorized officer of address change immediately.
8. Permittee shall observe all Federal, State, and local laws and regulations applicable to the premises and to erection or maintenance of signs or advertising displays including the regulations for the protection of game birds and game animals, and shall keep the premises in a neat, orderly, and sanitary condition.
9. Permittee shall pay the authorized officer, in advance, the lump sum of $0.00 for the period of use authorized by this permit or $ 0.00 , annually, as rental or such other sum as may be required if a rental adjustment is made.
10. Use or occupancy of land under this permit shall commence within months from date hereof and shall be exercised at least days each year.
11. Permittee shall take all reasonable precautions to prevent and suppress forest, brush, and grass fires and prevent pollution of waters on or in the vicinity of the lands.
12. Permittee shall not cut any timber on the lands or remove other resources from the land without prior written permission from the authorized officer. Such permission may be conditioned by a requirement to pay fair market value for the timber or other resources.
13. Permittee agrees to have the serial number of this permit marked or painted on each advertising display or other facility erected or maintained under the authority of such permit.
14. This permit is subject to the provisions of Executive Order No. 11246 of September 24, 1965, as amended, which sets forth the Equal Opportunity clauses. A copy of this order may be obtained from the signing officer.
15. Permittee acknowledges, by signing below, that he/she knows, understands and accepts the terms and conditions under which this permit is issued.
16. Special conditions (*attach additional sheets, if necessary*)

   See Attached

Permit issued for periods

From	8/30/02	05/01/2003
To	09/30/2002	09/30/2003

[signature] (Permittee)

Mervin C. Boyd (Authorized Officer)

Acting Field Manager (Title) 8-30-02 (Date)

INSTRUCTIONS

1. Submit, in *duplicate*, to any local office of the Bureau of Land Management having jurisdiction of the lands.
2. Applications for Land Use Permits will not be accepted unless a notification of the availability of the land for non-BLM use (*Notice of Realty Action*) has been published in the Federal Register and for 3 weeks thereafter in a newspaper of general circulation. This provision does not apply in those situations where the publication of a (*Notice of Realty Action*) has been waived by the authorized officer.
3. If the annual rental exceeds $250 dollars per year; costs of processing the application *must* be paid by the applicant in advance.
4. The authorized officer may require additional information to process an application. Processing will be deferred until the required information is furnished by the applicant.

The Paperwork Reduction Act of 1980 (44 U.S.C. 3501 et seq.) requires us to inform you that:
Information is needed to process application for land use authorizations, pursuant to 43 CFR Section 2920.
Information shows if the applicant and proposed use meet the requirements of 43 CFR Section 2920.1.
Applicant *must* respond before he/she can be g n authorization to use public lands.

☆U.S. GPO: 1999—774-502

Attachment A

Special Conditions/Stipulations for Land Use Permit AZA-32147

1. This permit only authorizes the use of federal lands administered by the Bureau of Land Management (BLM), Phoenix Field Office. It does not authorize the use of private lands, or lands owned or managed by other federal, state, tribal or local governmental agencies where BLM has no authority to issue such authorizations.

2. Humane Borders must maintain a minimum of $10,000,000.00 (ten million dollars) per occurrence worth of general liability insurance coverage, in a policy form acceptable to the Authorized Officer, for property damage, personal injury and comprehensive public liability resulting from action taken or caused by Humane Borders under this permit. The United States shall be named as an additional insured on the Certificate of Insurance. Humane Borders must furnish proof of insurance in the form of a Certificate of Insurance to the Authorized Officer prior to execution of the permit. Humane Borders must maintain the required insurance coverage for the life of the permit.

3. The period of use under the Special Use Permit is to be from date of permit approval through September 30, 2002 and May 1 through September 30, 2003. Under extenuating circumstances (such as prolonged drought or high temperatures), Humane Borders may apply to the Authorized Officer 30 days in advance to extend this time period.

4. Humane Borders is responsible for the training, monitoring, safety and security of its individual employees and volunteers including notifications about approaching individuals on BLM administered lands, biohazards or other safety precautions, off-road driving conditions, etc.

5. Any cultural and/or paleontological resource (historic or prehistoric site or object) discovered by the permittee, or any person working on its behalf, on BLM administered land must be immediately reported to the Authorized Officer. Humane Borders shall suspend all operations in the immediate area of such discovery until written authorization to proceed is issued by the Authorized Officer. An

evaluation of the discovery will be made by the Authorized Officer to determine appropriate actions to prevent the loss of significant cultural or scientific values. Humane Borders will be responsible for the cost of evaluation and the Authorized Officer will make any decision as to proper mitigation measures after consulting with the permittee.

6. While on BLM administered lands, Humane Borders will notify Phoenix Field Office Law Enforcement within two hours of: any encounters with the Border Patrol or calls to emergency service providers; any transportation of individuals for medical assistance, and any discovery of deceased persons or human remains. Upon receipt of any information under this paragraph, BLM Law Enforcement will make appropriate and necessary additional notifications to the U.S. Border Patrol and other responsible governmental agencies.

7. No commercial filming or photography is permitted. Humane Borders may not issue any news releases concerning the water stations without the express written approval of the Authorized Officer. The BLM requires notification of any media coverage that Humane Borders becomes aware of which discusses or mentions the permitted water stations. Any photographs taken by Humane Borders must only be used be for internal record keeping or internal training.

8. At each water station location: No vegetation will be trimmed, cleared or removed; no holes or pits will be excavated for footings; wildlife will not be harassed or harmed; and trash or debris, for which Humane Borders is responsible, will be removed. Trash and refuse collected by Humane Borders will be removed from the site to appropriate dumpsters or refuse sites.

9. The installation of water stations shall be coordinated with BLM staff at the Phoenix Field Office to ensure avoidance of sensitive areas and to ensure conformance with BLM regulations, policies, and planning. Arrangements with BLM staff shall be made no less than 48 hours in advance of proposed installation activities.

10. Humane Borders will maintain no more than two 60-gallon tanks at each station without further approval from the Authorized Officer. Humane Borders will provide GPS coordinates from each water station to the Phoenix Field Office, Pima County Sheriff's Office, and the Ajo Sector for the U.S. Border Patrol.

11. For the water station locations approved, Humane Borders will provide daily service and field inspections to ensure compliance with the following standards; no tanks are empty over a 24-hour period; water quality standards are tested and maintained equivalent to all applicable federal, state, and local governmental water quality standards; tanks will remain sealed and tamper proof and replaced immediately if needed due to tampering, punctures or similar flaws. The tanks authorized by this permit will not exceed 60 gallons each. A schedule of planned daily maintenance and servicing will be provided to the BLM.

12. BLM may immediately cancel the permit if tampering or sabotage occurs to one or more water stations. The Phoenix Field Office will cancel the permit if directed by the Arizona State Office or Washington Office based on new policies, regulations or advice of the Solicitor.

13. This permit may not be transferred or assigned without the written consent of the Authorized Officer.

14. Humane Borders will comply with all applicable federal, state and local governmental public health and sanitation standards and codes.

15. Installation of water stations without prior written authorization from the Authorized Officer is not allowed and may be considered a trespass against the United States.

16. All flags, flagpoles, rebar, and water tanks shall be removed within 30 days after expiration of this permit, cancellation of the permit by BLM, or return of the permit by Humane Borders prior to expiration of term. The Authorized Officer shall be notified upon completion of removal activities.

17. No cross-ccuntry access is authorized outside of the designated sites, as identified by this permit. All approved sites (see attached map) are within the Ajo Block under the jurisdiction of the Phoenix Field Office. All water station sites shall be accessed via existing routes of travel only. In these areas vehicles may pull off of existing roads no more than 10 feet from edge of roadbed. Water stations outside of these 10 feet shall be installed and maintained by foot travel.

18. The Authorized Officer may suspend or terminate this permit in whole or in part when, in his or her judgment, unforeseen conditions arise which result in the approved terms and conditions being inadequate to protect the public health, safety and welfare or to protect the environment.

19. As permittee of AZA-32147 Humane Borders agrees, without limitation, to indemnify the United States against any liability arising from the release of any hazardous substance or hazardous waste (as these terms are defined in the Comprehensive Environmental Response, Compensation and Liability Act of 1980, 42 U.S.C. 9601, et seq. or the Resource Conservation and Recovery Act of 1976, 42 U.S.C. 6901 et seq.) on BLM administered lands subject to this permit. This agreement applies without limitation to whether a release is caused by the permittee, its agent, or unrelated third parties.

20. Approval of this permit is not to be construed as approval or authorization of any action by the permittee, or its officers, agents or employees to violate any federal laws or regulations, including U.S. Immigration and Naturalization laws.

Authorized Official: ______________________________ Date: _______________

Aug-24-02 0:18am From-USDI-BLM Tucson FO tucson 1-520-258-7238 T-807 P.001 F-894

Bureau of Land Management

Tucson Field Office
12661 East Broadway Blvd.
Tucson, AZ 85748-7208
(520) 258-7200
Fax: (520) 258-7238

FAX TRANSMISSION COVER SHEET

Date: 8/24/02

To: Robin Doowe

Fax Number: 520-624-0890
520-624-1210

From: Shela McFarlin

Subject: Stips for permit

YOU SHOULD RECEIVE PAGE(S), INCLUDING THIS COVER SHEET.
IF YOU DO NOT RECEIVE ALL THE PAGES, PLEASE CALL (520) 258-7200.

Remarks:

Call when received
Shela cell ph 602-361-0379

HB 520 - 6?? - 0020
CF 520 - 624 - 1210

Special Use Permit - SPECIAL STIPULATIONS

Note: prior to approving the permit:

1) BLM will review the insurance binder

2) Humane Borders will review the permit stipulations

In addition to the standard stipulations marked on the permit, the following Special Stipulations will apply:

1. This permit only authorizes the use of federal lands administered by the Bureau of

Land Management (BLM), Tucson Field Office (TFO), at 4 (four) locations within or adjacent to the Ironwood Forest National Monument. It does not authorize the use of private lands, or lands owned or managed by other federal, state, tribal or local governmental agencies where BLM has no authority to issue such authorizations.

2. Humane Borders must maintain a minimum of $10,000,000.00 (ten million dollars) per occurrence worth of general liability insurance coverage, in a policy form acceptable to the Authorized Officer, for property damage, personal injury and comprehensive public liability resulting from action taken or caused by Humane Borders under this permit. The United States shall be named as an additional insured on the Certificate of Insurance. Humane Borders must furnish proof of insurance to the Authorized Officer in the form of a Certificate of Insurance prior to execution of the permit. Humane Borders must maintain the required insurance coverage for the life of the permit.

3. The period of use under the Special Use Permit is to be from date of permit approval through September 30, 2002 and May 1 through September 30, 2003. Under extenuating circumstances (such as prolonged drought or high temperatures), Humane Borders may apply to the Authorized Officer 30 days in advance to extend this time period.

4. Humane Borders is responsible for the training, monitoring, safety and security of its individual employees and volunteers including notifications about approaching individuals on BLM administered lands, biohazards or other safety precautions, off-road driving conditions, etc.

5. Any cultural and/or paleontological resource (historic or prehistoric site or object) discovered by the permittee, or any person working on its behalf, on BLM administered land must be immediately reported to the Authorized Officer. Humane Borders shall suspend all

opera ions in the immediate area of such discovery until written authorization to proceed is issue l by the Authorized Officer. An evaluation of the discovery will be made by the Authorized Offic r to determine appropriate actions to prevent the loss of significant cultural or scientific valu s. Humane Borders will be responsible for the cost of evaluation and the Authorized Offic r will make any decision as to proper mitigation measures after consulting with the perm ittee.

6. While on BLM administered lands, Humane Borders will notify Tucson BLM Law Enf rcement within two hours of any encounters with the U.S. Border Patrol or calls to eme gency medical service providers (e.g., Pima County Emergency Services, etc.); any tran portation of individuals for medical assistance; and any discovery of deceased persons or hum an remains. Upon receipt of any information under this paragraph, BLM Law Enforcement will make all appropriate and necessary additional notifications to the U.S. Border Patrol and oth r responsible governmental agencies.

7. No commercial filming or photography is permitted. Humane Borders may not issue any news releases concerning the water stations without the express written approval of the Au horized Officer. The BLM requires notification of any media coverage that Humane Borders bec mes aware of which discusses or mentions the permitted water stations. Any photographs tak n by Humane Borders must only be used for internal record keeping or internal training.

8. At each water station location: no vegetation will be trimmed, cleared or removed; no hol s or pits will be excavated for footings, wildlife will not be harassed or harmed; and trash or del ris, for which Humane Borders is responsible, will be removed. Trash and refuse collected by H mane Borders will be removed from the site to appropriate dumpsters or refuse sites.

9. The installation of water stations will be coordinated with BLM staff at the Tucson Field Office to ensure avoidance of sensitive areas and conformance with BLM regulations, policies, and planning. Arrangements with BLM staff shall be made no less than 48 hours in advance of proposed installation activities.

10. Humane Borders will maintain no more than two 60-gallon tanks at each water station without further approval of the Authorized Officer. Humane Borders will provide GPS coordinates from each water station to the Tucson Field Office, Pima County Sheriff's Office, and the Tucson Sector for the U.S. Border Patrol.

11. For the water station locations approved, Humane Borders will provide daily service and field inspections to ensure compliance with the following standards: no tanks are empty over a 24 hour period; water quality standards are tested and maintained equivalent to all applicable federal, state, and local governmental water quality standards; tanks will sealed and tamper proof and replaced immediately if needed due to tampering, punctures or similar flaws. The tanks authorized by this permit will not exceed 60 gallons each without prior approval of the Authorized Officer. A schedule of planned maintenance and servicing will be provided to the BLM.

12. BLM may immediately cancel the permit is tampering or sabotage occurs to one or more water stations. The Tucson Field Office will cancel the permit if so directed by the Arizona State Office or the Washington, D.C. Office, BLM, based on new policies, regulations, or advice of the Solicitor.

13. The permit may not be transferred or assigned without the written consent of the Authorized Officer.

14. Humane Borders will comply with all applicable federal, state, and local governmental public health and sanitation standards and codes.

15. Installation of water stations without prior written authorization from the Authorized Officer is not allowed and may be considered a trespass against the United States.

16. All flags, flagpoles, rebar, and water tanks shall be removed within 30 days after expiration of this permit, cancellation of the permit by BLM, or return of the permit by Humane Borders prior to expiration of term. The Authorized Officer shall be notified upon completion of removal activities.

17. No cross-country access is authorized outside of the designated sites, as identified in this permit. All approved sites (see attached map) are located within or adjacent to the Ironwood Forest National Monument and are under the jurisdiction of the Tucson Field Office. All water station sites shall be accessed via existing routes of travel only. In these areas vehicles may pull off of existing roads no more than 10 feet from edge of the roadbed. Water stations outside of this 10-foot zone shall be installed and maintained by foot travel.

18. The Authorized Officer may suspend or terminate this permit in whole or in part when, in his or her judgment, unforeseen conditions and/or circumstances arise which result in the approved terms and conditions being inadequate to protect the public health, safety and welfare, or the protect the environment.

19. As permittee of AZA-_____, Humane Borders agrees, without limitation or restriction, to indemnify the United States against any liability arising from the release of any hazardous substance or hazardous waste (as these terms are defined in the Comprehensive Environmental Response, Compensation and Liability Act of 1980, 42 U.S.C. 9601 et seq., or the

Reso urce Conservation and Recovery Act of 1976, 42 U.S.C. 6901 et seq.) on BLM-administered lands subject to this permit. This agreement applies without limitation to whether a release is caused by the permittee, its agent, or unrelated third parties.

20. Approval of this permit is not to be construed as approval or authorization of any action by the permittee, or its officers, agents or employees, to violate any federal laws or regulations, including U.S. Immigration and Naturalization laws.

Authorized Officer:____________________ Date: ______________

RIGHT OF ENTRY

Pima County Solid Waste Management, a division of Pima County Wastewater Management Department (the Grantor), hereby grants to Citizens for Humane Borders (the Grantee), permission to enter upon the following described land: The Sasabe - Arivaca Transfer Station (the Property) located at the junction of State Highway 86 and State Route 89.

This Right of Entry shall be for the purpose of a station to store and other provisions necessary as necessary for immigrants in need of assistance.

Conditions:

1. Grantee are responsible for repairing any damage to County's improvements. Any vegetation removed shall be replaced.
2. Grantee shall be responsible for acquiring all the permits necessary to conduct the requested activity and Grantee shall be responsible for complying with all zoning and code requirements that may apply, if any.
3. Grantee shall leave the Property free of trash and keep areas of the property used in reasonable good order.
4. Grantor shall have the right, without notice or payment of any compensation to Grantee, to sell, destroy, or dispose of any personal property left on the Property after Grantee has vacated or abandoned the Property or when this Right of Entry has been terminated.
5. Grantee shall indemnify, defend and hold harmless Grantor from any or all present or future claims, demands, causes of action or equity resulting from activities in connection with this Right of Entry.
6. This permission shall commence August 1, 2001 and terminate August 1, 2005 with the provision that the permission may be granted for subsequent five year periods as requested Grantee and agreed to by the Grantor.

PIMA COUNTY

Suzanne Shields

By: ______________________ ______________
Manager, Solid Waste Management Division Date

ACCEPTANCE:

By: Robin Hoover 8-2-01
Date

Title: President, Humane Borders

CONTRACT
NO. 11-30-H-129598-0601
AMENDMENT NO.
This number must appear on all invoices, correspondence and documents pertaining to this contract.

CONTRACT FOR THE PROVISION OF WATER DISTRIBUTION SERVICES IN REMOTE AREAS OF PIMA COUNTY
BETWEEN
PIMA COUNTY AND HUMANE BORDERS, INC.

THIS CONTRACT entered into between Pima County, a body politic and corporate of the State of Arizona, hereinafter called COUNTY; and Humane Borders, Inc., hereinafter called CONTRACTOR.

WITNESSETH

WHEREAS, A.R.S. § 11-251.02 authorizes the Board of Supervisors to use county resources in search or rescue operations involving the life or health of any person; and,

WHEREAS, on June 5, 2001, a State of Local Emergency was declared in Pima County due to the extreme peril faced by persons exposed to the high summer desert temperatures and limited water supply; and,

WHEREAS, COUNTY requires the services of a CONTRACTOR to provide water stations and potable water to various remote desert locations in Pima County to reduce the need for aggressive search and rescue operations; and,

WHEREAS, CONTRACTOR is qualified and willing to provide such services; and,

WHEREAS pursuant to Pima County Code 11.12.060, emergency procurement of services is authorized when there exists a threat to public health, welfare, property or safety;

NOW, THEREFORE, the parties hereto agree as follows:

ARTICLE I - TERM AND EXTENSION/RENEWAL

This Contract shall commence on the 5th day of June, 2001, and shall terminate on the 4th day of June, 2002 unless sooner terminated or further extended pursuant to the provisions of this Contract. The COUNTY shall have the option to extend this Contract for up to one additional one (1) year period(s) or any portion thereof. Any modification, or extension shall be by formal written amendment executed by the parties hereto.

ARTICLE II - SCOPE

2.1 Services to be provided by CONTRACTOR shall assure take reasonable steps to that hikers and others on foot in the desert regions of Pima County have access to potable water and shall include, but are not limited to:

a) Identification of appropriate locations for water stations, in consultation with local, state, and federal authorities;

b) Installation and maintenance of water stations at identified and approved sites;

c) Purchase of potable water in sufficient quantity to assure, to the extent possible, a constant supply of water at the water stations;
d) Transportation, delivery and installation of potable water at each water station at, to the extent possible, intervals sufficient to assure a constant supply of water;
e) Purchase, lamination, and delivery of area maps to be placed at each water station; and,
f) Printing and distribution of informational brochures in English and Spanish.

2.2 CONTRACTOR shall perform the work in accordance with the terms of the contract and to the best of CONTRACTOR'S ability.

ARTICLE III - PAYMENT

In consideration of the services to be provided under this Contract, the COUNTY agrees to pay CONTRACTOR twenty-five thousand dollars ($25,000.00) in a lump sum on or before August 31, 2001.

Total payment for this Contract shall not exceed $25,000.00.

ARTICLE IV - MONTHLY REPORTS

CONTRACTOR shall accurately report to COUNTY all activities performed under this CONTRACT in a format acceptable to COUNTY. Reports for activities conducted in June, July, and August 2001 shall be due no later than the 10th day of September 2001. Reports for each month thereafter shall be due no later than the 10th day of the following month.

ARTICLE V - INDEMNIFICATION

CONTRACTOR shall indemnify, defend, and hold harmless COUNTY, its officers, employees and agents from and against any and all suits, actions, legal administrative proceedings, claims or demands and costs attendant thereto, arising out of any act, omission, fault or negligence by the CONTRACTOR, its agents, employees or anyone under its direction or control or on its behalf in connection with performance of this Contract.

ARTICLE VI - COMPLIANCE WITH LAWS

CONTRACTOR shall comply with all federal, state, and local laws, rules, regulations, standards and Executive Orders, without limitation to those designated within this Contract. The laws and regulations of the State of Arizona shall govern the rights of the parties, the performance of this Contract, and any disputes hereunder. Any action relating to this Contract shall be brought in a court of the State of Arizona in Pima County. Any changes in the governing laws, rules, and regulations during the terms of this Contract shall apply, but do not require an amendment.

ARTICLE VII - INDEPENDENT CONTRACTOR

The status of the CONTRACTOR shall be that of an independent contractor. Neither CONTRACTOR, nor CONTRACTOR's officers agents or employees shall be considered an employee of Pima County or be entitled to receive any employment-related fringe benefits under the Pima County Merit System. CONTRACTOR shall be responsible for payment of all federal, state and local taxes associated with the compensation received pursuant to this Contract and shall indemnify and hold COUNTY harmless from any and all liability which COUNTY may incur because of CONTRACTOR's failure to pay such taxes. CONTRACTOR shall be solely responsible for program development and operation.

ARTICLE VIII - SUBCONTRACTOR

CONTRACTOR will be fully responsible for all acts and omissions of any subcontractor and of persons directly or indirectly employed by any subcontractor and of persons for whose acts any of them may be liable to the same extent that the CONTRACTOR is responsible for the acts and omissions of persons directly employed by it. Nothing in this contract shall create any obligation on the part of COUNTY to pay or see to the payment of any money due any subcontractor, except as may be required by law.

ARTICLE IX - ASSIGNMENT

CONTRACTOR shall not assign its rights to this Contract, in whole or in part, without prior written approval of the COUNTY. Approval may be withheld at the sole discretion of COUNTY, provided that such approval shall not be unreasonably withheld

ARTICLE X - NON-DISCRIMINATION

CONTRACTOR shall not discriminate against any COUNTY employee, client or any other individual in any way because of that person's age, race, creed, color, religion, sex, disability or national origin in the course of carrying out CONTRACTOR's duties pursuant to this Contract. CONTRACTOR shall comply with the provisions of Executive Orders 75-5, as amended by Executive Order 99-4, which are incorporated into this Contract by reference as if set forth in full herein.

ARTICLE XI - AMERICANS WITH DISABILITIES ACT

CONTRACTOR shall comply with all applicable provisions of the Americans with Disabilities Act (Public Law 101-336, 42 U.S.C. 12101-12213) and all applicable federal regulations under the Act, including 28 CFR Parts 35 and 36.

ARTICLE XII - AUTHORITY TO CONTRACT

Contractor warrants its right and power to enter into this Contract. If any court or administrative agency determines that COUNTY does not have authority to enter into this Contract, COUNTY shall not be liable to Contractor or any third party by reason of such determination or by reason of this Contract.

ARTICLE XIII - FULL AND COMPLETE PERFORMANCE

The failure of either party to insist on one or more instances upon the full and complete performance with any of the terms or conditions of this Contract to be performed on the part of the other, or to take any action permitted as a result thereof, shall not be construed as a waiver or relinquishment of the right to insist upon full and complete performance of the same, or any other covenant or condition, either in the past or in the future. The acceptance by either party of sums less than may be due and owing it at any time shall not be construed as an accord and satisfaction.

ARTICLE XIV - CANCELLATION FOR CONFLICT OF INTEREST

This Contract is subject to cancellation for conflict of interest pursuant to A.R.S. § § 38-511, the pertinent provisions of which are incorporated into this Contract by reference.

ARTICLE XV - TERMINATION

15.1 COUNTY reserves the right to terminate this Contract at any time and without cause by serving upon CONTRACTOR 30 days advance written notice of such intent to terminate. In the event of such termination, the COUNTY'S only obligation to CONTRACTOR shall be payment for services rendered prior to the date of termination.

15.2 This Contract may be terminated at any time without advance notice and without further obligation to the COUNTY when the CONTRACTOR is found by COUNTY to be in default of any provision of this Contract.

15.3 Notwithstanding any other provision in this Contract, this Contract may be terminated if for any reason, there are not sufficient appropriated and available monies for the purpose of maintaining COUNTY or other public entity obligations under this Contract. In the event of such termination, COUNTY shall have no further obligation to CONTRACTOR, other than to pay for services rendered prior to termination.

ARTICLE XVI - NOTICE

Any notice required or permitted to be given under this Contract shall be in writing and shall be served by delivery or by certified mail upon the other party as follows:

COUNTY:

Dennis Douglas, Director
Pima County Health Department
150 W. Congress, Suite 237
Tucson, AZ 85701

CONTRACTOR:

Reverend Robin Hoover
Humane Borders, Inc.
740 E. Speedway
Tucson, AZ 85719

ARTICLE XVII - NON-EXCLUSIVE CONTRACT

CONTRACTOR understands that this Contract is nonexclusive and is for the sole convenience of COUNTY. COUNTY reserves the right to obtain like services from other sources for any reason.

ARTICLE XIX - REMEDIES

Either party may pursue any remedies provided by law for the breach of this Contract. No right or remedy is intended to be exclusive of any other right or remedy and each shall be cumulative and in addition to any other right or remedy existing at law or at equity or by virtue of this Contract.

ARTICLE XX - SEVERABILITY

Each provision of this Contract stands alone, and any provision of this Contract found to be prohibited by law shall be ineffective to the extent of such prohibition without invalidating the remainder of this Contract.

ARTICLE XXI - BOOKS AND RECORDS

21.1 CONTRACTOR shall keep and maintain proper and complete books, records and accounts, which shall be open at all reasonable times for inspection and audit by duly authorized representatives of COUNTY.

21.2 In addition, CONTRACTOR shall retain all records relating to this contract at least 5 years after its termination or cancellation or, if later, until any related pending proceeding or litigation has been closed.

ARTICLE XXII - ENTIRE AGREEMENT

This document constitutes the entire agreement between the parties pertaining to the subject matter hereof, and all prior or contemporaneous agreements and understandings, oral or written, are hereby superseded and merged herein. This Contract may be modified, amended, altered or extended only by a written amendment signed by the parties.

IN WITNESS THEREOF, the parties have affixed their signatures to this Contract on the date written below.

PIMA COUNTY

C. Duhelbauer
County Administrator

Date: 8/15/01

CONTRACTOR

Robin Hoover, president
Name and Title

Date: 8-21-01

APPROVED AS TO CONTENT:

Enrique P. Serna
Department Head

APPROVED AS TO FORM:

Karen S. Friar
Deputy County Attorney

AMENDMENT NO. 1 TO AGREEMENT
NO. 11-30-H-129598-0601

I. The AGREEMENT between PIMA COUNTY and HUMANE BORDERS, INC., pertaining to the provision of water stations and potable water to various remote desert locations in Pima County, is hereby amended as follows:

A. Article I. is amended to extend the Agreement for a one-year period through June 4, 2003 as follows:

Pursuant to Article I., this Agreement is extended for a one-year period from June 5, 2002 through June 4, 2003.

B. Article III. is amended to increase the contract ceiling by $25,000.00 from $25,000.00 to $50,000.00 and to reflect the one-year extension payment due date of August 31, 2003 as follows:

"In consideration of the services to be provided under this Contract, the COUNTY agrees to pay CONTRACTOR Twenty-Five Thousand Dollars ($25,000) in a lump sum on or before August 31, 2003.

Total payment for this Contract shall not exceed $50,000.00."

II. The effective date of this Amendment is June 5, 2002.

III. All other elements of the original AGREEMENT not amended by Amendment No. 1 remain unchanged.

IN WITNESS WHEREOF, the parties do hereby agree to carry out the terms of this Amendment to the AGREEMENT.

PIMA COUNTY

By:____________________
Sharon Bronson, Chair
Board of Supervisors

HUMANE BORDERS, INC.

By: Rev. Robin Hoover, Ph.D.
Contractor

APPROVED AS TO CONTENT

By:____________________
Dennis W. Douglas, Director
Pima County Health Department

ATTEST

By:____________________
Clerk of the Board

APPROVED AS TO FORM

By: Karen S. Friar
Karen S. Friar
Deputy County Attorney

PERMISSIVE USE AGREEMENT 7/3/01

THIS AGREEMENT made and entered into this 20th day of July, 2001 by and between Rio Rico Properties Inc., an Arizona corporation, having its principal office at 275 Rio Rico Drive, Rio Rico, Arizona 85648, hereinafter called "LESSOR" and Humane Borders, Inc., whose address is 740 East Speedway, Tucson, Arizona 85719, hereinafter called "LESSEE"; and

WHEREAS, LESSOR is the owner of certain lands in Rio Rico, Santa Cruz County, Arizona, more particularly described in Exhibit "A" ("lands" or "property") attached hereto and made a part hereof; and,

WHEREAS, LESSEE is desirous of obtaining permission to use, as hereinafter provided, the lands of the LESSOR.

NOW, THEREFORE, in consideration of the covenants to be kept and performed by each of the parties hereto, and the sum of One Dollar ($1.00) cash in hand paid by the LESSEE to the LESSOR, receipt of which is hereby acknowledged, and further consideration as herein provided, it is agreed as follows:

(1) LESSOR, subject to the conditions herein expressed, does hereby grant unto the LESSEE the non-exclusive privilege and license to use the lands during the period beginning 8:00 a.m. on June 25, 2001, and ending 12:00 p.m. on June 14, 2003, said license and privilege herein granted to be exercised in accordance with the laws of the State of Arizona and the United States of America and the rules and regulations of any other duly constituted body having authority to make rules and regulations covering the use of the lands by LESSEE.

LESSEE shall pay a rental of Ten ($10.00) Dollars, net of any applicable tax, payable on or before June 25, 2001, for said license and privilege.

(2) The license and privilege granted LESSEE under this Agreement shall be exercised only on the demised property of LESSOR and upon no other property.

The property may be used only by LESSEE for the purposes of erecting and maintaining a drinking water relief station.

(3) LESSEE agrees to indemnify and save harmless LESSOR from and against all

M:\LEGAL\AGREEMENT\PUA\Humane.doc

This instrument prepared by:

DENNIS J. GETMAN, ESQUIRE
12th Floor, 201 Alhambra Circle
Coral Gables, Florida 33134

claims of whatever nature arising from any act, omission or negligence of LESSEE or LESSEE'S contractors, licensees, agents, invitees, guests, servants or employees, or arising from any accident, injury or damage whatsoever caused to any person or to the property of any person during the term hereof in or about the lands where such accident, damage or injury results or is claimed to have resulted from any act or omission on the part of LESSEE or LESSEE'S agents or employees. This indemnity and hold harmless agreement shall include indemnity against all costs and expenses, including attorney fees incurred in or in connection with any such claim or proceedings brought thereon and the defense thereof.

LESSEE agrees to maintain in full force during the term hereof a policy of public liability insurance under which LESSOR is named as additionally insured and under which the insurer agrees to indemnify and hold LESSOR harmless from and against all costs, expenses and liability arising out of or based upon any and all personal injuries sustained and accidents occurring in or about the lands. The minimum limits of such insurance shall be ONE MILLION ($1,000,000) DOLLARS per occurrence for bodily injury and/or death and ONE HUNDRED THOUSAND ($100,000) DOLLARS per occurrence for property damage. A duplicate or certificate of said public liability and property damage insurance coverage from a reputable insurance carrier, licensed to conduct business in the State of Arizona, and having a Best's rating of at least A VI, shall be delivered to LESSEE within ten (10) days after the issuance and each renewal of said policy. Such evidence of insurance shall name the LESSOR as additional insured and shall provide that said insurance will not be cancelled without giving LESSOR thirty (30) days prior written notice.

(4) LESSEE shall not incur any indebtedness giving right to a lien of any kind upon the LESSOR'S interest in and to the above-described lands. LESSOR'S interest shall not be subject to liens for improvements made by the LESSEE on the above-described lands. In the event any liens are filed, due to improvements made by the LESSEE, the LESSEE shall immediately discharge said lien by such manner as permitted by law.

(5) Nothing herein contained shall be construed as limiting the LESSOR from having the full use and enjoyment of its lands, save only as to the rights granted to the LESSEE by the terms of this Agreement, and nothing herein contained shall be construed or

interpreted as granting anything to LESSEE other than use of the property provided herein.

(6) In the event of any breach or non-performance of any of the covenants, agreements, terms or conditions to be performed by LESSEE, and said breach or non-performance continues for three (3) days, LESSOR has the right to declare this Agreement terminated and to re-enter the demised property and remove LESSEE and its property therefrom, and LESSEE agrees to peacefully vacate said demised property and pay all costs, including reasonable attorney's fees, that may be incurred by LESSOR in enforcing the covenants, agreements, terms and conditions of this Agreement.

(7) It is understood and agreed that this Agreement sets forth all of the covenants, agreements, terms and conditions between the parties and that there are no other oral or written agreements between them.

(8) It is further understood and agreed that no subsequent amendments, alterations or additions to this Agreement shall be binding upon the parties hereto unless reduced to writing and executed by said parties.

(9) LESSOR and LESSEE agree that this Agreement shall be governed by and construed under the laws of the State of Arizona.

(10) LESSEE shall not transfer or assign the interest or right provided in this Agreement, nor attempt to grant any sublease or sub-license to any persons whomsoever without the written consent of the LESSOR. The consent of the LESSOR shall be at the LESSOR'S sole discretion.

(11) The parties hereto agree that time is of the essence in this Agreement.

(12) All notices or requests between the parties shall be in writing and shall be served or mailed Certified Mail (Return Receipt Requested) at the addresses above set forth or such address as the applicable party shall designate in writing.

(13) This Agreement and all of its terms and conditions shall extend to and be binding upon the parties hereto and upon their respective heirs, executors, administrators, successors and assigns.

(14) The invalidation of any provision or clause in whole or in part by judgment or court order shall in no way affect any of the other provisions or clauses, which shall remain

in full force and effect.

(15) It is understood between the parties hereto that the property has been inspected by the LESSEE and that the property is being accepted in an "As Is" condition.

(16) The LESSEE shall, upon the expiration of this Agreement, quit and surrender the property so that the property is in the same order, condition and state of repair as when LESSEE took possession. The property shall be broom clean when surrendered by the LESSEE.

(17) Nothing contained in this Agreement shall be deemed to constitute or be construed to create the relationship of principal and agent, partnership, joint venturer or any other relationship between the parties hereto, other than the relationship of LESSEE/LESSOR.

(18) The prevailing party in any litigation brought to enforce rights hereunder shall be entitled to reimbursement of all reasonable costs and expenses, including, but not limited to, court costs, fees, and attorneys' fees of in-house and outside counsel at all judicial levels.

(19) Notwithstanding anything to the contrary herein, the LESSOR reserves the right to terminate this Agreement upon sixty (60) days written notice, which notice shall be in the sole discretion of the LESSOR.

IN WITNESS WHEREOF, the LESSOR and LESSEE have executed this Agreement as of the date and year first above written.

WITNESSES

[signature]

[signature]

RIO RICO PROPERTIES INC.
LESSOR

By: [signature]
Dennis J. Getman, Executive Vice President

WITNESSES

Margaret M. Schmidt

Carol J. Hall

HUMANE BORDERS, INC.
LESSEE

By: Rev. Robin Hoover, PhD

M:\LEGAL\AGREEMEN\PUA\Humane.doc

Mexican Military Incursions

<u>March 9, 1999</u>

San Miguel Gate: U.S. Customs agents fired on by Mexican military smuggling marijuana.

<u>April, 2000</u>

Menagers Dam: cattle truck drove into the village with Mexican soldiers armed with machine guns.

<u>January 6, 2002</u>

GuVo: soldiers with machine guns smuggled 2,000 lbs. of narcotics; ran an intersection colliding with another vehicle killing two innocent people and two soldiers.

<u>May 17, 2002</u>

Papago Farms: soldiers pursued Ranger officer on foot while protecting a large drug load.

<u>February 7, 2003</u>

Serapos Gate 6:45am: soldiers in uniform crossed into the village with a pickup, suspected of protecting a drug load.

Proposed Interdiction Patrol Corridor

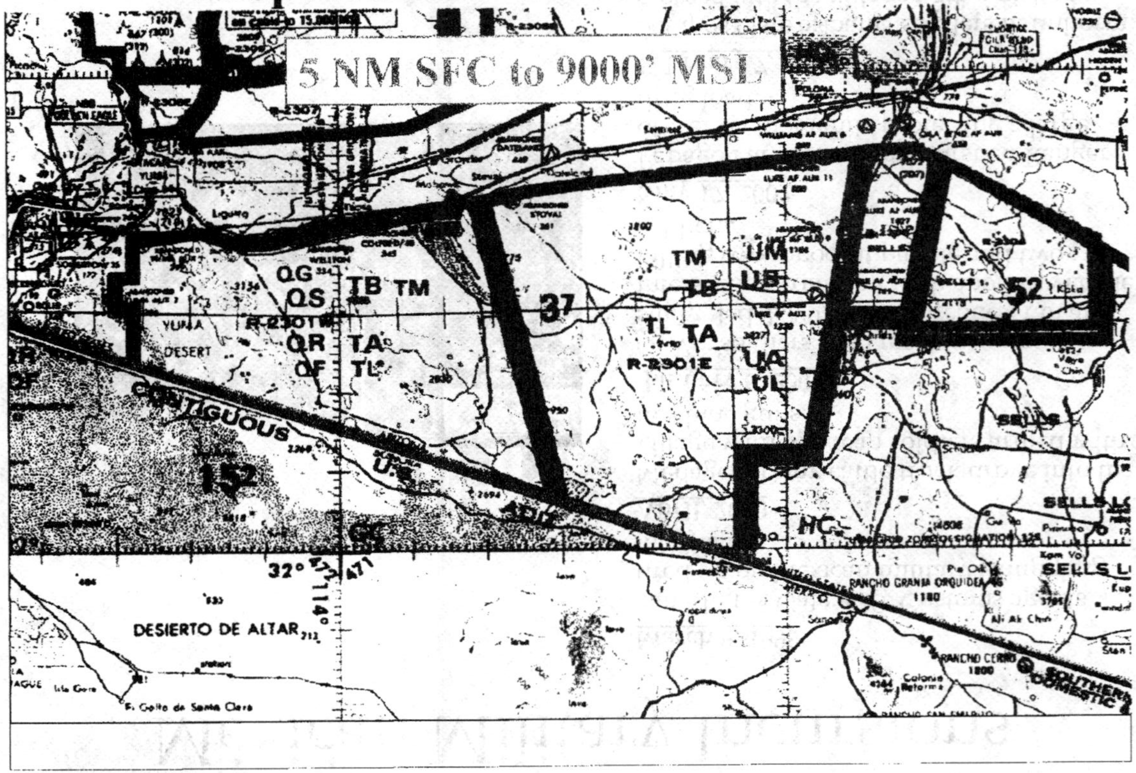

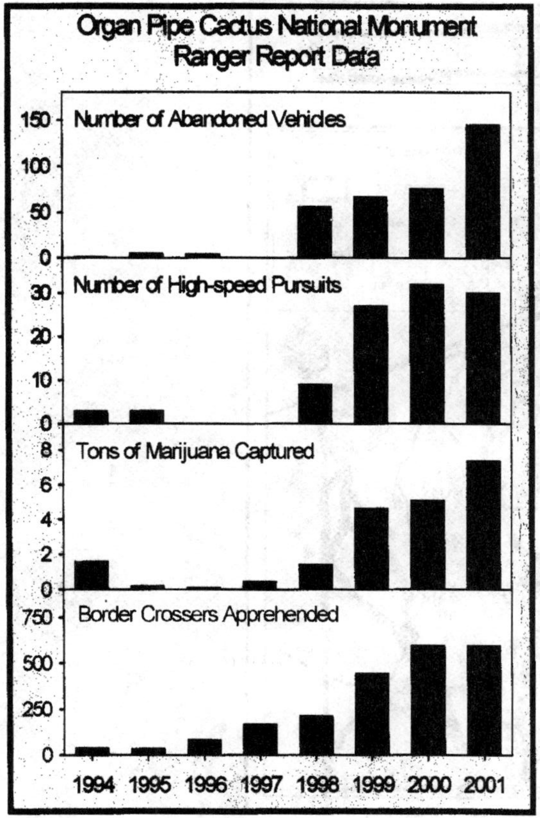

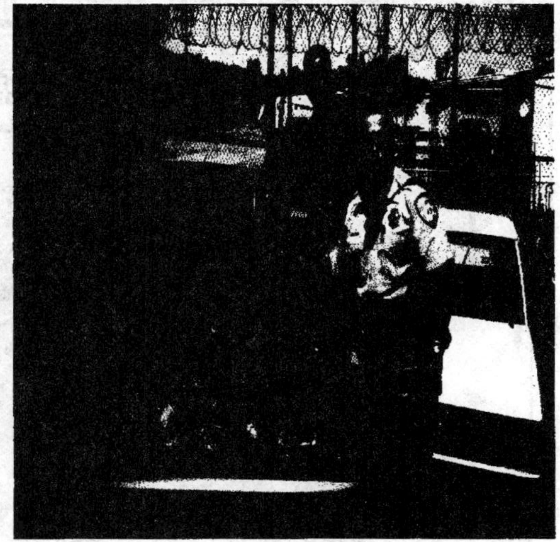

Marijuana seizure at Organ Pipe

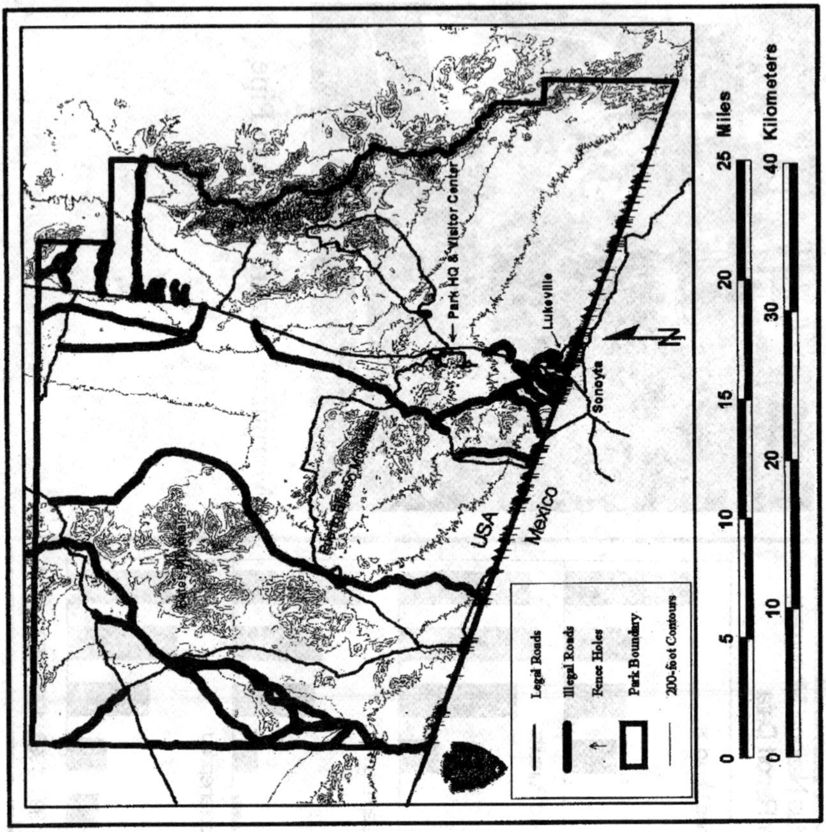

Park HQ & Visitor Center
Lukeville
Sonoyta
USA
Mexico
N
Legal Roads
Illegal Roads
Fence Holes
Park Boundary
200-foot Contours
0 5 10 15 20 25 Miles
0 10 20 30 40 Kilometers

Agents net 20 smugglers, marijuana

BY BILL HESS
HERALD/REVIEW

DOUGLAS — Twenty drug-smuggling Mexican nationals carrying 1,612 pounds of marijuana were taken into custody early Friday morning in the Carr Canyon area of the Huachuca Mountains, said Lee Morgan, resident agent in charge of the Immigration and Customs Enforcement office in Douglas.

"We had received information that a group would be coming through carrying dope," Morgan said Friday afternoon.

Border Patrol agents of the recently created Bureau of Customs and Border Protection joined the new Department of Homeland Security's Bureau of Immigration and Customs Enforcement in the operation slightly after midnight on Friday, he said. This is the first case in which the two new bureaus, formed from Immigration and Naturalization Service, Customs Service and Border Patrol assets that came into existence on March 1, have had a successful operation anywhere along the country's border, Morgan said.

Based on intelligence garnered from informants, the ICE team and Border Patrol agents watched the canyon area as the drug smugglers were walking, Morgan said.

They had come over the Huachuca Mountains into Carr Canyon, "and that's where we surprised them," he said. The smugglers were told to stop, and the agents identified themselves as federal law enforcement officers.

"As the agents challenged them, shining lights from flashlights at them, most of them fled," Morgan said, adding all in the group were apprehended.

Border Patrol air units helped locate the suspected smugglers.

The 20 suspects were taken to the Border Patrol's Naco Station for processing and identification, he said. None were

See MARIJUANA, Page A13

MARIJUANA: *Two of the suspects were juveniles*

FROM PAGE A1

found to be wanted on any criminal warrant in the United States.

Two of those apprehended were juveniles, Morgan said.

The 18 adults were charged with numerous drug-related federal felonies, including smuggling, possession with intent to sell and conspiracy.

The first joint action by the two new Homeland Security bureaus "went very well," Morgan said, adding he personally sees a new and stronger strategy along the border to stop illegal activities.

Paying informants for information that provides good intelligence is part of the strategy, Morgan said. Friday's case is an example of how good information is needed in stopping illegal activities along the border.

"We pay pretty nice sums," Morgan said.

Information on smuggling operations in which people are being brought across the border is especially critical, he said.

Individuals who wish to provide information, which will be kept confidential, are asked to call 1-800-Be-Alert, or 1-800-232-5378, or Morgan's office in Douglas at 364-1218.

Canyon homeowners' tranquility disrupted

LEE M. SPINKS
Essay report

"America's Most Wanted," a popular network television program for many years, visited southeastern Arizona with a camera crew not long ago, to record footage related to possible criminal activity contained within the exodus of foreign nationals, illegally immigrating across the Mexican-American border.

The production schedule called for a few hours of assignment in Cochise County. That element of the production was extended to several days as camera crews kept reeling-in footage of high-impact images showing groups of 40-50 people running along foot paths and trails through mountain terrain and desert plains, in open defiance of existing border management agencies.

The segment broadcast on the program ran approximately seven minutes.

The script for the video footage stated among the massive number of intruders were many drug smugglers and many additional people from countries other than Mexico.

It was the people from those "other countries" who were described as potential terrorists in the broadcast.

Testimony was presented in the video by "coyotes" who organized and operated the regional illegal human trade cargo business, as to the characteristics of their customers and clients. Those from countries other than Mexico were cast in a clandestine role described as being insular, apart, separate, individual cells or clusters, people with some purpose agents of foreign-sponsored terrorism aimed against the United States.

This was not the first contact with *MVN* on this matter by Griffin.

In February she also notified *MVN* she was aware and concerned with potentially dangerous situations being observed in areas near Carr, Miller, Stump and Ramsey Canyons.

Since that time she said she had been photo-documenting the transit of UDAs, drug traffickers and suspicious persons in the area, trespassing on private property and across personal homesteads.

Griffin showed a collection consisting of dozens of photographs pointing out discarded clothing, comfort items, survival items, of transients making the trek from Mexico.

Griffin also showed pictures of large black plastic wrappers, burlap gunny sack bags and discarded backpacks used in the transport of marijuana, cocaine and other controlled substances, in her opinion.

Griffin mentioned 800 pounds of marijuana being seized recently in Ramsey Canyon by an area task force.

Griffin said she had been conducting a personal neighborhood watch in one of the popular canyon areas and had seen for herself late-night and early morning exchanges of suspicious nature.

She said she was informed by residents that "scouts" or "spotters" carrying "big guns," described as Uzis, listened to police scanners to alert others as to possible interdiction in drug exchanges at 4 a.m.

in the United States.

Those customers were willing to pay as much as $60,000 each for safe delivery and entrance into the U.S.A., said subjects in the television report and subsequent testimony to authorities.

Videotape copies of the program are presently circulating among homeowners, builders, residents and occupants of mountain resorts, canyon homes, and wilderness retreats, in the Sierra Vista area.

Previously, the lowlands of Naco, Douglas, Agua Prieta and Nogales were the focus of attention for border crossings and illegal trespass, according to reports from Border Patrol and the Cochise County Sheriff's Office.

More recently the flight of foreigners has taken to higher ground, a claim substantiated by several U.S. Forest Rangers in accounts regarding the possible causes for the Ryan and Oversite Fires in the Coronado National Park forest lands.

Incident Commanders and District Forest Service Rangers have stated it is their opinion, based on observation of fire-origin sites, transient undocumented aliens (UDAs) were responsible for igniting the wildfires which have destroyed more than 40,000 acres at a cost of millions of dollars in emergency response funds.

On June 3, former two-term Arizona Legislator Gail Griffin, a real estate agent and licensed Associate Broker in Sierra Vista, contacted *Mountain View News* to express her concerns regarding these matters, particularly the aspects of drug smugglers and entry of possible insurgent

tered in Casa Grande, said Griffin, pulled along an open roadway, beeped its horn a few times to signal backpackers hiding in the forested shoulders and received several large packages wrapped in black plastic.

She said she had seen other vehicles driving at high-speeds following exchanges with other trespassing individuals on posted property.

Griffin told *MVN* she had spoken with homeowners who told her they were upset and concerned about their welfare and safety.

Griffin told how in one instance a property owner, in an expensive upper canyon estate, had seen a group of 40 or 50 people crossing his property and notified the Sheriff's Office.

Following his call to authorities Griffin said he told her he heard his name and address being broadcast on a portable scanner held by the intruders.

The intruders had police and sheriff's frequencies programmed on radio receivers.

That, said Griffin, was enough to convince the homeowner to relocate for the sake of personal safety.

The passage of hundreds of thousands of illegal entrants is well documented by law enforcement authorities in Cochise County. The claims of monumental drug smuggling also find substance in police logs.

The possible entrance of "terrorists" into the U.S.A. through Cochise County is a newer claim, but one which has at least some foundation in fact.

Congressman Jim Kolbe (Rep. Dist. 8) when asked about this possibility in February by *Mountain View*

See TERRORISTS p.6

Wednesday, June 12, 2002

RRORISTS from p.1

ws replied he doubted was the case.

Kolbe's opinion terror- would not be sneaking rough the back roads of ise County, but through urnstiles of international rts, posing as certifiable ors, students or business ons.

ked about the possible ence of automatic as- weapons observed in anyon areas Kolbe said ch was the case in actu- it was most likely ily armed drug smug- , not terrorists.

be also said, in his opin- drug smugglers were ter- ts, but of a different na- han those involved with ctions of September 11.

ffin has questions:

iere documentation re- [illegible]

those apprehended by Bor- der Control and U.S. Cus- toms? How many known fel- ons have been arrested and deported? How many repeat offenders have crossed and recrossed into the U.S.A.? How many of those appre- hended have criminal records of violent crimes? How many people are car- rying communicable dis- eases into the U.S.A.?

In a recent news release Rep. Kolbe stated the efforts to reorganize the Immigra tion and Naturalization Ser vice would not take place prior to the 2002 Primary and General Elections

Griffin said she and others were surprised at that [illegible] tion. She said that the [illegible] is as important [illegible] election debates and [illegible] cal discussions [illegible] been and should [illegible]

Griffin has asked that other citizens and property own- ers, who are concerned and involved with illegal tresspass, remember to no- tify authorities for each in- stance they see or possible drug smuggling.

Contact Naco Border Patrol at 432-5121; 24 hours a day. Call Cochise County Sheriff's Office at 432-9500 during normal business hours and 432-9501 other times. Contact U.S. Customs 1-800-973-2877 or Douglas branch of Customs at 364- 1218.

[redacted]

Rev. Robin Hoover, Ph.D.
Pastor, First Christian Church
President, Humane Borders
740 E. Speedway
Tucson, Arizona 85719

Church Office	520-624-8695
Humane Borders	520-628-7753
Robin's Cell	520-360-7818

DATE: March 11, 2003

TO: Mr. Nick Coleman

Dear Nick,

In response to the request from Congressman Shadegg at the recent field hearing in Sells, Arizona, we are submitting to your office one sample of a federally issued permit to erect and maintain water stations on federally managed lands, a copy of the contract with Pima County Government establishing Humane Borders, Inc. as a provider of water stations, and a sample private land owner agreement.

PERMISSIVE USE AGREEMENT 7/3/01

THIS AGREEMENT made and entered into this 20th day of July, 2001 by and between Rio Rico Properties Inc., an Arizona corporation, having its principal office at 275 Rio Rico Drive, Rio Rico, Arizona 85648, hereinafter called "LESSOR" and Humane Borders, Inc., whose address is 740 East Speedway, Tucson, Arizona 85719, hereinafter called "LESSEE"; and

WHEREAS, LESSOR is the owner of certain lands in Rio Rico, Santa Cruz County, Arizona, more particularly described in Exhibit "A" ("lands" or "property") attached hereto and made a part hereof; and,

WHEREAS, LESSEE is desirous of obtaining permission to use, as hereinafter provided, the lands of the LESSOR.

NOW, THEREFORE, in consideration of the covenants to be kept and performed by each of the parties hereto, and the sum of One Dollar ($1.00) cash in hand paid by the LESSEE to the LESSOR, receipt of which is hereby acknowledged, and further consideration as herein provided, it is agreed as follows:

(1) LESSOR, subject to the conditions herein expressed, does hereby grant unto the LESSEE the non-exclusive privilege and license to use the lands during the period beginning 8:00 a.m. on June 25, 2001, and ending 12:00 p.m. on June 14, 2003, said license and privilege herein granted to be exercised in accordance with the laws of the State of Arizona and the United States of America and the rules and regulations of any other duly constituted body having authority to make rules and regulations covering the use of the lands by LESSEE.

LESSEE shall pay a rental of Ten ($10.00) Dollars, net of any applicable tax, payable on or before June 25, 2001, for said license and privilege.

(2) The license and privilege granted LESSEE under this Agreement shall be exercised only on the demised property of LESSOR and upon no other property.

The property may be used only by LESSEE for the purposes of erecting and maintaining a drinking water relief station.

(3) LESSEE agrees to indemnify and save harmless LESSOR from and against all

M:\LEGAL\AGREEMEN\PUA\Humane.doc

This instrument prepared by:

DENNIS J. GETMAN, ESQUIRE
12th Floor, 201 Alhambra Circle
Coral Gables, Florida 33134

claims of whatever nature arising from any act, omission or negligence of LESSEE or LESSEE'S contractors, licensees, agents, invitees, guests, servants or employees, or arising from any accident, injury or damage whatsoever caused to any person or to the property of any person during the term hereof in or about the lands where such accident, damage or injury results or is claimed to have resulted from any act or omission on the part of LESSEE or LESSEE'S agents or employees. This indemnity and hold harmless agreement shall include indemnity against all costs and expenses, including attorney fees incurred in or in connection with any such claim or proceedings brought thereon and the defense thereof.

LESSEE agrees to maintain in full force during the term hereof a policy of public liability insurance under which LESSOR is named as additionally insured and under which the insurer agrees to indemnify and hold LESSOR harmless from and against all costs, expenses and liability arising out of or based upon any and all personal injuries sustained and accidents occurring in or about the lands. The minimum limits of such insurance shall be ONE MILLION ($1,000,000) DOLLARS per occurrence for bodily injury and/or death and ONE HUNDRED THOUSAND ($100,000) DOLLARS per occurrence for property damage. A duplicate or certificate of said public liability and property damage insurance coverage from a reputable insurance carrier, licensed to conduct business in the State of Arizona, and having a Best's rating of at least A VI, shall be delivered to LESSEE within ten (10) days after the issuance and each renewal of said policy. Such evidence of insurance shall name the LESSOR as additional insured and shall provide that said insurance will not be cancelled without giving LESSOR thirty (30) days prior written notice.

(4) LESSEE shall not incur any indebtedness giving right to a lien of any kind upon the LESSOR'S interest in and to the above-described lands. LESSOR'S interest shall not be subject to liens for improvements made by the LESSEE on the above-described lands. In the event any liens are filed, due to improvements made by the LESSEE, the LESSEE shall immediately discharge said lien by such manner as permitted by law.

(5) Nothing herein contained shall be construed as limiting the LESSOR from having the full use and enjoyment of its lands, save only as to the rights granted to the LESSEE by the terms of this Agreement, and nothing herein contained shall be construed or

interpreted as granting anything to LESSEE other than use of the property provided herein.

(6) In the event of any breach or non-performance of any of the covenants, agreements, terms or conditions to be performed by LESSEE, and said breach or non-performance continues for three (3) days, LESSOR has the right to declare this Agreement terminated and to re-enter the demised property and remove LESSEE and its property therefrom, and LESSEE agrees to peacefully vacate said demised property and pay all costs, including reasonable attorney's fees, that may be incurred by LESSOR in enforcing the covenants, agreements, terms and conditions of this Agreement.

(7) It is understood and agreed that this Agreement sets forth all of the covenants, agreements, terms and conditions between the parties and that there are no other oral or written agreements between them.

(8) It is further understood and agreed that no subsequent amendments, alterations or additions to this Agreement shall be binding upon the parties hereto unless reduced to writing and executed by said parties.

(9) LESSOR and LESSEE agree that this Agreement shall be governed by and construed under the laws of the State of Arizona.

(10) LESSEE shall not transfer or assign the interest or right provided in this Agreement, nor attempt to grant any sublease or sub-license to any persons whomsoever without the written consent of the LESSOR. The consent of the LESSOR shall be at the LESSOR'S sole discretion.

(11) The parties hereto agree that time is of the essence in this Agreement.

(12) All notices or requests between the parties shall be in writing and shall be served or mailed Certified Mail (Return Receipt Requested) at the addresses above set forth or such address as the applicable party shall designate in writing.

(13) This Agreement and all of its terms and conditions shall extend to and be binding upon the parties hereto and upon their respective heirs, executors, administrators, successors and assigns.

(14) The invalidation of any provision or clause in whole or in part by judgment or court order shall in no way affect any of the other provisions or clauses, which shall remain

in full force and effect.

(15) It is understood between the parties hereto that the property has been inspected by the LESSEE and that the property is being accepted in an "As Is" condition.

(16) The LESSEE shall, upon the expiration of this Agreement, quit and surrender the property so that the property is in the same order, condition and state of repair as when LESSEE took possession. The property shall be broom clean when surrendered by the LESSEE.

(17) Nothing contained in this Agreement shall be deemed to constitute or be construed to create the relationship of principal and agent, partnership, joint venturer or any other relationship between the parties hereto, other than the relationship of LESSEE/LESSOR.

(18) The prevailing party in any litigation brought to enforce rights hereunder shall be entitled to reimbursement of all reasonable costs and expenses, including, but not limited to, court costs, fees, and attorneys' fees of in-house and outside counsel at all judicial levels.

(19) Notwithstanding anything to the contrary herein, the LESSOR reserves the right to terminate this Agreement upon sixty (60) days written notice, which notice shall be in the sole discretion of the LESSOR.

IN WITNESS WHEREOF, the LESSOR and LESSEE have executed this Agreement as of the date and year first above written.

WITNESSES

RIO RICO PROPERTIES INC.
LESSOR

By: [signature]
Dennis J. Getman, Executive Vice President

WITNESSES

HUMANE BORDERS, INC.
LESSEE

By: [signature]

M:\LEGAL\AGREEMENT\LA\Humane.doc

PIMA COUNTY HEALTH DEPARTMENT
150 WEST CONGRESS • TUCSON, AZ 85701-1333

March 27, 2003

Reverend Robin Hoover
Humane Borders, Inc.
740 East Speedway Blvd.
Tucson, Arizona 85719

Subject: Family Planning Homeless Youth Program

Dear Rev. Hoover:

The Pima County Health Department is contracting with Humane Borders, Inc., for the provision of water stations and potable water to various remote desert locations. Enclosed are three (3) originals of the proposed agreement for your review and signature. Once signed, please return all three (3) originals to the following address:

Contracts & Grants Office
Pima County Health Department
150 W. Congress Street, Room 253
Tucson, Arizona 85701

An original agreement will be returned to your attention once it has been fully executed. Please contact our office at (520) 740-3681 with any inquiries or comments you may have.

Sincerely,

John F. Thomas, Contracts & Grants Manager
Pima County Health Department

JT:lr

Enclosures
cc: file

GENERAL SERVICES CONTRACT $100,000 or Less Per Year
Water Distribution Services in Remote Areas of Pima County

THIS CONTRACT entered between Pima County, a body politic and corporate of the State of Arizona, hereinafter called COUNTY; and Humane Borders, Inc., hereinafter called CONTRACTOR.

WITNESSETH

WHEREAS, A.R.S. § 11-251-02 authorizes the Board of Supervisors to use county resources in search or rescue operations involving the life or health of any person; and,

WHEREAS, on June 5, 2001, a State of Local Emergency was declared in Pima County due to the extreme peril faced by persons exposed to the high summer desert temperatures and limited water supply; and.

WHEREAS, pursuant to Pima County Code 11.12.060, emergency procurement of services is authorized when there exists a threat to public health, welfare, property or safety; and,

WHEREAS, CONTRACTOR was selected to provide water stations and potable water to various remote desert locations in Pima County to reduce the need for aggressive search and rescue operations; and,

WHEREAS, Pima County Contract No. 11-30-H-129598-0601 was entered into on June 5th, 2001; and,

WHEREAS, Article I of the Agreement provides an ability to extend the term of the Agreement for one additional (1) one year period, or any portion thereof; and,

WHEREAS, the County Administrator was authorized to sign and did sign said Agreement; and,

WHEREAS, the Pima County Board of Supervisor has amended Pima County Code and Board Policy to remove the County Administrator's signature authority and to vest the Procurement Director with the authority to sign contracts up to $100,000.00; and,

WHEREAS, said Agreement now falls under the signature authority of the Procurement Director; and,

WHEREAS, a new Agreement is appropriate to acknowledge the Board of Supervisor's directives on contract authorization;

NOW, THEREFORE, the parties hereto agree as follows:

ARTICLE I - TERM AND EXTENSION/RENEWAL

This Contract shall commence on the 5th day of June, 2002, and shall terminate on the 4th day of June, 2003 unless sooner terminated or further extended pursuant to this Contract. Any modification, or extension shall be by formal written amendment executed by the parties hereto.

ARTICLE II - SCOPE

A. Services to be provided by CONTRACTOR shall assure that reasonable steps are taken so that hikers and others on foot in the desert regions of Pima County have access to potable water and shall include, but are not limited to:

1. Identification of appropriate locations for water stations, in consultation with local, state, and federal authorities;
2. Installation and maintenance of water stations at identified and approved sites;
3. Purchase of potable water in sufficient quantity to assure, to the extent possible, a constant supply of water at the water stations;
4. Transportation, delivery and installation of potable water at each water station at, to the extent possible, intervals sufficient to assure a constant supply of water;
5. Purchase, lamination, and delivery of area maps to be placed at each water station; and,
6. Printing and distribution of informational brochures in English and Spanish.

B. CONTRACTOR shall accurately report to COUNTY all activities performed under this Contract in a format acceptable to COUNTY. Reports for activities conducted for each month are due no later than the 10th day of the following month.

CONTRACTOR shall perform the work in accordance with the terms of the Contract and to the best of CONTRACTOR'S ability.

ARTICLE III - PAYMENT

In consideration of the services specified in this Contract, the COUNTY agrees to pay CONTRACTOR a lump sum of Twenty Five Thousand Dollars ($25,000) for services rendered during the period from June 5, 2002 through June 4, 2003. Payment will be made by COUNTY within 60 days after execution of this Contract.

Total payment for this Contract shall not exceed Twenty Five Thousand Dollars ($25,000).

ARTICLE IV – INSURANCE

CONTRACTOR shall obtain and maintain at its own expense, during the entire term of this Contract the following type of insurance:

A. If required by law, workers' compensation coverage including employees' liability coverage.

ARTICLE V - INDEMNIFICATION

CONTRACTOR shall indemnify, defend, and hold harmless COUNTY, its officers, employees and agents from and against any and all suits, actions, legal administrative proceedings, claims or demands and costs attendant thereto, arising out of any act, omission, fault or negligence by the CONTRACTOR, its agents, employees or anyone under its direction or control or on its behalf in connection with performance of this Contract.

ARTICLE VI - COMPLIANCE WITH LAWS

CONTRACTOR shall comply with all federal, state, and local laws, rules, regulations, standards and Executive Orders, without limitation to those designated within this Contract. The laws and regulations of the State of Arizona shall govern the rights of the parties, the performance of this Contract, and any disputes hereunder. Any action relating to this Contract shall be brought in a court of the State of Arizona in Pima County. Any changes in the governing laws, rules, and regulations during the terms of this Contract shall apply, but do not require an amendment.

ARTICLE VII - INDEPENDENT CONTRACTOR

The status of the CONTRACTOR shall be that of an independent contractor. Neither CONTRACTOR, nor CONTRACTOR'S officers agents or employees shall be considered an employee of Pima County or be entitled to receive any employment-related fringe benefits under the Pima County Merit System. CONTRACTOR shall be responsible for payment of all federal, state and local taxes associated with the compensation received pursuant to this Contract and shall indemnify and hold COUNTY harmless from any and all liability which COUNTY may incur because of CONTRACTOR'S failure to pay such taxes. CONTRACTOR shall be solely responsible for program development and operation.

ARTICLE VIII - SUBCONTRACTOR

CONTRACTOR will be fully responsible for all acts and omissions of any subcontractor and of persons directly or indirectly employed by any subcontractor and of persons for whose acts any of them may be liable to the same extent that the CONTRACTOR is responsible for the acts and omissions of persons directly employed by it. Nothing in this contract shall create any obligation on the part of COUNTY to pay or see to the payment of any money due any subcontractor, except as may be required by law.

ARTICLE IX - ASSIGNMENT

CONTRACTOR shall not assign its rights to this Contract, in whole or in part, without prior written approval of the COUNTY. Approval may be withheld at the sole discretion of COUNTY, provided that such approval shall not be unreasonably withheld.

ARTICLE X - NON-DISCRIMINATION

CONTRACTOR shall not discriminate against any COUNTY employee, client or any other individual in any way because of that person's age, race, creed, color, religion, sex, disability or national origin in the course of carrying out CONTRACTOR'S duties pursuant to this Contract. CONTRACTOR shall comply with the provisions of Executive Orders 75-5, as amended by Executive Order 99-4, which are incorporated into this Contract by reference as if set forth in full herein.

ARTICLE XI - AMERICANS WITH DISABILITIES ACT

CONTRACTOR shall comply with all applicable provisions of the Americans with Disabilities Act (Public Law 101-336, 42 U.S.C. 12101-12213) and all applicable federal regulations under the Act, including 28 CFR Parts 35 and 36.

ARTICLE XII - AUTHORITY TO CONTRACT

Contractor warrants its right and power to enter into this Contract. If any court or administrative agency determines that COUNTY does not have authority to enter into this Contract, COUNTY shall not be liable to Contractor or any third party by reason of such determination or by reason of this Contract.

ARTICLE XIII - FULL AND COMPLETE PERFORMANCE

The failure of either party to insist on one or more instances upon the full and complete performance with any of the terms or conditions of this Contract to be performed on the part of the other, or to take any action permitted as a result thereof, shall not be construed as a waiver or relinquishment of the right to insist upon full and complete performance of the same, or any other covenant or condition, either in the past or in the future. The acceptance by either party of sums less than may be due and owing it at any time shall not be construed as an accord and satisfaction.

ARTICLE XIV - CANCELLATION FOR CONFLICT OF INTEREST

This Contract is subject to cancellation for conflict of interest pursuant to ARS § 38-511, the pertinent provisions of which are incorporated into this Contract by reference.

ARTICLE XV - TERMINATION

COUNTY reserves the right to terminate this Contract at any time and without cause by serving upon CONTRACTOR 30 days advance written notice of such intent to terminate. In the event of such termination, the COUNTY'S only obligation to CONTRACTOR shall be payment for services rendered prior to the date of termination.

This Contract may be terminated at any time without advance notice and without further obligation to the COUNTY when the CONTRACTOR is found by COUNTY to be in default of any provision of this Contract.

Notwithstanding any other provision in this Contract, this Contract may be terminated if for any reason, there are not sufficient appropriated and available monies for the purpose of maintaining COUNTY or other public entity obligations under this Contract. In the event of such termination, COUNTY shall have no further obligation to CONTRACTOR, other than to pay for services rendered prior to termination.

ARTICLE XVI - NOTICE

Any notice required or permitted to be given under this Contract shall be in writing and shall be served by personal delivery or by certified mail upon the other party as follows:

COUNTY:

Dennis W. Douglas, Director
Pima County Health Department
150 West Congress, Suite 237
Tucson, Arizona 85701

CONTRACTOR:

Reverend Robin Hoover
Humane Borders, Inc.
740 East Speedway
Tucson, Arizona 85719

ARTICLE XVII - NON-EXCLUSIVE CONTRACT

CONTRACTOR understands that this Contract is nonexclusive and is for the sole convenience of COUNTY. COUNTY reserves the right to obtain like services from other sources for any reason.

ARTICLE XVIII - REMEDIES

Either party may pursue any remedies provided by law for the breach of this Contract. No right or remedy is intended to be exclusive of any other right or remedy and each shall be cumulative and in addition to any other right or remedy existing at law or at equity or by virtue of this Contract.

ARTICLE XIX- SEVERABILITY

Each provision of this Contract stands alone, and any provision of this Contract found to be prohibited by law shall be ineffective to the extent of such prohibition without invalidating the remainder of this Contract.

ARTICLE XX - BOOKS AND RECORDS

CONTRACTOR shall keep and maintain proper and complete books, records and accounts, which shall be open at all reasonable times for inspection and audit by duly authorized representatives of COUNTY.

In addition, CONTRACTOR shall retain all records relating to this contract at least 5 years after its termination or cancellation or, if later, until any related pending proceeding or litigation has been closed.

ARTICLE XXI - ENTIRE AGREEMENT

This document constitutes the entire agreement between the parties pertaining to the subject matter hereof, and all prior or contemporaneous agreements and understandings, oral or written, are hereby superseded and merged herein. This Contract may be modified, amended, altered or extended only by a written amendment signed by the parties.

IN WITNESS THEREOF, the parties have affixed their signatures to this Contract on the date written below.

PIMA COUNTY

____
Procurement Director
Date: ____________

CONTRACTOR

____
Name and Title
Date: ____________
Federal Tax ID # ________________

APPROVED AS TO CONTENT

____
Department Head
Date: __________

APPROVED AS TO FORM

Paula J. Perrera
Deputy County Attorney
Date: 3-24-03

657-03

Resolution 2001 - 146

**RESOLUTION OF THE
PIMA COUNTY BOARD OF SUPERVISORS
TO PROCLAIM THE EXISTENCE OF CONDTIONS OF
EXTREME PERIL TO THE HEALTH AND SAFETY
OF PERSONS IN PIMA COUNTY**

WHEREAS, on June 5, 2001, the Pima County Board of Supervisors declared the existence of conditions of extreme peril to the health and safety of persons in Pima County; and

WHEREAS, the conditions of limited water supply, extreme desert temperatures, high probability for hikers and others on foot to become lost, deplete of water, and subject to life threatening conditions have created a situation of extreme peril to the health and safety of persons, particularly in the desert regions of Pima County; and

WHEREAS, A.R.S. § 26-311 authorizes the Chairman of the Pima County Board of Supervisors, when an emergency is deemed to exist, to declare a local emergency.

NOW, THEREFORE, BE IT RESOLVED, that the Chairman of the Pima County Board of Supervisors has authorization to impose a proclamation, effective immediately, that a condition of local extreme peril to the health and safety of persons exists within Pima County. Let it also be resolved, Pima County requests the State of Arizona provide emergency funding to reimburse local response agencies, the medical examiner, and health care providers for cost of responses to rescue, resuscitation and returning to health or medical examining services for person(s) rescued or recovered from the desert regions of Pima County.

PASSED and ADOPTED this 3rd day of July, 2001, at Tucson, Pima County, Arizona.

PIMA COUNTY BOARD OF SUPERVISORS

____
Raul Grijalva, Chairman

ATTEST:

____
Lori Godoshian, Clerk of the Board

APPROVED AS TO FORM:

Karen S. Frias
Deputy County Attorney

United States Department of the Interior

BUREAU OF LAND MANAGEMENT
Tucson Field Office
12661 East Broadway
Tucson, AZ 85748-7208

(520) 258-7200

In reply refer to:

2920 AZA 32153 (600)

October 11, 2002

CERTIFIED MAIL No. 7002 0860 0000 2909 6900
RETURN RECEIPT REQUESTED

DECISION

Humane Borders, Inc.
740 East Speedway Boulevard
Tucson, Arizona 85719

: Land Use Permit
: AZA 32153

PERMIT DATE EXTENSION

On August 30, 2002, the Humane Borders, Inc., was issued a land use permit authorized under 43 CFR 2920 to locate and place water stations on public lands. The permit was issued for a one-year period from the date of issuance of August 30, 2002 to September 30, 2002, and then from May 1, 2003 through September 30, 2003. On October 1, 2002, the Tucson Field Office received a written request from the permittee to extend the permit date to October 30, 2002.

An extension of the permit date is hereby approved to October 30, 2002. This approval is offered subject to the terms and conditions under the original permit dated August 30, 2002.

Shela A. McFarlin
Field Manager

HB 520-624-0010
CF 520-624-1210

Special Use Permit - SPECIAL STIPULATIONS

~~Note: prior to approving the permit:~~

~~1) BLM will review the insurance binder~~

~~2) Humane Borders will review the permit stipulations~~

In addition to the standard stipulations marked on the permit, the following Special Stipulations will apply:

1. This permit only authorizes the use of federal lands administered by the Bureau of

Land Management (BLM), Tucson Field Office (TFO), at 4 (four) locations within or adjacent to the Ironwood Forest National Monument. It does not authorize the use of private lands, or lands owned or managed by other federal, state, tribal or local governmental agencies where BLM has no authority to issue such authorizations.

2. Humane Borders must maintain a minimum of $10,000,000.00 (ten million dollars) per occurrence worth of general liability insurance coverage, in a policy form acceptable to the Authorized Officer, for property damage, personal injury and comprehensive public liability resulting from action taken or caused by Humane Borders under this permit. The United States shall be named as an additional insured on the Certificate of Insurance. Humane Borders must furnish proof of insurance to the Authorized Officer in the form of a Certificate of Insurance prior to execution of the permit. Humane Borders must maintain the required insurance coverage for the life of the permit.

3. The period of use under the Special Use Permit is to be from date of permit approval through September 30, 2002 and May 1 through September 30, 2003. Under extenuating circumstances (such as prolonged drought or high temperatures), Humane Borders may apply to the Authorized Officer 30 days in advance to extend this time period.

4. Humane Borders is responsible for the training, monitoring, safety and security of its individual employees and volunteers including notifications about approaching individuals on BLM administered lands, biohazards or other safety precautions, off-road driving conditions, etc.

5. Any cultural and/or paleontological resource (historic or prehistoric site or object) discovered by the permittee, or any person working on its behalf, on BLM administered land must be immediately reported to the Authorized Officer. Humane Borders shall suspend all

opera ions in the immediate area of such discovery until written authorization to proceed is issue l by the Authorized Officer. An evaluation of the discovery will be made by the Authorized Offic r to determine appropriate actions to prevent the loss of significant cultural or scientific valu s. Humane Borders will be responsible for the cost of evaluation and the Authorized Offic er will make any decision as to proper mitigation measures after consulting with the perm ittee.

6. While on BLM administered lands, Humane Borders will notify Tucson BLM Law Enfc rcement within two hours of any encounters with the U.S. Border Patrol or calls to eme gency medical service providers (e.g., Pima County Emergency Services, etc.); any tran portation of individuals for medical assistance; and any discovery of deceased persons or hum an remains. Upon receipt of any information under this paragraph, BLM Law Enforcement will make all appropriate and necessary additional notifications to the U.S. Border Patrol and oth r responsible governmental agencies.

7. No commercial filming or photography is permitted. Humane Borders may not issue any news releases concerning the water stations without the express written approval of the Au horized Officer. The BLM requires notification of any media coverage that Humane Borders bec mes aware of which discusses or mentions the permitted water stations. Any photographs tak n by Humane Borders must only be used for internal record keeping or internal training.

8. At each water station location: no vegetation will be trimmed, cleared or removed; no hol s or pits will be excavated for footings, wildlife will not be harassed or harmed; and trash or del ris, for which Humane Borders is responsible, will be removed. Trash and refuse collected by Hi mane Borders will be removed from the site to appropriate dumpsters or refuse sites.

9. The installation of water stations will be coordinated with BLM staff at the Tucson Field Office to ensure avoidance of sensitive areas and conformance with BLM regulations, policies, and planning. Arrangements with BLM staff shall be made no less than 48 hours in advance of proposed installation activities.

10. Humane Borders will maintain no more than two 60-gallon tanks at each water station without further approval of the Authorized Officer. Humane Borders will provide GPS coordinates from each water station to the Tucson Field Office, Pima County Sheriff's Office, and the Tucson Sector for the U.S. Border Patrol.

11. For the water station locations approved, Humane Borders will provide daily service and field inspections to ensure compliance with the following standards: no tanks are empty over a 24-hour period; water quality standards are tested and maintained equivalent to all applicable federal, state, and local governmental water quality standards; tanks will sealed and tamper proof and replaced immediately if needed due to tampering, punctures or similar flaws. The tanks authorized by this permit will not exceed 60 gallons each without prior approval of the Authorized Officer. A schedule of planned maintenance and servicing will be provided to the BLM.

12. BLM may immediately cancel the permit is tampering or sabotage occurs to one or more water stations. The Tucson Field Office will cancel the permit if so directed by the Arizona State Office or the Washington, D.C. Office, BLM, based on new policies, regulations, or advice of the Solicitor.

13. The permit may not be transferred or assigned without the written consent of the Authorized Officer.

14. Humane Borders will comply with all applicable federal, state, and local governmental public health and sanitation standards and codes.

15. Installation of water stations without prior written authorization from the Authorized Officer is not allowed and may be considered a trespass against the United States.

16. All flags, flagpoles, rebar, and water tanks shall be removed within 30 days after expiration of this permit, cancellation of the permit by BLM, or return of the permit by Humane Borders prior to expiration of term. The Authorized Officer shall be notified upon completion of removal activities.

17. No cross-country access is authorized outside of the designated sites, as identified in this permit. All approved sites (see attached map) are located within or adjacent to the Ironwood Forest National Monument and are under the jurisdiction of the Tucson Field Office. All water station sites shall be accessed via existing routes of travel only. In these areas vehicles may pull off of existing roads no more than 10 feet from edge of the roadbed. Water stations outside of this 10-foot zone shall be installed and maintained by foot travel.

18. The Authorized Officer may suspend or terminate this permit in whole or in part when, in his or her judgment, unforeseen conditions and/or circumstances arise which result in the approved terms and conditions being inadequate to protect the public health, safety and welfare, or the protect the environment.

19. As permittee of AZA-_____, Humane Borders agrees, without limitation or restriction, to indemnify the United States against any liability arising from the release of any hazardous substance or hazardous waste (as these terms are defined in the Comprehensive Environmental Response, Compensation and Liability Act of 1980, 42 U.S.C. 9601 et seq., or the

Reso irce Conservation and Recovery Act of 1976, 42 U.S.C. 6901 et seq.) on BLM-administered land: subject to this permit. This agreement applies without limitation to whether a release is caus d by the permittee, its agent, or unrelated third parties.

20. Approval of this permit is not to be construed as approval or authorization of any actic n by the permittee, or its officers, agents or employees, to violate any federal laws or regu ations, including U.S. Immigration and Naturalization laws.

Aut orized Officer:____________________ Date: ______________

The Tohono O'odham Nation & Homeland Security

Edward D. Manuel
Chairman

Henry A. Ramon
Vice-Chairman

This is the first line of defense for
Homeland Security.
The Tohono O'odham are the second.

Tohono O'odham Nation: General Background

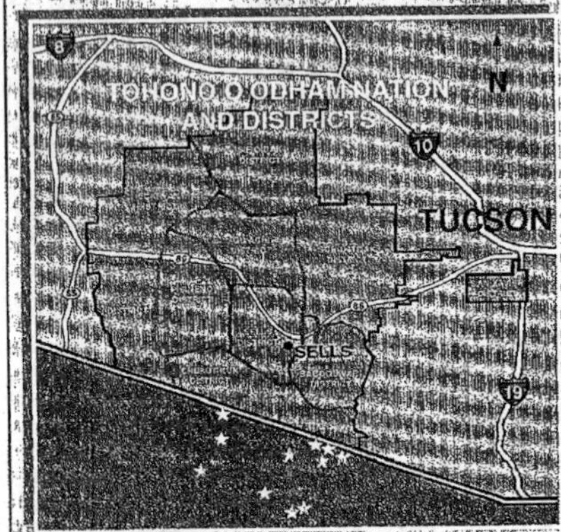

- 4 Separate Land Areas comprised of 2.86 million acres
- 3 Counties (Pima, Pinal, and Maricopa)
- 28,000 members
- 75 Miles Contiguous With Mexico
- Nine Villages in Mexico

Tohono O'odham Border Statistics: Fiscal Year 2002

Narcotics Seizures:

2002: 65,000 lbs.

2001: 45,000 lbs.

2000: 35,000 lbs.

1999: 27,500 lbs.

Illegal Immigrant Traffic: Over 1,500 daily; TOPD assists Border Patrol with over 800 cases per month

Vehicle Towing: 30-40 per day

Refuse: Each immigrant leaves behind over 8 lbs. per day (equal to 6 tons per day)

Undocumented Immigrant Apprehensions on the Nation December 2002- January 2003: 5400

TOPD Border Expenditures: Fiscal Year 2002

Immigrant Exposure Deaths/ Autopsies:
85 Cases; $266,050

Drug Smuggling Cases:
140 Cases; $642,880

Other Death Investigations (Homicides, Traffic):
12 incidents; $260,000

Vehicle Towing: nearly 4,500 vehicles; $180,000

Immigrant Interaction Cases:
over 15 cases/day; $1.4 million

Sells Indian Hospital: treatment of illegal immigrants over 50 cases monthly summertime over $500,000

Total Cost to the Nation:
$6.5 million - $7 million

(Figures are conservative and do not include fence repair, well repair, gas, vehicle upkeep, garbage removal, etc.)

Not just Mexican Nationals

- In 2002, over 200 undocumented immigrants were apprehended on the Nation that were not Mexican Nationals.
- August 6, 2002; TOPD Drug Enforcement Officers found a plane ticket stub dated August 21, 2001. The plane ticket was for Yousif Abdelkaber and was paid for in cash.

Mexican Military Incursions

__March 9, 1999__
San Miguel Gate: U.S. Customs agents fired on by Mexican military smuggling marijuana.

__April, 2000__
Menagers Dam: cattle truck drove into the village with Mexican soldiers armed with machine guns.

__January 6, 2002__
GuVo: soldiers with machine guns smuggled 2,000 lbs. of narcotics; ran an intersection colliding with another vehicle killing two innocent people and two soldiers.

__May 17, 2002__
Papago Farms: soldiers pursued Ranger officer on foot while protecting a large drug load.

__February 7, 2003__
Serapos Gate 6:45am: soldiers in uniform crossed into the village with a pickup, suspected of protecting a drug load.

Nation's Priorities for Strengthening Homeland Security

1. Homeland Security Funding Directly to the Nation
2. Protection of the Border:
   - Presence & Barriers
3. Hospital Services

1. Homeland Security Funding Directly to the Nation

- Federal and State funding should come directly to the Nation.
- Nation should be included in strategic planning for all border related issues.

2 – Protection of the Border

- Tohono O'odham Police is manned and equipped to serve the Nation as a community based police force.
- Approximately 55% of our resources are expended to provide Federal national security.
- Nation needs recurring federal funding for additional manpower and resources. Examples:
    1. Vehicle Barrier Fence
    2. Construct a border road to make more accessible for law enforcement agencies
    3. Border Patrol resources to be increased and stationed along the border

3. Hospital Services

- Hospital in Sells is the first respondent to emergencies and the only hospital in the region.
- Hospital is finitely funded exclusively for local Native Americans.
- Federal funding is crucial
  - Expanded facilities
  - Specialized equipment
  - Trained medical staff

*Bills recently introduced in the Senate and House include allotments made to border hospital agencies for reimbursements of services rendered to undocumented immigrants, including IHS

Tohono O'odham Nation's Border/ Immigrant Statistics

Illegal Immigrant Traffic

- Total immigrant deaths on the Nation from 01-01-02 to 9-30-02: **85**
- 1,500-2000 people crossing the Nation's lands daily (over 45,000 per month, 547,500 per year)
- TOPD (Tohono O'odham Police Dept.) assisted with over 4,000 immigrants between January and May, 2002
- On average, TOPD currently assists with 800 immigrants per month (apprehensions, search and rescues, etc.). In 1999, the TOP assisted with 100 per month.
- Estimated that each person leaves behind 8.5 lbs of litter daily on the Nation. (12,750 pounds per day, 4.6 million pounds per year)

Numbers October, November, December: 4

TOPD:

Narcotics Seized (mostly marijuana):

- 1999- 27,500 lbs.
- 2000- 35,000 lbs.
- 2001- 45,000 lbs.
- 2002- up to the end of September – 65,000 lbs., including 16,000 lbs. in April alone
- Number of vehicles towed per day: 30-40
- Total cost to TOPD for all border related issues: **$2.5- $3 million annually**

Hospital/ Ambulance Services

Total Number of Undocumented Immigrants Served at Sells Indian Health Center

- 10/97-10/99 – 90
- 10/99-7/00 – 404 (Includes disaster of March 8, 2000 330 seen-snow storm)
- 7/00-10/01 – 579 (Includes disaster of 260 during cold spell at Baboquivari High)
- 10/01-4/02 – 198
- 2002 cost is estimated at $500,000, which has come from hospital's operating budget as of May 2002.

Proposed Solutions

A. Increase Border Patrol and Customs presence on the Nation, agents to be stationed along the border.
B. Construct a road along Nation's 76-mile international boundary, between Sasabe and Lukeville, for Border Patrol use (enabling easier access to border).
C. Provide Homeland Security funding for the Nation. Uses include increasing the number and improving the training of TOPD officers, environmental cleanup, etc.
D. Increase federal funding for the Indian Health Service hospital in Sells and its ambulance services.

TOHONO O'ODHAM NATION POLICE DEPARTMENT
BORDER SECURITY SPENDING

Cost estimates incurred for fiscal year 2002

Exposure Deaths/ Autopsies		
Autopsy	$	1,450
2002 Immigrant Deaths on the Nation		85
Total Autopsy Costs	$	**123,250**
Personnel Opportunity Cost	$	28/ hourly
60 Hours Minimum Per Case		x60
Total Per Case	$	1,680
Total Personnel Costs	$	**142,800**
Grand Total	$	**266,050**
Drug Smuggling Cases		
Personnel Opportunity Cost	$	28/hourly x 2 Officers = 56
Minimum Hours Per Case		82
Total Personnel Opportunity Cost Per Case	$	4,592
Total of Cases Handled by the TOPD		140
Grand Total	$	**642,880**
Traffic Related Fatality Cases		
3 Separate Incidents Involving Mexican Nationals		
9 Deaths, 16 Injuries		
Personnel Opportunity Cost	$	28/ hourly x 4 Officers = 112
Total Hours Spent on Cases		90 x 3 cases = 270
Grand Total	$	**30,240**
Homicide Investigations		
Personnel Opportunity Cost	$	28/ hourly x 2 Officers = 56
Total Hours Spent on Two Cases		2,000
Grand Total	$	**112,000**
Vehicle Towing		
Personnel Opportunity Cost	$	28/ hourly
Minimum Hours Per Tow		1.5
Total Number of Cases		3,516
Grand Total	$	**147,672**
Immigrant Interaction Cases		
Includes apprehensions (which are turned over to Border Patrol), residential break-ins, Etc.		
Personnel Opportunity Cost	$	42 (time and ½) hourly x 2 Officers = 84
Minimum Hours Per Case		3
Total Cost Per Interaction	$	252
Total Cases YTD		5,400
Grand Total	$	**1,360,800**
Grand Total of all Border Related Costs Incurred by the Tohono O'odham Nation	$	**2,559,642.00**

These costs do not include gas, vehicle maintenance and all other administrative costs related to the Border. The Tohono O'odham Nation Police Department budget for fiscal year 2002 is $6 million. The budget for FY 2001 was $9 million. During the fiscal year of 2002, the Tohono O'odham Nation Police Department was responsible for the seizure of approximately 65,000 lbs of illegal narcotics. These seizures resulted in the arrest of over 100 individuals on tribal, state and federal charges. The Nation estimates it spent $6.5- $7 million in 2002 for Border related activities, with $3 million being spent on the police department alone.

O